Raised Right

The Cultural Lives of Law
Edited by Austin Sarat

Raised Right

Fatherhood in Modern American Conservatism

Jeffrey R. Dudas

Stanford Law Books
An Imprint of Stanford University Press
Stanford, California

Stanford University Press
Stanford, California

Printed in the United States of America on acid-free, archival-quality paper

Library of Congress Cataloging-in-Publication Data

Names: Dudas, Jeffrey R., author.
Title: Raised right : fatherhood in modern American conservatism / Jeffrey R.
   Dudas.
Description: Stanford, California : Stanford Law Books, an imprint of Stanford
   University Press, 2017. | Includes bibliographical references and index.
Identifiers: LCCN 2016027402 (print) | LCCN 2016029529 (ebook) | ISBN
   9781503600188 (cloth : alk. paper) | ISBN 9781503601727 (pbk. : alk. paper) |
   ISBN 9781503601734
Subjects: LCSH: Conservatives—Family relationships—United States. | Fami-
   lies—Political aspects—United States. | Civil rights—United States—Phi-
   losophy. | Fathers and sons—United States. | Conservatism—United States.
   | Buckley, William F., Jr., 1925–2008—Family. | Reagan, Ronald—Family. |
   Thomas, Clarence, 1948– —Family.
Classification: LCC JC573.2.U6 D835 2017 (print) | LCC JC573.2.U6 (ebook) |
   DDC 320.52092/273—dc23
LC record available at https://lccn.loc.gov/2016027402

For Mary, Connor, and Andrew

Contents

Preface

I began this book in earnest in summer 2007. Our youngest child was not yet two years old; our firstborn was four years old and just beginning preschool. We were still relatively new parents, and our lives were dominated by, on one hand, the daily joys of seeing the children discover with new eyes the things that we adults take for granted (sidewalks! butterflies! snow!) and, on the other hand, by the deep exhaustion and chronic sleep deprivation that is common to the parents of many young children. This is not a book about the political effects of depicting the American nation according to *those* parent/child dynamics.

Instead, the major question with which this book is concerned— How does it matter that a major American political movement, modern conservatism, is consumed with the paradoxical struggles of children to at once honor and escape the legacies of the nation's fathers?—is better suited to the passage of personal time. Such concerns about filial autonomy and loyalty inform manifold family struggles and tensions, and they emerge first in adolescence. Families, of course, tend to be much more than simply sites of struggle—even families like ours that now, ten years down the road, have adolescents in them. Amid new challenges and frustrations, many families remain sites of comfort, joy, and growth.

But what is remarkable about the families that are depicted in this book—especially the families of modern American conservatism's most celebrated leaders—is that they are consistently described in negative terms, not as balanced between joy and tension at all. These families are like funhouse mirrors: they reflect some of the ordinary tensions of stable family life but also distort those tensions until they are grotesque and overwhelming. Sometimes, sadly, the evidence suggests that the distortions are basically accurate; sometimes, happily, the evidence suggests a more complicated telling. Yet the personal and public narratives of family life that are presented in this book emphasize struggle and dysfunction;

if there are positive, nurturing elements of these families, they are rarely acknowledged. And so my own interpretations of these narratives—the discursive and conceptual stuff of modern American conservatism—tends toward the tragic.

Given the frequently dour tone of what follows, I am especially happy to start with a more pleasing endeavor and to acknowledge the many folks who have helped me bring this book to fruition. I am grateful to Renée Cramer, who encouraged me at the outset and throughout my writing, read and commented on multiple chapter and proposal drafts, gently prodded me when it seemed that things were taking too long, and was always available for enlivening chats. I am similarly indebted to Claire Rasmussen and Susan Burgess, each of whom wrote multiple times in support of this project, engaged me in spirited discussions over the book's long gestation period, and contributed their own important scholarship that has helped me along the way. Paul Passavant has been both the best conference roommate imaginable and a source of consistent encouragement and engagement over the years.

So many scholars affiliated with the Law and Society Association have been helpful over the nearly ten years that I have been laboring on this book; I despair that I may neglect to mention all of them. But here goes anyway: thank you to George Lovell, Anna Maria-Marshall, Scott Lemieux, Jon Goldberg-Hiller, Austin Sarat, Eve Darian-Smith, Chuck Epp, Helena Silverstein, Jon Gould, Patricia Ewick, William Haltom, Scott Barclay, John Gilliom, Jeb Barnes, Tom Burke, Christine Harrington, John Brigham, and Laura Hatcher. Joseph Mello and Sarah Hampson have emerged as part of a new generation of Law and Society scholars (along with Shauna Fisher, Josh Wilson, and Amanda Hollis-Brusky); their success is gratifying. And my enduring gratitude goes to Michael McCann. Michael is a titan of the Law and Society community who has encouraged and inspired me to develop a distinctive scholarly voice; his continued support means the world to me.

I am thankful for my colleagues at the University of Connecticut, especially the inimitable Stephen Dyson, who is always interested in going for lunch with me and talking about scholarship; Stephen's own prodigious scholarly record is a source of both envy and inspiration. Virginia Hettinger, Vin Moscardelli, Kristin Kelly, David Yalof, Jane Gordon, Ernie Zirakzadeh, Michael Morrell, Paul Hernson, Jeremy Pressman, and Heather Turcotte (now at UMASS-Dartmouth) are great colleagues and I am proud to work in the same building as they do. And, finally, I am thankful to the many UConn graduate and undergraduate students who have engaged bits and pieces of the perspectives that inform this book.

This book was largely finished at the University of Connecticut's Humanities Institute, where I had the great fortune of serving as a faculty fellow during the 2014–2015 academic year. The community of scholars and staff at the Humanities Institute welcomed me into their space and made me feel at home. The institute's director, Michael Lynch, and associate director, Brendan Kane, were wonderful hosts, and its marvelous staff, including Dorothy Ludwig and Jo-Ann Waide, made certain that I had everything that I needed. I am grateful to the other faculty fellows— especially Joseph McAlhany, Frank Costigliola, and Fiona Somerset—for their engagement with this work and their own stimulating scholarship. And I'm appreciative for Greg Semenza, who first identified this book as something that the Humanities Institute might be interested in and who encouraged me to apply for the faculty fellowship.

I regret that several scholars who encouraged and inspired me did not live to see this book's completion. At the University of Connecticut, first Howard Reiter and then Garry Clifford passed away; each shared some of their wealth of knowledge with me over a decade or so, and I miss them. At the University of Washington, David Olson died suddenly; he left many great friends and admirers, myself among them. Finally, Stuart Scheingold's death leaves an enduring void.

Michelle Lipinksi is an extraordinary editor, and I am thankful to have worked with her while bringing this book to publication at Stanford University Press. From our first meeting, Michelle was fully engaged and interested in this book; she was patient when I blew past several deadlines, and she worked diligently to ensure that the review and publication process went smoothly. Thank you, Michelle! Thanks also go to Nora Spiegel and Tim Roberts for production assistance and to the great design team at Stanford University Press for the wonderful and evocative cover that adorns this book.

My final and most important acknowledgments are for my family: for my parents, John and Diane, and my brother, Jay; for my in-laws, Frank and Anne; and, especially, for my wife, Mary, and our sons, Connor and Andrew. I could not have written this book without Mary and our boys. So much of what appears in these pages has conviction only because of their presence in my life. I am beyond grateful for each of them; I dedicate this book to them.

Raised Right

1

Raised Right

William F. Buckley Jr.'s task in 1970 was no less daunting than it is now. The "patron saint"[1] of modern American conservatism, Buckley had taken it on himself to expose "the flesh and blood of conservatism in America." On one hand, the felt need for an exploration of "the conservative position: its attitudes, its tones" was testament to the improbable success of American conservatism over the previous fifteen years—a success that was rooted in his 1955 founding of the definitive conservative periodical, the *National Review*.[2] Defying the predictions of mainstream, Cold War–era commentators who insisted that a liberal "consensus" had overtaken American life, Buckley and his colleagues had stood "athwart history, yelling Stop."[3] Indeed, by 1970, those consensus voices, so ubiquitous in the 1950s, had disappeared, lost in the domestic and international turmoil of the 1960s. Far from marginal, the American conservative movement in 1970 was soon to reach full flight. A taking of stock was thus in order.

But, on the other hand, Buckley knew that articulating a satisfying definition of American conservatism was perhaps a fool's errand. After all, conservatism was, like all other viable social movements, made up of a dizzying array of constituents and approaches to governance—most of them in tension, and sometimes in outright rivalry, with one another. Buckley's intent when founding the *National Review* was to make American conservatism intellectually rigorous and respectable; he meant to provide American conservatism with a distinctly *modern* identity. But given the fractious nature of its members, this was no small feat. How, exactly, to distill a common essence from the motivating impulses of large corporate interests, small-government libertarians, social and racial traditionalists, and, eventually, evangelical Christians? What did these populations have in common? What made them all identifiably "conservative"?

The answers to these questions, Buckley knew, were critical. Without a common set of commitments around which to gather—without something, or *someone*, to believe in—the burgeoning American conservative movement was in constant danger of implosion. And so, Buckley, wary but undaunted, set about to define "what conservatism is."[4]

Buckley's definition of American conservatism proceeded according to "processes of exclusion." And because he knew "who is a conservative less surely than I know who is [not],"[5] Buckley was confident in his exclusions: Ayn Rand and the followers of her atheistic dogma of "objectivism"; Robert Welch and the conspiracy-mad denizens of his John Birch Society; the anarchist, state-hating followers of economist Murray Rothbard; and, most painful, former *National Review* authors such as Max Eastman and Garry Wills, who had both criticized Buckley's characteristic sanctification of American conservatism with Christian principle.[6] These exclusions allowed Buckley to sketch "the confines of contemporary conservatism" so that after twenty-three pages of text, he was able to deliver on his goal of defining American conservatism. Modern conservatives, he declared, shared a "spirit of defiance" that issued "from distinctively American patterns of thought, from the essence of the American spirit." American conservatives, Buckley opined, "dragg[ed] their feet, resist[ed], kick[ed], complain[ed], hugg[ed] on to our ancient moorings."[7]

Those "ancient moorings," it turned out, were built with specifically *paternal* anchors. Indeed, the "American spirit" transmitted the "faith of our fathers" to the present day, bringing their paternal disapproval, in particular, to two of the twentieth century's most troubling trends: its "beatification" and concomitant "integration" of the state "as a member of the American household" and its reigning intellectual cynicism, which gave rise to the "trauma of self-doubt." Modern American conservatism accordingly channeled the "certitudes" of the American fathers; it "intellectualized" paternal desire in order to resist "the twentieth century's" attempts to rearrange the "American household." Linking conservative purpose to the spectral dictates of "the founders of the American republic," Buckley rejoiced:

In the past fifteen years in America a literature has emerged which taken together challenges root and branch the presumptions of the twentieth century. The intuitive wisdom of the founders of the American republic . . . is being rediscovered. . . . The meaning of the spirit of the West is being exhumed; impulses that never ceased to beat in the American heart are being revitalized.[8]

But what was this "intuitive wisdom of the founders of the American republic"? What were the "certitudes" and "rediscovered . . . impulses" that fired the "faith of our fathers" and coursed through the defiant "American spirit"? Buckley identified them in 1955 as the "fixed postulates having to do with the meaning of existence, with the relationship of the state to the individual, of the individual to the neighbor, so clearly enunciated in the enabling documents of our Republic."[9] They were, in short, the *individual rights* that are sacralized in our founding documents—the rights according to which American government was founded and legitimized. Cocksure, nontraumatic belief in the dictates of both paternal influence and individual rights: this, according to its undisputed intellectual founder, was the distinctive, unifying creed of modern American conservatism.

But this is curious. Paternal influence, with its spectral transmission of the timeless certitudes of the fathers, stands for external domination; the self-governance championed by Enlightenment notions of individual rights stands instead for autonomous self-creation. The one gestures toward control, the other toward freedom.

What are we to make of a political movement that celebrates both submission to paternal will *and* defiance to ascendant social, cultural, and political orders? A movement that not only champions such a paradoxical creed but, according to its "patron saint," *requires its presence* as the catalytic force that harmonizes its fractious member populations? More: What does it mean for those public figures whom the movement champions as its heroes, who both contain within themselves and publicly articulate such warring impulses? Indeed, what does it mean that modern American conservatism is founded on, and regenerates itself, paradoxically, through a paternal demand for rights?

Raised Right approaches these questions through an interrogation of the shared meanings that inform American life. In so doing, it eschews study of the formal, institutional dynamics—the elections, interbranch relations, and legislative and judicial debates about the proper scope of governmental authority—that are the typical subjects of scholarship on American law and politics. Instead, it offers a specifically cultural analysis of modern American conservatism, arguing that the otherwise uncomplimentary actors who make up the movement mutually celebrate a series of iconic public figures (including especially the trinity of William F.

Buckley Jr., former president Ronald Reagan, and current US Supreme Court justice Clarence Thomas). What makes these figures iconic is that they each employ(ed) a common familial and legal discourse—one that identified, as did Buckley Jr., the timeless certitudes of paternal authority and individual rights as the warp and weft of modern American conservatism's intellectual weave.

Indeed, these iconic conservatives celebrated citizens who were reared in conventional domestic and family circumstances. As we will see, Buckley Jr., Reagan, and now Thomas were especially fond of households in which fathers exercised unstinting authority and mothers were supportive and nurturing but never overbearing, or smothering of, their (especially) male children. From such families emerged the vaunted citizens of republican nations—the citizens who were disciplined and responsible enough to be trusted with the rights that confirmed them as autonomous, self-governing subjects. The seedbeds of self-governance, such patriarchal family units were said to prepare the way for the mature, rights-bearing subjects who were needed for modern democratic practice.

The effects of this paternal rights discourse, I will argue, radiate in multiple and paradoxical directions. The discourse, on one hand, is the common denominator of modern American conservatism; as such, it both defines the conservative movement's goals and has a salutary effect on the movement itself, working to smooth the jagged edges of conservatism's discontinuous elements. But as will become increasingly clear as this book's chapters unfold, the hortatory and catalytic impulses of modern American conservatism's central creed exert a heavy toll: on the intellectual coherence of the conservative movement, its iconic figures (whose own personal histories call into question the supposed virtues of stern paternal authority), and, especially, American conservatism's stated goal of creating autonomous, rights-bearing citizens. The process according to which modern American conservatism at once defines and rejuvenates itself—its cultural, discursive regeneration through rights—thus carries within it the seeds of the movement's instability—an instability whose marks escape the confines of American conservatism and surface in contemporary American politics writ large.

Scholarly and Methodological Principles

Although its approach is, as I have suggested, unconventional to most political analysis, *Raised Right* relies on two premises about rights discourse that are well established by scholars who work in the area of law, society, and politics. The first of these premises is that the discourse of the self-governing, rights-bearing citizen—exactly that lexicon that in part animates American conservatism—is a distinctive, and perhaps the defining, American political discourse.[10] Yet in spite of that discourse's claims to universality—all Americans, it holds in principle, are properly vested with and can employ rights—commentators of all partisan positions have conventionally placed conditions on the attainment and exercise of rights. The most prominent restriction has been that only those persons who exercise self-discipline, and the autonomy that it is said to enable, are fit for rights.[11] *Raised Right* builds on this well-established scholarly premise. Indeed, it finds that the conventional American preconditions for rights, self-discipline and autonomy, are themselves frequently held to be attainable only when particular kinds of domestic and familial circumstances—strong paternal and weak, or missing, maternal authority—are present.

Thus, written into the facially egalitarian discourse of individual rights is a qualifying, exclusionary logic that conditions rights on particular familial and gendered dynamics. And as we will see, these exclusionary dynamics frequently align with racial and class-based inequities such that those persons disqualified from rights are marked not only by supposed family dysfunction but also by racial and class difference. Gendered, bleached, and classed, the "normal" rights-bearing American citizen has conventionally been emblematic of white male privilege.

The second scholarly premise on which this book rests, however, maintains that although the accreted weight of historical and cultural practice emphasizes the limits of American rights discourse, that discourse is not simply disabling. Instead, its cultural legibility has consistently made it a powerful vocabulary for all Americans, including those historically denied the benefits of American democracy. Indeed, one of the outstanding characteristics of the previous sixty years of American history is the expansion of rights discourse, and the valued identities that it transmits, to include many nonwhite male Americans who had previously been marked as lacking the self-discipline and autonomy required for proper rights practice.[12]

But isn't this odd? How is it that our rights discourse can transmit, without undermining its own legitimacy, such a deeply ambivalent, even puzzling message? How can our dialect of rights point to both universal entitlement and the boundaries of personal and social (especially family) circumstance? The paradox that animates our rights discourse—it at once legitimates individual autonomy and heteronomous limit, individual liberation and social constraint—is derived, it turns out, from the character of modern law and politics itself.

According to Peter Fitzpatrick, the assemblage of legal and political practices that we call "modernity" is united by a rejection of the superstitions of the premoderns (of myth) and a celebration of its own supposed universality (of antimyth). This modern pretension toward transcendence and rationality is itself the artifact of an underlying horror of, and paradoxical attraction to, all manner of difference and particularity—to "myth." Refracted through the still-prevalent tropes of personhood that inform Anglo American colonial and imperial imaginations, modernity represses the racial and sexual desires of socially dominant, "civilized" populations, which it then demonizes and projects onto the "savage" bodies, minds, families, and cultures of colonial and imperial subjects. Thus is modernity's repulsion of myth and insistence on its own rational, transcendent character—its denial of the exotic and erotic desires that constitute it—both its distinctive mark and the key to understanding how modern "law transcends society yet is of society."[13] This "myth of transcendence" is, in Ewick and Silbey's more recent formulation, at the center of how most Americans, for example, believe without contradiction in the apparently irreconcilable "before the law" and "with the law" forms of legal consciousness.[14]

So, too, it seems, is there something of this forbidden desire for difference in what Scheingold called the American "myth of rights." Scheingold's innovation, the one that propelled multiple generations of scholars, was to see how modern law's distinctive pathologies could be mobilized as political resources by "empire's children"[15]—by those on whom the Anglo American imagination projected its own desires and fears: by women, racial and sexual minorities, and other disdained peoples of all sorts. Evoking the entrenched, constitutive desire for transcendence, these marked others leveraged their subjugated statuses as resources for political insurgency that, at least occasionally, successfully gained for them some of the long-denied benefits of democratic citizenship. The "politics of rights"—the mobilization of a culturally salient, if deeply ambivalent discursive convention—is thus a hallmark of both modern law and the modern configuration of politics itself. Paradoxical though it is, a politics of rights simply makes sense to most Americans most of the time.[16]

These insights provide the historical and conceptual backdrop for my interrogation of modern American conservatism. Indeed, the instability of rights discourse—the simultaneous signification *and* troubling of undemocratic privilege that is derived from modern law and politics itself—lends to conservative politics, ironically, its vitality. Articulation and defense of the "normal," paternally disciplined, rights-bearing citizen thus works as the conservative movement's catalytic and harmonizing force; it is the cultural source of the movement's seemingly limitless capacity to regenerate itself as a relatively cohesive, unified movement in spite of ongoing internal tensions.

Given these core scholarly premises and commitments, I engage in a particular form of investigation and employ a particular set of methods in order to conduct that investigation. The source material, or "data," on which this book relies is contained primarily in chapters 3 to 5, which explore the trio of public figures whom movement conservatives consider to be their most important representatives: William F. Buckley Jr. (in Chapter 3), Ronald Reagan (in Chapter 4), and Clarence Thomas (in Chapter 5). Each of these chapters interprets the distinctive, paternal rights discourse with which these figures articulated their visions of the American nation, the sorts of family structures necessary for the production of virtuous citizens, and the acts of governance that would best reflect the nation's core commitment to autonomous self-governance. In short, each of these chapters interrogates the presence, and the effects, of the paternal rights talk that distinguishes, rejuvenates, and troubles modern American conservatism.

As such, I rely on methods of inquiry that are drawn from *interpretive* approaches to the social sciences and the humanities. My interpretive account fixates, in particular, on the effects of language—effects that register in the domains of both the conceptual and the epistemological. Indeed, interpretive scholars are concerned with how a culture's common vernaculars at once reflect and constitute the widely shared meanings with which people make sense of themselves, others, and the possibilities of action that do and do not exist at any particular time. It is through the habitual speaking and hearing of such commonly held discursive conventions that we become meaningful; they lead us to know who we are (and are not), what we desire (and what we fear), and which practices are best suited (or not) for realizing our goals.[17]

Language is thus not simply descriptive verbiage; we do not carry around in our heads with us fully formed, intuitive senses of our identities and our interests that are waiting to be born in a swaddle of intentionally chosen words. Instead, the commonly shared languages that we speak operate on us recursively; the words that we use are at once reflective and generative of our understandings: of who we are (and are not), of what we desire (and fear), and of how best (or worst) to pursue our goals. To the extent that our beliefs, fears, desires, and ambitions have meaning—to the extent that we can make ourselves intelligible to both ourselves and others—we have our commonly shared languages, our discursive conventions, to thank for it.[18]

Interpretive analyses pinpoint the meaning-making activities of human beings, and especially our capacity for language. Given the cultural specificity of such meaning-making activities (every culture in every era of human existence, after all, has its own stories of self that are told in its own inflections), interpretive analyses tend to avoid making strict causal claims about how the influence of statically fixed, isolate, and cross-cultural "independent variables" (e.g., income inequality, level of educational attainment, partisan identification) "cause" particular outcomes. Indeed, "interpretation begins from the postulate that the web of meaning constitutes human existence to such an extent that it cannot ever be meaningfully reduced to constitutively prior speech acts, dyadic relations, or any predefined elements."[19] Thus do interpretive scholars, according to Cramer, "use their work in order to . . . see connections . . . to situate particular phenomena within a cultural context that helps it to be more legible."[20]

My examination of modern American conservatism is thus appropriately interpretive in character. It investigates, on one hand, the discursive conventions according to which prominent conservatives make sense of their selves, their desires, their fears, and the possibilities of action that attend contemporary American politics. It investigates, on the other hand, the many culturally specific connections between prominent conservatives, the movement of which they are a part, and the American polity they have frequently succeeded in remaking in their image. And it argues, finally, that the paradoxical discursive conventions that animate modern

American conservatism—the distinctive vocabulary that at once champions paternal dictate and individual rights—work both to rejuvenate and unify a political movement and give rise to a paternal politics that ultimately troubles conservatism's own stated goal of creating and promoting autonomous, rights-bearing citizens.

On Metaphor: Father Knows Best

Generous readers may be willing to grant the centrality of meaning-making activity to human life and thus be further willing to grant the political importance of the taken-for-granted languages with which we make sense of our lives with one another. But it's one thing to claim that a distinguished, rarified discourse such as the language of individual rights exerts constitutive effects on the conduct of American citizenship.[21] Isn't it another thing altogether to assert that references, on one hand, to the nation's "founding fathers" and, on the other hand, to the nation's biological fathers, however obsessive such references might be, themselves do crucial work in the building, the sustaining, and, ultimately, the troubling of modern American conservatism?

Perhaps. As Corey Robin argues, conservatives of all sorts—old and new, American and otherwise—have consistently defended society's prevailing orders of rule from potential subversion. And, according to Robin, the countersubversive tendencies of conservatives are especially pronounced when confronted with attacks on "private" sphere hierarchies—those that animate the workplace and, especially, the family. Fearing that "every great political blast . . . is set off by a private fuse," conservatives have believed that discipline starts at home, and so they have worked to shore up the "private life of power."[22]

It is thus unsurprising that modern American conservatives compulsively testify on behalf of paternal authority.[23] Nor is it surprising that these tributes are consistently yoked to narratives of family trauma told by iconic conservative figures about their own lives and the lives of others. But isn't all of this *just* verbiage? Isn't it just linguistic cover for the *real* interests of conservatism—just pleasing nostalgia that hides modern American conservatism's attempts to fortify conventional but eroding asymmetries of social power? Does it really matter, in a distinctively political sense, that American conservatives portray their mission as the arrangement of the American nation according to the desires of fathers past and present?

What difference does it make that American conservatism is infatuated with paternal authority rather than some other totem of American life?

It makes, in short, a great deal of difference. Much language is, in fact, metaphoric in character. But as I have already implied, to identify language as metaphoric is not to strip it of its power to make worlds. Instead, as do all widely shared discourses, metaphors register at once in conceptual and normative domains: they both offer an explanation for how the world works and, accordingly, suggest a series of preferred and proscribed behaviors. The paternal authority discourse/metaphor does not neutrally describe or comment on an already existing reality; instead, it "partially constitutes [that] reality . . . [it] constructs, interprets, and reflects [reality]."[24] By representing reality, it helps to constitute the possibilities of action that are widely present (because intelligible) or absent (because unintelligible) to most Americans most of the time.[25]

Accordingly, *Raised Right* pursues an analysis of modern American conservatism that pays equal heed to the paternal authority and rights discourses that infuse the movement and whose interplay, indeed, characterizes and propels it. In order to illuminate the centrality of these discursive conventions to modern conservatism, this book relies on substantive insights that are derived from feminist critical (especially psychoanalytic) and legal theory. In particular, it traces the negated, oppositional, and yet always intersubjective grounds of individual identity—grounds that, in the United States at least, tend to be inflected with gender and race-based dynamics.[26] Indeed, the practice of "virtuous" citizenship—and the self-disciplined, autonomous subject of American lore who is capable of engaging in such practice—depends on a constant and thoroughgoing repression of those characteristics in one's self (weakness, immaturity, irrationality, dependence, indolence, licentiousness) that are typically envisioned as barriers to autonomy. It involves also the projection of those disavowed personal characteristics onto a demonized, typically gendered and raced "other," such that the characteristics that are ever present but forbidden in one's self are employed as markers of illegitimacy.[27] Jane Caputi makes the point: "'Otherness,' the basis of oppression, is created when the self is split, and what is disowned, feared, and denied in the self is projected onto another being or group. The 'other' is then stigmatized and warred against."[28] Disavowal, projection, and stigmatization thus frequently sit at the leading edge of identity, including that of the autonomous subject who is the champion of conservative visions of American citizenship.

And as contemporary feminist theory, in particular, has established, the modern self's identity as a mature, self-governing subject frequently relies on the suppression of the maternal realm and its avatars and the elevation of the paternal realm and its avatars. Indolence, dependence, immaturity, emotional attachment, sensuous orality, innocence, and nostalgia for the bliss of mother-infant (or "dual") unity: all become human characteristics and states that are internalized negatively (or at least ambivalently), repressed into the unconscious, and identified with feminine influence. At the same time, the self-discipline that is said to mark a mature, modern state of autonomy is celebrated and associated with paternal influence.[29]

While the gendered basis of modern subjectivity tends to be general,[30] it is especially constitutive of possibilities of action in a society such as the United States. First, Americans have conventionally designated child rearing to be women's work that is confined to a "private" sphere of home and family that is hermetically sealed from the "public" masculine-coded world of business, politics, and influence. Second, as generations of commentators have noted, Americans have typically proclaimed that self-reliant, individualistic behavior is the key to worldly success and virtuous citizenship.[31] American children, especially boys, thus tend to be conversant at an early age in a discourse that emphasizes how both worldly influence and legitimacy of self depend on leaving and overcoming the maternal world of sentiment, attachment, and nourishment and entering the paternal, public world of competition, where rational calculation and unsentimental logic are the coins of the realm.[32] Accordingly, the maternal is a culturally ambivalent site: it speaks to both half-conscious desires of nostalgia, comfort, safety, and emotional attachment *and* to horror over the possibility of a maternal "reengulfment" and domination that would threaten the capacity of masculine autonomy that is said to animate virtuous American citizenship. DiStefano summarizes:

Difference and separation from a female (m)other characterize a boy's quest for self within a familial and outlying social setting that is organized in segregated and hierarchical gendered terms. A concomitant aspect of this process is that the (m)other poses a significant threat to [an autonomy] acquired in rigid opposition to her.[33]

I appreciate that it is a potentially long distance from how gendered binaries give rise to a specifically masculinist identity in usually male children and adolescents to an appraisal of modern American conservatism. The problem is this: the personal and political narratives that are offered by iconic conservative figures (including the trio of Buckley, Reagan, and Thomas analyzed in this book) and mimicked by conservative intellectuals emphasize self-control, self-discipline, personal maturity, and, above all, the suppression of sentimental attachment in favor of logic and reason. Their narratives of successful American citizenship, that is, emphasize the suppression of the values associated with the maternal realm and the embrace of values associated with paternal influence. Their narratives also *explicitly* locate the discipline necessary for productive citizenship and legitimate rights practice in proper child rearing and family relations—in the positive influence of strong fathers (who are said to prepare children [boys especially] for a productive, self-disciplined, and, thus, autonomous life) and the negative influence of weak or absent fathers and neglectful or domineering mothers (who are said to smother children and so leave them undisciplined and vulnerable to noxious outside influences).[34]

This gendered discourse of family success and dysfunction recurs compulsively in the personal and political narratives of the American conservative icons that occupy the coming pages. The discourse is at times metaphorical and at other times literal in character, but it works for American conservatism, no matter its character, as both a bedrock explanation of the virtues and vices of the American nation and as a normative seedbed for what is to be done. This is a book, accordingly, that interprets modern American conservatism's core belief that father knows best.

Chapter Overview

Raised Right unfolds, following this introductory chapter, over the course of five additional chapters. Chapter 2 investigates the large body of scholarship that details the rise of the modern conservative movement in post–World War II America. This scholarship persuasively accounts for the trajectory of the movement and the internal divisions that beset it. While this scholarship implies that the success and vitality of American conservatism depend on the ability of prominent movement figures to at once appeal to a mass public and gild the fractious tendencies of its own member populations, the accumulated scholarship offers little in the way of understanding how this feat has been accomplished. *Raised Right*— which finds that rights discourse, and the patriarchal commitments that animate it, is the catalytic force of American conservatism—thus provides a new component to the existing scholarship on modern American conservatism.

Chapters 3 through 5 explore the presence and the effects of the paternal rights discourse that propels modern American conservatism. In particular, these three chapters offer finely grained analyses of conservatism's most prominent and celebrated figures: William F. Buckley Jr., Ronald Reagan, and Clarence Thomas. Although they are distinct in their institutional locations, their formal affiliations with American government, and their intellectual styles, these three figures share an exalted status as conservative icons among both dispassionate observers and movement activists. Their acclaimed status comes in large part from the shared discourse that they employ. Chapters 3 through 5 thus focus on the paternal rights discourse common to Buckley, Reagan, and Thomas. In so doing, these chapters trace the multiple effects of that discourse: on their own political visions, the conservative movement, and the American polity.

Chapter 3 investigates Buckley's substantial intellectual and personal legacy. It does so, in particular, by illuminating an almost entirely neglected aspect of Buckley's career: the best-selling Blackford Oakes spy novels that he produced between 1976 and 2005. Though certainly not his most acclaimed writings, the Oakes novels stand apart from the rest of Buckley's oeuvre precisely because their fictional form allowed him to present his vision of virtuous American citizenship in crystalline terms— terms that were unencumbered by the contemporary, parochial concerns that tended to dominate his more explicitly political writing. Indeed, filtered through the hypermasculine and sexually voracious Cold War–era adventures of a protagonist with whom Buckley shared particular biographical (and especially family) elements, these novels contain some of their author's starkest ruminations on the character of the American nation. As such, they stand as Buckley's clearest articulation of the desires and fears that are central to modern American conservatism's paternal rights discourse. And the Oakes novels, it so happened, prepared the way in fiction for the Reagan Revolution of the 1980s that brought American conservatism to new heights of prominence.

Chapter 4 turns specifically to those heights. The chapter explores the effects of Ronald Reagan's yoking of the discourses of paternal authority and individual rights—a central, though frequently neglected, feature of his nearly thirty-year political career—on the trajectory of both American conservatism and American politics writ large. Chapter 4 first engages a trove of Reagan's handwritten speeches, letters, and radio broadcasts in order to produce a close reading of his political vision. This vision, which had roots in Reagan's own unstable childhood, was the unifying thread of his career in electoral politics. Conjoining childhood submission to paternal authority with the mature and responsible practice of rights later in life, Reagan's normative vision of American citizenship led him to at once champion the rights of America's "average" citizens and attack the rights of the nation's subversives—its "welfare queens," "wild animals," and "little criminals."

Second, Chapter 4 interprets the major moments of Reagan's time, first, as governor of California and, second, as president of the United States in light of his abiding commitment to this distinctive paternal rights discourse. The discourse infused Reagan's responses to political crises in each role and led him to pursue a particular, but frequently troubling and ineffective, strategy of governance: those citizens whom he thought paternally disciplined and thus responsible users of their rights would benefit from either the largesse or the inaction of government; those who were improperly disciplined at home and so later turned into immature, subversive users of rights would face, in the form of law and order, the full wrath of American government's oversight. However, as evidenced by his handling of student protesters while governor and his later conduct of the Contra war while president, the deliverance of American law and order had deeply ambivalent consequences for Reagan's own stated desire of converting these subversive citizens into responsible users of rights. Even so, Chapter 4 finds that Reagan's characteristic focus on rights, self-discipline, and conventional familial relationships that were marked by strong paternal authority was generative. It was a political vision that served, in spite of the tangled and frequently self-defeating politics that it produced, as a potent intellectual, electoral, and governing template for American conservatism—as is evidenced by both recent calls for a "new Reagan" to lead the conservative movement and the continued articulation of Reagan's political vision by his intellectual acolytes, none of whom are more prominent than is the subject of Chapter 5.

Chapter 5 turns to Justice Clarence Thomas. Thomas has been anointed by many conservative movement activists as Reagan's heir—as, indeed, "the leading conservative in America today." Although he is often characterized as the "silent justice" because of his refusal to ask questions during the Supreme Court's oral arguments, he has produced a rich corpus of off-court speeches, interviews, and memoirs that are highly revealing.

Using this primary source material to explore Thomas's personal, political, and legal visions, Chapter 5 finds that Thomas's characteristic, familial-based rights discourse, on one hand, unites him with the fathers of modern American conservatism (figures such as Buckley and Reagan) but, on the other hand, has ambivalent consequences for Thomas himself. Indeed, these consequences manifest in Thomas's life and in his jurisprudential philosophy; they evoke the abiding tension inherent in American conservatism's paternal rights discourse, especially in regard to its stated method of using stern, dominating paternal influence in order to produce autonomous, self-governing citizens.

This tension between paternal domination and self-governance, I have already noted, courses through American conservatism writ large. And it raises a final question that is the subject of Chapter 6, the book's concluding chapter. Indeed, considering the paradoxical, troubling consequences that the paternal rights discourse exerts on modern American conservatism, why is it the movement's defining creed? To which deeply seated fears and desires does the movement's devotion to paternal authority point? How, finally, are we to account for the paternal rights discourse that haunts modern American conservatism?

Conclusion

"Ideas rule the world," wrote William F. Buckley Jr. in 1955.[35] And so, as did the other iconic conservatives who appear in the coming pages, Buckley dedicated his career to infusing American conservatism with a very particular idea: they all sought to imbue American conservatism, and so American politics as a whole, with a distinctive "American spirit" that yoked paternal desire to self-governance. Buckley, as did Reagan and Thomas after him, believed that modern American conservatism thrived at the intellectual altar of paternal authority, on one hand, and the rights of man, on the other hand.

We will see here that the American spirit that Buckley identified continues to distinguish and unify modern conservatism. But this spirit also haunts. For, despite their political prescience, neither Buckley nor his peers gave any indication that they appreciated the paradoxical, disruptive character of an animating creed that gestures at once to the timeless dictates of the fathers and the self-determination rights of the children. It is left for us, then, to untangle the family drama that American conservatism's own patriarchs left unacknowledged. Let us begin.

2

Something to Believe In: Modern American Conservatism and the Paternal Rights Discourse

Scholarly investigation of modern American conservatism moves in two directions. There is, on one hand, scholarship that explores the theoretical underpinnings of conservatism's political vision. These works compare and contrast the modern forms with previous versions of American and continental conservatism.[1] There is, on the other hand, scholarship that points less to the presuppositions of modern American conservatism and more to its historical origins and developmental trajectories. It is the latter scholarship—on origins and trajectories—that works as my primary scholarly springboard.

Indeed, that scholarship at once develops the motley, fragmented character of modern American conservatism and suggests that its abiding tensions would have long ago caused the movement's implosion if not for the integrative and catalytic efforts of a few charismatic leaders. My contribution to this scholarship is to highlight the crucial role that the distinctive and shared paternal rights discourse of these leaders has played in the constitution of modern American conservatism, and especially in its capacity to gild the fractious tendencies of its member populations. I highlight the means according to which conservatism's most prominent figures have been so charismatic.

My account of modern American conservatism draws inspiration from Corey Robin's 2011 injunction that scholars acknowledge that "differences on the right are real" but that, nonetheless, "there is an underlying affinity that draws those differences together." Scholars should "look to the underlying arguments, the idioms and metaphors, the deep visions, and metaphysical pathos evoked" across the spectrum of modern conservative practice. Here, Robin argues, are found the bits of evidence that point to the movement's "animating purpose."[2]

I also draw inspiration from the substance of Robin's analysis and, in particular, from his conviction that conservatism (modern and historical) amounts to a countersubversive defense of eroding orders of rule in the most intimate, private spheres of life, especially the family.[3] Accordingly, this chapter registers in multiple domains: it traces the scholarship on the development of modern American conservatism among fractious concerns and constituents, identifies the shared idioms and metaphors voiced by conservatism's most prominent leaders, and interprets the distinctive paternal rights discourse with which these idioms and metaphors are articulated.

This discourse, we will see, collapses into one another public and private anxieties over the erosion of conventional, undemocratic hierarchies and the formerly hegemonic meanings that naturalized them. In so doing, the paternal rights discourse articulates what Lauren Berlant calls the "intimate public sphere" that organizes the American nation, where "private" matters define the normative value of American citizenship. At the heart of this intimate public sphere, argues Berlant, is "a scandal of ex-privilege . . . [that] can include [both] rage at the stereotyped peoples who have appeared to change the political rules of social membership" and nostalgia for the formerly uncontested values upon which privilege rested. Such troubled values, Berlant further notes, underwrote an "order of things deemed normal, an order of what was felt to be a general everyday intimacy" that was nowhere more evident than in the performance of conventional family roles. Accordingly, and broadly speaking, this chapter traces how conservatism's paternal rights discourse—its celebration of biological and mythical American fathers—became its most potent resource for entrenching the "view that the intimacy of citizenship is something scarce and sacred, private and proper, and only for members of families."[4]

It is, in fact, no surprise that conservatives' work of convincing both the citizenry and themselves "that the core context of politics should be the sphere of private life" has been performed with rights discourse.[5] After all, rights discourse, according to multiple generations of law and society scholars, is the preeminent American political vernacular.[6] A broadly persuasive language that spans historical, social, and partisan boundaries, American rights discourse transmits the defining attributes of American self-consciousness; it is, in the parlance of D. H. Lawrence, the "democratic and idealistic" clothing in which Americans dress themselves.[7] And so, while we are more familiar with the contemporary use of rights discourse by those who were historically denied the benefits of American democracy, they are not the only Americans who in modern times have found in rights discourse an animating and motivating impulse. Investing it with the paradoxical desires for individual autonomy and paternal authority that course through the nation's intimate public sphere, American conservatives have made their own use of our rights heritage.

Origins

Scholars trace the origins of modern American conservatism to a confluence of apparently unrelated mid-twentieth-century trends: early opposition by corporate executives to Franklin Roosevelt's New Deal programs; the contemporaneous emergence of a group of young conservative intellectuals and their publications; the post–World War II growth of a libertarian, antigovernment ethos that was particularly prominent in the sunbelt states of Arizona, California, and Texas; and reactions by Southern whites, as well as by their working-class counterparts in the North and Midwest, to the various rights movements of the 1950s and 1960s. The scholarship then portrays the development of the modern conservative movement as the story of how prominent leaders managed the frequently unruly prerogatives inherent in these source materials.

Corporate executives (such as the heads of the DuPont and Goodrich families) played an important role in the constitution of the nascent conservative movement. These executives virulently opposed the governmental regulation of the American economy that animated Franklin Roosevelt's New Deal programs; they funded established organizations such as the National Association of Manufacturers (NAM) and created new organizations such as the Foundation for Economic Enterprise , each of which sought to popularize the free market theories of prominent economists such as Ludwig Von Mises and Friedrich Hayek. Ayn Rand—who would later author such popular novels as *The Fountainhead* and *Atlas Shrugged* and become a monumental, if controversial, figure for American conservatives—was involved in many of these corporate-funded organizations. But principled free market opposition to New Deal programs occasionally gave way to conspiratorial fears that American government was actively subverting individual freedom. Such fears were easily discredited by New Deal supporters, even as they failed to gain popular traction with the electorate and generally left the impression that conservative opposition to Roosevelt was not serious.[8]

By the 1950s, however, corporations such as General Electric began to present their free market philosophies in a more positive fashion that emphasized the virtues of individual freedom, creativity, and responsibility. In GE's case, such messaging was helped along greatly by the corporation's sponsorship of *General Electric Theater* (a popular television series hosted by Ronald Reagan) and the efforts of GE Vice President Lemuel Boulware, who trained senior-level employees in the theories of Hayek and Von Mises and then sent Reagan himself on plant tours to bring the message to GE's rank-and-file workers.[9] Similarly, business organizations such as the Chamber of Commerce presented a unified voice that trumpeted the virtues of American business and soft-pedaled critiques of governmental regulation and labor union interests.

Corporate executives soon found a potent ally in William F. Buckley Jr., whose founding of the *National Review* in 1955 marked a watershed moment in the history of contemporary American conservatism. The magazine fused free market economic principles to a virulent anticommunism and fidelity to conventional social values, all presented in Buckley's uniquely terse and combative style. In addition to Buckley's own writings, the *National Review* offered a forum for the writings of other conservative intellectuals such as Whittaker Chambers and Richard Weaver, whose writings had greatly inspired Buckley in the first place.[10]

Though contemporary scholars generally credit the *National Review* as the most important of the post–World War II conservative periodicals, it was not the only one. Nor were all influential conservative intellectuals affiliated with it. Irving Kristol's rival magazine, the *Public Interest*, which featured the articles of Daniel Bell, Nathan Glazier, and Kristol's wife, Gertrude Himmelfarb, was launched in 1965.[11] The *Intercollegiate Review*—a scholarly journal that would eventually provide publishing opportunities for conservative academics such as Robert Bork, Russell Kirk, Elizabeth Fox-Genovese, Leo Strauss, and Eric Vogelin—was also launched in 1965.[12]

Corporate executives and conservative intellectuals articulated a critique of modern American society that was born in opposition to New Deal governmental programs. The development of sunbelt conservatism, conversely, was primarily the result of impersonal, structural alterations in American life: massive population growth in the American Southwest and the transformation of the American economy from a producer to a consumer model. These structural alterations fostered a libertarian, anti-government ethos that inspired a cadre of grassroots activists to affiliate themselves with conservative movement politics.

Governmental programs designed to integrate soldiers returning from World War II into the postwar American economy and to fight the Cold War were, ironically, largely responsible for the demographic and economic shifts that would eventually produce this antigovernment ethos. In particular, the low-interest mortgages, educational incentives, and career training programs made available by the GI Bill made social mobility for the first time a legitimate possibility for a generation of white working-class families located in urban centers. Contemporaneously, massive governmental defense spending indirectly led to many of the technological innovations that spurred the conversion of the manufacturing-based American economy into what Hurley calls a "consumer's paradise" full of color television sets, home appliances, and fuel-efficient automobiles (the ubiquity of which would soon be reflected in the pursuit of another enormous governmental project: the Eisenhower interstate system).[13] The biggest regional beneficiary of these economic changes, as well as of the government spending that underwrote those changes, was the American Southwest and especially the "sunbelt" states of California, Arizona, and Texas.

Indeed, with its attenuated taxation policies, its compliant local governments, and its vast tracts of undeveloped land, the American Southwest was an ideal location for both the migration of newly mobile people from more densely populated areas (who could now realize the American dream of home ownership) and for the building of new missile bases, airfields, armaments manufacturing plants, and, eventually, the nation's space industry. The American Southwest became the epicenter of what President Dwight Eisenhower, in his 1961 farewell address to the nation, called the American "military-industrial complex": an integrated network of private industry, governmental contracts, and international Cold War prerogatives and logics.[14]

It is thus ironic that the American Southwest emerged during the 1950s and 1960s as the source of a libertarian, antigovernment ethos that was promoted by a growing network of activists and organizations. This network provided important material and electoral support for like-minded public officials (such as Barry Goldwater and, later, Reagan) even as it sought to transform American conservative politics and the Republican Party in the antigovernment image. Indeed, conservative activists gained logistical control of Young Americans for Freedom, which had begun a decade earlier as a Buckley Jr. enterprise, and used it as a base from which to woo Goldwater and eventually secure his nomination as the 1964 Republican Party presidential candidate.[15]

Finally, and perhaps most prominent, scholars source the emergence of contemporary American conservatism in white reaction to the many rights-based struggles of the postwar era, especially in reaction to the African American civil rights movement. The conventional story, which has been complemented and sometimes corrected by recent scholarship, highlights the self-conscious move by the Republican Party in the late 1960s to cultivate the electoral support of resentful white Southern voters. A segment of these voters had first displayed their willingness to abandon long-standing loyalties to the Democratic Party by voting in droves for Goldwater in the 1964 presidential election. Richard Nixon's 1968 Southern strategy, according to conventional renderings, was the culminating event of this political dance macabre. That strategy was masterminded by Nixon advisor Kevin Phillips (before he became the well-known public intellectual that he is today) and employed South Carolina senator Strom Thurmond as go-between. Nixon assuaged the ongoing fears of Southern white voters with coded bromides about his commitments to limited government and states' rights—commitments that would, he implied, prevent his administration from aggressively enforcing national civil rights laws (especially as they applied to public school desegregation) and also lead him to nominate a host of Southern judges to the federal judiciary.[16]

Although Nixon implied that he would not support the use of governmental power to enforce civil rights law, enforcement of "law and order" was another matter. Inspired by the success of Alabama governor George Wallace's racially coded appeals on behalf of law and order (which was especially important to enforce when Southern blacks resisted racist laws and governmental policies[17]), Nixon bemoaned the presence of street crime in American cities and promised, as in his acceptance of the Republic Party's 1968 presidential nomination, to invigorate the nation's "peace forces." This politics of law and order occupies, according to much scholarship, a crucially important place in the transformation of the South's regional political loyalties away from the Democratic Party and toward the Republican Party.[18]

It was not simply a one-sided Republican recruitment of white Southern loyalties. Indeed, many Southern politicians and other prominent public figures tethered their concerns about the erosion of white supremacy to the core conservative concerns of limited government and conventional social values that were increasingly influencing Republican Party politics. Politically moderate Southern governors, according to Walker, were particularly adept at depicting the configurations of economic and political power that made up the Southern racial caste system (or the Jim Crow system) not as manifestations of white supremacy but rather as the legitimate products of Southern fidelity to the conventional American principles of limited government and states' rights. Kruse, for example, details how Atlanta's economic and political elites presented their efforts at maintaining racially segregated residential patterns as nothing more than forthright defenses of the property rights of white home owners. Sokol treads similar ground, exploring how white moderates attempted to maintain the "Southern way of life" (itself inextricably linked to white supremacy) through principled appeals to property rights, traditional social conventions, and a virulent anticommunism that attributed civil rights protest to supposed communist infiltration. This last appeal, which yoked communist subversion to movements for social justice, was particularly potent in the postwar South.[19]

Not that resistance to civil rights protest through coded appeals to "moderate" tropes of law and order, property rights, limited government, and anticommunism was limited to the Deep South. Instead, this politics was central to the growth of suburban communities in what Lassiter calls the "Sunbelt South": North Carolina, Virginia, Maryland, and the other states conventionally designated as mid-Atlantic states.[20] Stripped of their racist antecedents and linked to the paternal rights discourse, such arguments enjoyed significant resonance with middle- and upper-middle-class whites in Midwest and Northeastern industrial states.[21]

Scholars thus present modern American conservatism as an amalgam of regional, philosophic, economic, and political imperatives. Significant friction between these imperatives, given their diversity, would be expected. It would seem, for example, difficult to maintain belief in the libertarian, antigovernment ethos with a belief that government should strongly support conventional social and racial values (frequently by the expansion of the American criminal justice system). Indeed, scholars have puzzled over how the apparently discordant origins of contemporary American conservatism were overcome so that by the late 1970s, the conservative movement was enjoying substantial success at the ballot box and in the everyday management and pursuit of public policy. The scholarly answer to this puzzle points in two directions at once: to the emergence of a series of charismatic leaders whose appeals glossed the unruly origins of contemporary conservatism and to the sustained efforts of conservative organizations and think tanks to promote these leaders and thereby entrench the only tenuously coherent conservative political vision in the mainstream of American culture.

Articulating Conservatism

Scholars trace the appearance of a cadre of electable conservative political candidates to the conservative movement's mid-1960s capture of the Republican Party. Formerly the stronghold of moneyed, Eastern industrialists, the Republican Party was, we have seen, the target of a campaign orchestrated by young conservatives affiliated with Young Americans for Freedom. This campaign came to fruition in the party's nomination of the decidedly unelectable Goldwater as its presidential candidate in the 1964 election.[22] The nomination was a disastrous first step; Goldwater was manifestly out of place on the campaign trail and was easily defeated in the general election by President Lyndon Johnson.[23]

Discouraged but not defeated by Goldwater's collapse, conservative activists redoubled their efforts. They focused, in particular, on recruiting candidates who could at once take the harsher edges off conservatism's antigovernment, free market principles and better integrate the discordant elements that constituted the new conservative movement. As it turned out, they did not have to look far. Ronald Reagan, who over the previous decade had made the transition from acting in Hollywood movies to serving as both the host for the weekly *General Electric Theater* and as the primary spokesperson for General Electric itself, revealed himself as a promising political figure. A thirty-minute televised address that Reagan offered on behalf of Goldwater near the end of the presidential election campaign, which has since become known as "The Speech," thrilled conservatives and announced Reagan's arrival on the national political stage.[24] Enthused conservative activists wooed Reagan, eventually convincing him to enter the 1966 California gubernatorial race.[25]

While Reagan won the gubernatorial election and so began his steady political rise, another figure, back from the political dead, emerged to carry forward the conservative message. Richard Nixon, last seen proclaiming his retirement from electoral politics during his infamous "last press conference" following a failed bid to be California's governor in 1962, was quick to read the changing landscape within the Republican Party.[26] He befriended high-ranking party delegates and barnstormed the nation on behalf of conservative Republican congressional candidates in the 1966 election cycle. By the time that Nixon unveiled his Southern strategy, he had made himself into the party's preferred nominee for the 1968 presidential election. Although he was not a figure who was ever trusted by prominent conservatives (Buckley Jr., for example, endured a fraught relationship with Nixon), Nixon's labors on behalf of the Grand Old Party allowed his candidacy for the Republican nomination to withstand a late charge by Reagan himself.[27]

Yet Reagan remained the favorite of conservatives. Even his botched run for the Republican presidential nomination in 1976 did little to harm the esteem in which conservatives held him. Indeed, conservatives had correctly judged Reagan as exactly the sort of candidate that a fractious, multifaceted movement required: a candidate who had the intellectual capacity to synthesize internal tensions and the oratorical skills to present this synthesis to a broad-based electoral coalition. Taking advantage of an economic, cultural, and political environment that was especially challenging for the electoral fortunes of the Democratic Party,[28] Reagan cruised to a landslide victory over the embattled incumbent, Jimmy Carter, in the 1980 presidential election.[29]

It is difficult to overstate Reagan's prominence in contemporary scholarship about modern American conservatism.[30] There is, however, scholarship that portrays the successes of the American conservative movement not simply as the ascent to power of prominent conservatives such as Reagan but also as the product of long-term efforts by conservative activists, organizations, and think tanks to entrench the conservative political vision (and its prominent spokespersons) in American politics and culture.

Entrenching Conservatism

The early 1970s saw the emergence of a variety of prominent conservative "think tanks," including the American Enterprise Institute and the Heritage Foundation, and, in the area of law and courts, the Federalist Society. Rather than facilitate direct access to policymakers and coordinate electoral participation, as was the strategy of more conventional conservative interest groups such as NAM, the Chamber of Commerce, and (later) the Free Congress Foundation, the mission of these newer organizations was to fund the research of conservative scholars. The resulting intellectual product was then employed as a resource for conservative activists and policymakers in their efforts to entrench into mainstream American law and politics conservatism's vision of limited government, on one hand, and governmental support of conventional social values, on the other hand. Another important conservative foundation, the Pacific Legal Foundation, conversely, was designed to initiate, fund, and otherwise support litigation on behalf of conservative causes.[31]

Also in the 1970s, Christian evangelicals across the nation, and particularly in the South, were shedding their historic reticence of partisan politics. Enraged by a 1978 Internal Revenue Service policy that required Christian private schools to cease all forms of racial discrimination in order to maintain their tax-exempt status, scores of evangelical leaders and parishioners, encouraged by Jerry Falwell (who would himself, with the 1980 founding of the Moral Majority, soon become the nominal leader of conservative evangelical politics), began to politically mobilize.[32] Williams acknowledges the importance of the IRS episode, but locates the roots of evangelical political mobilization in earlier (and sometimes much earlier) campaigns, such as in the antigay rights campaign engaged in by Miami-based gospel singer Anita Bryant in 1977, on one hand, and in Cold War–era campaigns against supposed communist infiltration of American society, on the other hand.[33]

Scholars argue that this evangelical political mobilization introduced yet another unruly element into conservative movement politics. Fidelity to Christian values was neither a new nor uncontroversial presence in modern conservative politics. Indeed, Buckley Jr.'s *God and Man at Yale*, itself a founding document of contemporary conservatism, simultaneously made a strong case for the elevation of religion in the American public sphere and enraged the movement's more libertarian supporters—some of whom veered, like Ayn Rand, toward atheism and the vast majority of whom, even if personally religious themselves, tended to look askance at any sort of governmental contact with organized religion. Yet the frequently singular focus of evangelicals on ensuring governmental support (not just neutrality) for their positions on "private" sphere matters—including reproductive health policy, gay rights, and governmental funding for religious schools—aggravated the existing tensions between limited and big government that are inherent in modern American conservatism.[34]

All told, recent scholarship on modern American conservatism tells a coherent story: about conservatism's varied origins, about the fractious nature of its members and the occasionally conflicting political visions that those members articulate, and about the concerted efforts of its most talented activists and practitioners to gloss these differences and present the movement and its political vision as unified and stable. Accordingly, the scholarship suggests that the success of the conservative movement relies on its ability to cultivate and promote charismatic leaders—like William F. Buckley, Jr., Ronald Reagan and, surprisingly (given his reputation for public reticence), Clarence Thomas—who possess the unique ability to gild the fractious tendencies that animate it.

The scholarship, as far as it goes, is compelling. Its illumination of the historical and structural development of modern conservatism is indeed persuasive, but this focus begs multiple questions. Most pressing is, What makes conservatism's leaders so charismatic? What makes the Buckleys, Reagans, and Thomases of the movement so appealing to movement activists? How do they manage to convince American conservatives of varying orientations that they have common beliefs and goals when, as the scholarship makes clear, they frequently do not? The answer, we will see, is that they speak a shared language—one full of "metaphors . . . deep visions, and metaphysical pathos."[35] It is a discourse that is catalytic and unifying precisely because it is dressed in America's most "democratic and idealistic clothes," precisely because it is a language of rights.

"The law is real," wrote Stuart Scheingold, "but it is also a figment of our imaginations."[36] This basic insight provoked a generation of "rights mobilization" scholarship, including my own previous work.[37] It is a scholarship that follows Scheingold's lead by insisting that law and rights constitute the "symbolic life" of American politics; they "condition perceptions, establish role expectations, provide standards of legitimacy, and account for the institutional patterns of American politics."[38]

Indeed, the elemental American "myth of rights" voices a "call" to which most Americans are responsive; the myth expresses a widespread faith "in the political efficacy and ethical sufficiency of law as a principle of government."[39] The myth's supposition that the "realization of rights is tantamount to meaningful change" is only partially accurate; but widespread belief in the myth of rights enables a whole range of political activities anyway.[40] This is because the myth works ideologically, making it "possible to capitalize on the perceptions of entitlement associated with rights to initiate and to nurture political mobilization."[41] Thus does the myth of rights generate a "politics of rights."

Scheingold and his immediate successors were mostly interested in politics of rights that were pursued by progressive left social movements of the 1970s and 1980s.[42] More recent rights mobilization scholarship, however, takes seriously how the cultural salience of rights makes them an animating impulse for most Americans and most causes, including those associated with modern American conservatism.[43] Moreover, critical legal scholars have interrogated the intersections between the conscious values of the American dream life—those expressed, for example, in the myth of rights and articulated in the founding documents of the American republic—and the fantasies that lie barely articulate in the national imagination.[44]

This book mines these intellectual veins. Tethering conservative reverence for rights to obsession with biological and historical fathers, conservatives claim that their distinctive paternal rights discourse has alchemical properties, working as seedbed for the development of the autonomous, self-governing American citizen. This discourse gained currency in Cold War–era America, at the dawning of modern American conservatism. But it was not until the 1970s—in response, first, to anxieties over the subversive effects of missing fathers on American law and order and, later, to anxieties over the proliferation of narcissistic selves—that modern conservatism's discursive catalyst, its politics of rights, emerged in full bloom.

Rights, Fathers, Subversion, and Narcissism

Widely shared Cold War desires influenced civil rights practice in the post–World War II United States. Indeed, anxieties over international perceptions of the conduct of American democracy, especially race relations, were prominent in the calculations of American diplomats and elected officials.[45] These officials feared that the systematic exclusion of racial minorities from the benefits of American democracy undermined the nation's ability to effectively combat communist appeals. But the relationship between the Cold War and civil rights was ambivalent. In addition to pressuring national officials to occasionally support civil rights activism, Cold War anxieties also made Americans sensitive to the possibility of communist aggression at home. These anxieties in turn catalyzed efforts to identify domestic subversives, with civil rights activists themselves emerging as likely suspects.[46] Frequently accused of disorderly, criminal behavior that undermined the American nation, civil rights activists were placed in the crosshairs of a potent countersubversive politics that fused a commitment to law and order with anticommunism.

Murakawa's perceptive study, for example, reveals that both Northern and Southern public officials frequently defended Jim Crow segregation policies following World War II by claiming that racial integration would "increase black-on-white crime."[47] Linking race reform to criminal activity, public officials throughout the 1950s fretted that racial integration and other shows of respect for black civil rights would unleash an elemental American nightmare: black domination—social, political, and sexual—of whites as punishment for the sins of slavery.[48] Segregation was thus widely understood as necessary in order to forestall the collapse of law and order—to stave off the racial reckoning—that would be the inevitable by-product of integration.[49] Accordingly, electoral appeals to the specters of disorder made in the 1960s by such prominent figures as Goldwater, Nixon, Reagan, and Wallace relied on an already well-established linkage between black civil rights protest and criminal disorder.[50]

Black disorder was, moreover, frequently believed to be the outcome of the sinister influence of domestic and international communists.[51] The view that blacks and reds were conspiring to undermine American law and order was not limited, as one might expect, to the white South. In fact, Southern public officials were successful in exporting nationwide this defense of race hierarchy. Benefiting "from a cold war political climate in which almost any manner of social nonconformity could be construed as a threat to fundamental American values," Southern segregationists made claims about the subversive nature of civil rights protests that seemed plausible to a wide swath of increasingly anxious Americans.[52] Joining racist fantasy of black vengeance to fear of communist subversion, the "Southern red scare"[53] found a frequently receptive nationwide audience.

But reactionary opinion ultimately sourced black disorder and the misuse of rights not in communist doctrine but in a missing paternal authority that made blacks susceptible to communist influence. Consider, for example, the infamous 1965 Department of Labor report entitled *The Negro Family* (better known as the Moynihan Report after its author, Daniel Patrick Moynihan). A comprehensive analysis of black inequality that Buckley Jr. (among many other prominent conservatives) found to be illuminating[54], Moynihan sourced racial inequality in the "tangle of pathology" that suffused black life and originated in the disordered black family. Following the arguments of sociologist E. Franklin Frazier, Moynihan noted that by 1965, the black family had been devastated by the brutalities of slavery, white racism, and lack of economic opportunity. Such structural forces produced comparatively high rates of separation, abandonment, illegitimate births, and welfare dependency; they emasculated the black family, removing paternal influence and authority from black society and generating instead a "matriarchal" structure.[55]

The family dysfunction that removed fathers from black society and substituted excessive maternal influence, Moynihan emphasized, doomed black pursuits of equality. The problem was, in part, "semantic." Moynihan here channeled the earlier pronouncements of Buckley and Reagan (pronouncements that Clarence Thomas would later reiterate): whereas equal rights had typically protected equality of opportunity for advancement, blacks now sought equality of results—a goal that denied the longstanding American understanding that inequality based upon achievement was legitimate.

Equality of opportunity now has a different meaning for Negroes than it has for whites. It is not (or at least no longer) a demand for liberty . . . to not be excluded from the competitions of life . . . [but] for . . . a distribution of achievements among Negroes roughly comparable to that among whites.[56]

But black children, though enthralled by these new (vaguely communist) expectations, were deprived of fatherly influence and so were incapable of achieving either equality of results or equality of opportunity, for "negro children without fathers flounder—and fail." They were deprived of the paternal discipline that would allow them to "delay immediate gratification of their desires"—they couldn't learn the self-discipline necessary for economic advancement—and were thus prone to "immature, criminal, and neurotic behavior." Especially criminal behavior—for black men were so disheartened and alienated by their inability to provide for the women and children (by their inability to express the "very essence of the male animal . . . to strut") that they gave in to despair and acted out their rage. Thus, in spite of an admitted lack of reliable evidence, Moynihan averred that "it is probable that at present a majority of the crimes against the person, such as rape, murder, and aggravated assault are committed by Negroes."[57]

"The single most important social fact of the United States today," the disorganized black family undermined black dreams of equality of results, generated immature and unproductive citizens, and menaced the bodies of American citizens (black and white) with violent crime. Social disorder spread like a virus from its source in black familial pathology to the rest of the nation. A call to action was thus necessary, Moynihan concluded, both for bringing blacks "to full and equal sharing in the responsibilities and rewards of citizenship" and for the integrity of American bodies (literally in the case of vulnerable citizens and metaphorically in the case of the American body politic). Indeed, if "the stability and resources of the Negro American family" were not enhanced, "there will be no social peace in the United States for generations."[58]

Black disorder, and the threat that it presented to American law and order writ large, was thus a product of missing paternal authority that deprived black youth of the capacity for self-discipline. Fatherless youth, claimed Moynihan Report–enthusiast Richard Nixon in 1969, "are denied the authority, the discipline, the love that come with having a father in the home."[59] Denied these building blocks of maturity, black youth were especially unprepared to handle the disappointment associated with the fact of unequal results. This immaturity made them, as it did the student protesters whom Ronald Reagan battled when governor of California (see Chapter 4), susceptible to alien, communist control. Encouraged by communist (and other militant) subversives, black youth raged against law and order and the legitimate patterns of privilege that it upheld.

Moynihan's linkage of social disorder to black deficiencies in self-discipline was a specific reaction to the challenges that the many forms of egalitarian activism of the 1960s presented to the American status quo. It was a reaction that was widely shared. For example, George Gilder—a conservative intellectual and occasional presidential speechwriter whose 1981 book, *Wealth and Poverty*, championed "supply-side" economics and who became a trusted, if unofficial, adviser to President Reagan[60]—endorsed

Moynihan's explanation of black disorder, even as he expanded its familial logic to explain social breakdown writ large. Tracing economic inequality to "the breakdown of family responsibilities among fathers" and, so, to the proliferation of female-headed households, Gilder argued that poverty was "governed by the rhythms of tension and release that characterize the sexual experience of young single men." Indeed, prosperous, "civilized" society itself depended on

the submission of the short-term sexuality of young men to the extended maternal horizons of women. This is what happens in monogamous marriage; the man disciplines his sexuality and extends it into the future through the womb of a woman. The woman gives him access to his children . . . a unique link to the future; he gives her faithfulness and a commitment to a lifetime of hard work.

But when a man does not engage in sexual self-discipline, "on the average, his income drops by one-third and he shows a far higher propensity for drink, drugs, and crime." Thus, the intractable problem of inequality was sourced not in the structural prerogatives of capitalism or racism, but instead in the lascivious sexual practices of undisciplined young men. "The problem" with poverty, and the disorder and lawlessness that it spawned in affected communities "is neither race nor matriarchy in any meaningful sense":

It is familial anarchy among the concentrated poor . . . in which flamboyant and impulsive youths rather than responsible men provide the themes of aspiration. The result is that male sexual rhythms tend to prevail, and boys are brought up without authoritative fathers in the home to instill in them the values of responsible paternity: the discipline and love of children and the dependable performance of the provider role.[61]

Gilder, the intellectual guru of Reaganomics, thus emphasized traditional family morality (a morality removed from the explicitly racialized context invoked by Moynihan) rather than governmental action as the engine of economic mobility and social tranquility.

Offering family dysfunction as explanation for structural injustice, Gilder exonerated American racism of its continuing impacts. His analysis also exemplified Berlant's claim that modern American conservatism is defined in large part by its obsession with intimate personal relations. Indeed, the linkage of sexual self-discipline to economic prosperity and sexual promiscuity to poverty and disorder was a widely shared explanation on the Right for the breakdown in American law and order evinced in the 1960s and 1970s. But the tethering of personal virtue to public success is embedded within the American grain; the intimate public sphere that Berlant locates in modern American conservatism also articulates with historic tropes of American citizenship.

Self-discipline of the sort celebrated by Moynihan and Gilder in fact has long been the primary value associated with the representative American citizen-subject.[62] Self-discipline—the capacity to resist leisure and license, to harness one's capabilities, and to achieve worldly success—is the essential marker of autonomous American citizenship. Its possession constitutes the subject as meritorious, as deserving of whatever material and cultural goods that one possesses. The self-disciplined citizen is the virtuous citizen because he or she has earned their way; the person has *made* his or her self.[63] The virtuous American subject understands, as did Reagan, that "there just 'ain't no such thing as free lunch'" and that one's privilege is legitimate only to the extent that it is the product of self-exertion and the discipline that makes such exertion possible.[64] It follows that self-disciplined individuals deserve the blessings—the rights and privileges—of American citizenship, for they have been earned. Yet the converse is also true: if those who practice self-discipline deserve the material and cultural benefits of American citizenship, then so too must those who lack discipline deserve not to possess such benefits.[65]

Accordingly, the understanding that Cold War–era egalitarian protest was a species of social disorder that was borne of a lack of self-discipline resonated with historic practices of American inequality. Moreover, the autonomous, self-disciplined subjectivity is a designation freighted with racial, gender, and class-based significances. Nonwhites, women, gays and lesbians, and poor people have been historically envisioned by America's political and cultural leaders as lacking the sort of self-discipline and mastery that constitute the autonomous American citizen. Existing in an immature state of narcissistic (frequently erotic) freedom, these people refused order, even as they tempted the self-disciplined with dangerous fantasies of license and sexual perversion.[66] Embodiments of moral turpitude, they were figured as constant reminders that self-discipline and control was integral to moral virtue and good citizenship. By negative example, they proved, again in Reagan's words, that "true freedom is the freedom of self-discipline—the freedom to choose within acceptable standards. Take that framework away and you lose freedom."[67]

Indians, blacks, women, gays and lesbians, poor people, and other so-called deviants were thus thought to refuse the discipline necessary for hard work and worldly success. Significantly, this refusal was frequently understood by political and cultural elites (as it was by Moynihan and the conservative thinkers who extolled his report) as both a moral failure and an emblem of personal immaturity. And such immaturity authorized governmental action in multiple domains. On one hand, the disorderly tendencies of the undisciplined threatened the interests and the bodies of virtuous citizens and so were subject to coercive governmental control. On the other hand, their disorder opened a potential site for governmental intervention. With guidance, support, and, above all, a firm hand, the undisciplined might learn self-control and attain maturity, as parental oversight in the form of a "Great Father" could transform unruly children into productive, rights-bearing adults.[68] Accordingly, the forms of control exercised on undisciplined people could be justified as necessary for both the protection of the already virtuous and the possibility that those lacking self-discipline might one day become autonomous—that they might one day become deserving of rights. It follows that the patterns of material inequality that were built on the American mythology of self-discipline, as well as the governmental actions that enforced those patterns, could be understood as legitimate.

Given its supposedly legitimate roots, such inequality was seen as properly recognized and protected in law. And, as Goodrich argues, the modern legal order traditionally has been envisioned in paternal terms, such that illegality is figured as both a product of actual paternal lack and an affront to the symbolic fatherly authority (the law and order) with which the state protects the fruits of mature, disciplined citizenship.

The social image of a divine figure whose paternal authority legitimated all other laws suffuses the Western legal tradition . . . the primacy of the image of the father is significant. . . . Thus, law is the speech of the father or, more technically, speech "in the name of the father." The same image of paternity provides the model for the social family and the domestic family. . . . According[ly], a law is legitimate if it is issued by, traceable to, or promulgated in the name of the father.[69]

Because it is "predicated both internally and externally upon images of social paternity and upon the application of legal rules in the name of the father" law and order thus offers both fatherly protection of privilege that is earned through legitimate means (self-disciplined effort, in the

American context) and stern rebuke of the unruly elements who threaten both that privilege and the authority that recognizes it.[70]

But law and order, and the privilege that it recognized, was widely understood as under attack in the Cold War era. It was perhaps unsurprising that such patricidal attacks would come from those who had been traditionally portrayed as deficient in self-discipline, or, as Moynihan and Gilder argued, those who were the products of a fractured family structure. What was seen as alarming, however, was that attacks on law and order were being engineered by an increasing number of traditionally advantaged white citizens. And while white liberal elites could be understood as having been duped by communist propaganda into supporting subversive attacks on American law and order, the behavior of increasing numbers of affluent college students was perplexing.

Indeed, the protests emanating from college campuses, including from some of the nation's most prestigious academic centers, were deeply troubling. Reagan voiced this anxiety frequently, such as when he asked an audience in the late 1960s: "How could this [protest be happening] on the campus[es] of . . . great Universit[ies]?"[71] Student protesters insisted that the denial of equal results, not simply the denial of equal opportunities, was a violation of right. It seemingly didn't matter to students that the privilege that they questioned (which was, in many cases, paying for their own college attendance) had been seemingly earned through the ascetic, disciplined self-exertion of virtuous Americans; protesters mocked the ideals of hard work and self-discipline.[72] In so doing, they denied the "right of man to achieve above the capacity of his fellows," condemning the American nation for the very qualities for which it had traditionally been celebrated: that in America "to a degree unequalled any place in the world, we unleashed the individual genius of man, recognized his inherent dignity, and rewarded him commensurate with his ability and achievement."[73] Student protesters thus mocked the characteristics that were understood to animate and distinguish autonomous American citizens; in so doing they dismissed the cultural markers according to which American privilege was legitimized.[74]

Reagan, as Chapter 4 will make clear, interpreted student protest along familiar lines: the protesters had themselves suffered from emasculated, if not entirely absent, paternal authority, and so they had not gained the character qualities necessary for autonomous, rights-based American citizenship. There was, though, a complementary explanation for their subversive behavior, particularly when it continued well into adulthood. Although it never held great appeal for Reagan, by the 1970s conservative and other right-leaning commentators had begun to argue that the deviant selves who protested in America's streets and campuses in the 1960's were, by the 1970s, stuck in the trappings of a vaguely defined but paralyzing narcissism. According to this perspective, writes the historian Natasha Zaretsky, "the 1970's were essentially shaped by political retreat, a turn to personal preoccupations, and narcissistic self-indulgence."[75] Fathers and rights—or, rather, missing fathers and the misuse of rights—were, as usual, at the heart of the matter.

Indeed, conservatives sourced the narcissistic personality in changing family dynamics, especially in declining paternal authority and an attendant, overwrought maternal oversight that was alleged to deprive children of the stern influence that they needed to become disciplined, mature selves. Once they were in the grip of narcissism, the road to political estrangement proceeded in multiple stages. First, narcissism encouraged its practitioners to express immature political demands and engage in unreasonable, often criminal behavior, such as was seen in the "filthy speech" movement and in the other supposed depravities that took place on the campus of the University of California-Berkeley in the late 1960s and early 1970s and bedeviled Governor Reagan.[76] Then, once those afflicted with the condition realized the impracticality of their politics, their narcissism, ironically, encouraged public disengagement and eventual political estrangement.

This narcissism explanation, most notably associated with disaffected liberal Christopher Lasch,[77] had roots in earlier condemnations of the rights movements of the 1960s, whose challenges to America's reigning configurations of power were, we have seen, accosted as immature, undisciplined, and criminal affronts to law and order. The deviance of the "new" political left was most in evidence, according to critics, in the way that activists perverted the conventional meaning of rights themselves.[78] Yoking rights to their own immature and unrealistic demands, activists were said to employ rights as vehicles for pursuing their narcissistic desires. It was a revaluation, conservative critics believed, that threatened the foundations of American democracy itself.

Indeed, conservative panic over the forms of national subversion accomplished by narcissistic selves reached an ambivalent apogee in contrasting visions of law and rights. On one hand, poorly reared, immature citizens had a corrosive, misunderstood relationship with rights. Instead of seeing them as bulwarks against overreaching governmental authority that guaranteed that self-disciplined citizens could, as in Reagan's formulation, "fly as high and as far as [their] own talent[s] and energ[ies] would take [them]," narcissistic selves viewed rights in a doubly subversive way: as both entitlements to a society based on the perfect equality of outcomes and as tools of disorder should such a society not be quickly forthcoming.[79] On the other hand, such an inversion led conservatives to view themselves as the defenders of rights conventionally understood. It set, according to Buckley Jr., the agenda for modern American conservatism:

> Order has been challenged, and the conservatives have always believed in the blessings of order. . . . So the conservatives find themselves defending the rights of the authorities . . . over against the mobcratic demands of [those] who wish to leapfrog the authorities so as to have their way, instantly.[80]

Consider, for example, Irving Kristol's "Republican Virtue versus Servile Institutions," a 1974 essay that originally appeared in the *Alternative* (which was renamed the *American Spectator* in 1975).[81] The essay reflected on the nature of student unrest at America's most prominent universities. By the 1970s, Kristol, as did other prominent conservatives, saw that unrest as both a precursor and an icon of all that troubled the American nation. Yet it was a 1968 essay that appeared in the *New York Times Magazine* that provided the backdrop for Kristol's later essay.[82] In this earlier essay, he diagnosed the "New Politics" that suffused student radicalism and black militancy as a symptom of the increasingly poor job that the nation's "nonpolitical" institutions—family, church, and school—were doing instilling the traditional American moral order of self and social discipline. Significant portions of the nation's youth, argued Kristol, had been taught to relentlessly critique the organization of those nonpolitical institutions, seeing them as "mere incarnations of power and prejudice." "Thoroughly instructed in their rights as Americans but hardly at all in their obligations as Americans," the nation's youth were inadvertently deprived of "any sense of personal moral purpose." Accordingly, their New Politics amounted to little more than a "wild explosion of moral outrage" over the failure of governmental institutions to compensate for the failures of family, church, and school to properly rear them. Even worse, the failures of America's domestic institutions threatened the nation itself.[83]

The American political tradition explicitly leaves the governance of moral life to our nonpolitical institutions—to the family, the churches, the schools. Ours is a limited government of a free society, and it is rooted in the assumption that it is the task of government to reconcile conflicting interests in a reasonable way. But this assumption, in turn, is only valid if our nongovernmental institutions see to it that the American people, no matter how diverse, all do behave in a reasonable way—i.e., a self-disciplined way. And this kind of discipline is learned in the home, in church, in school.[84]

Fueled by the "general breakdown of individual and social discipline" that fostered a narcissistic rights consciousness, the New Politics struck at the vitals of the American nation; it constituted the most serious threat to America "since the Civil War."

By 1974 Kristol had turned his critique into an attack on all American institutions (including governmental institutions) for the ways in which their "servility," their unwillingness to instill the building blocks of traditional moral order, had eroded the American nation's historical commitment to "republican virtue." At the root of the problem, Kristol thought, was a paradox: although Americans were, in a prolonged period of postwar prosperity, much more capable of "satisfying material grievances" than ever before, such capacity did "not seem to calm people or make them more reasonable." Instead, this affluence easily translated into a narcissistic demand for unlimited fulfillment and thus represented a "grave threat to the spirit of our institutions." For the failure of American institutions to demand that citizens recognize limits and, so, practice the "self-government" that constituted "republican virtue" had created a situation of "perpetual crisis." The narcissistic expectation that institutions satisfy every material demand at once discouraged self-discipline and eroded respect for traditional institutions:

People do not respect institutions which are servile; people only respect a society which makes demands on them, which insists that they become better than they are. Without such a moral conception of the self, without a vivid idea as to the kind of person a citizen is supposed to become, there can be no self-government.[85]

The cultural cancer that originated in the weakness of America's domestic institutions and in the concomitant, narcissistic resignification of rights metastasized; it produced the immature, undisciplined, and, eventually, estranged citizens whose subversive uses of rights dishonored the "faith of our fathers" and eroded the possibility of mature democratic governance.[86]

Thus did conservative intellectuals habitually argue that the turbulence of American society was sourced in the failures of America's private sphere—especially in changing family dynamics. These failures prompted the serial abuses of rights that undermined the American nation. Prominent conservatives tethered rights to the allegedly subversive and narcissistic character of post–civil rights American society; in so doing, rights themselves, as well as the intimate public sphere in which rights-bearing citizens were raised, became essential sites of political contest.

Indeed, American conservatives increasingly associated fortification of the traditional meaning of rights—of their paternal character, I mean—with the defense of "what is best in America." The alternative, averred Buckley Jr., was to give in to the subversive, immature rights-claims of the nation's undisciplined "enem[ies]."[87] American society, declaimed Ronald Reagan, "must be defended" from the rights claims of "little monsters," "wild animals," and "welfare queens."[88] Their "redefinition[s] . . . of freedom and rights," their "legal claim[s] to receive and demand something," were, Clarence Thomas summarized, "attack[s] . . . [on] individual rights" that defiled the "qualities of self-discipline [and] self-respect" that "informed the world of our founders."[89]

Conclusion

Scholars have beyond question established that modern American conservatism is, as are all social movements, an amalgam of competing principles, interests, and governing visions.[90] The movement is, they argue, more of a front than it is an organic whole; it performs unity and coherence where otherwise there would be dysfunction. My analysis in this chapter argues that in spite of these ongoing differences, modern American conservatives do have something in common in which they believe. Indeed, the movement's compulsive paternal rights discourse is both its unifying principle and the primary means by which it covers over its scar tissue.

Paternal rights discourse, we have seen, is not only balm for modern American conservatism's internal wounds. It works also as a conceptual resource with which to diagnose, and potentially cure, the supposed ills of American society. As such, their paternal rights discourse gives American conservatives both something and someone to believe in.

Indeed, Chapters 3, 4, and 5 explore modern American conservatism's devotion to the nation's real and spectral fathers. Conservatives believed that the nation's fathers were in need of defending, for as this chapter has argued, they detected paternal dishonor in the supposedly subversive rights claims of the nation's deviant citizens. William F. Buckley Jr., for example, sought to defend beleaguered paternal authority—to "defend what is best in America"—by creating in fiction an American hero who embraced the long shadow of America's fathers. His hero, Blackford Oakes, would be a "shining example," a "complete American" who would simultaneously redeem the American nation from the narcissism and cynicism of modern times and prepare the way in fiction for the coming "Reagan Revolution" of the 1980's. Chapter 3 explores Buckley's creation.

3

Penetrating the Inner Sanctum:
William F. Buckley Jr., Paternal Desire,
and the Rights of Man

I was born inclined toward the service of my own opinions which, happily, tend to coincide with those of our Founding Fathers.
—William F. Buckley Jr.

William F. Buckley Jr., according to biographer Lee Edwards, "was the maker of the American conservative movement." He was a "master fusionist" who "purged the conservative movement of its extremist elements and united the rest."[1] "Had it not been for Buckley," affirms another of his biographers, "conservatism would not be what it is today."[2] He was "Mr. Right," eulogized *Newsweek*; "our revered founder," concurred the *National Review*.[3] Upon his 2008 death, dispassionate journalists hailed him as the "intellectual father" who "wove the tapestry of what became the new American conservatism."[4] "For more than half a century," summarized *Newsweek*, "William F. Buckley, Jr. largely inspired and held together the conservative movement."[5] Buckley, added Rush Limbaugh, was a "founding father."[6] He was, to President Ronald Reagan, simply "the most influential journalist and intellectual of our era—he changed our country, indeed our century."[7]

It is surprising, then, to learn that the "intellectual godfather" of modern American conservatism was in 1975, at the age of forty-nine, hopelessly bored by American politics.[8] Buckley's boredom emerged in spite of the fact that his twenty years serving as editor-in-chief of the *National Review* had already made him the undisputed intellectual voice of modern American conservatism; he had become the "keeper of the tablets,"[9] in both his and in the general estimation. And so, at first blush, Buckley's apparent mid-1970s disinterest, occurring as it did at a time when one might instead expect his continued ascendance in the political realm, is puzzling.

Yet there were good reasons why Buckley had, momentarily anyway, lost interest in politics. There was, for one, the matter of Watergate and his ambivalence about Richard Milhous Nixon. Always skeptical of the now disgraced ex-president, Buckley had come to an uneasy peace with Nixon in the early 1970s when Nixon appointed him to serve as a delegate to the United Nation's Third Committee (on Human Rights) in 1973. The trauma of his association with Nixon dovetailed with a second source: Buckley's frustration over the general pathos that had come to distinguish the American nation in both politics and culture. Replete with self-denunciation and taking Nixon's own paranoiac, corrupt core as its exemplar, the intellectual tenor of mid-1970s America—found in academic texts, popular press accounts, and Hollywood movies—emphasized the hypocrisy of conventional American ideals such as equality, fairness, and, especially, the individual rights that were the intellectual and emotional keystones of the nation's founding fathers. Employing Nixon as antihero, the intellectual classes articulated the nation's erupting "legitimation crisis"; they pointed to the nation's contemporary history of racism and sexism, its imperialist fantasies in Southeast Asia and Latin America, and its intractable class boundaries and empty consumerism at home and concluded that the bromides of American democracy were little more than cover for a repressed and raging collective id. Buckley recoiled at this intellectual trend, and especially at its intimations that America had no claim of moral superiority over Soviet Russia; he rebelled against the reigning antinationalism that brooked no distinction between the virtuous, rights-infused American creed for which the nation's fathers, its "supermen,"[10] stood and the noxious, poisonous creed of Soviet communism.

But there was, finally, a third, deeper and crystallizing explanation for Buckley's self-imposed alienation from American politics: his long-standing tendency to, and disdain of, the state of boredom. Buckley's memoirs and interviews are scattered with the revelation that boredom was, for him, a constant and "painful" companion. There were, it turned out, many things that Buckley found boring and, so, painful; the long list, indeed, barely commenced with the mid-1970s state of American politics and culture. For example, although he was a lifelong advocate of capitalism, discussions about it were, nevertheless, "boring" to him. Even apart from the conventional themes of American conservative politics, Buckley found himself bored by many things that people of letters such as himself typically find invigorating. He was thus bored by the intellectual pursuits of writing and reading. He was afflicted even by apparent real-life adventure, ennuied in his short stint serving as an undercover CIA agent as a young man. But most of all, William F. Buckley Jr. was bored by foreplay and sex. Capitalism, he opined, was "like sex": boring; and the process of writing was "painful . . . [like] foreplay."[11]

This last antipathy—toward foreplay and sex; or, rather, as we will see, toward sex that was nonprocreative and/or involved feminine pleasure—is critically important. It is, I will argue here, the key to understanding Buckley's midlife self-alienation from, and his subsequent reengagement with, American politics (conservative and otherwise). It is also, and most important for my purposes in this book, at the center of his contemporary and lasting appeal to the American conservative movement itself. Indeed, as we shall see, Buckley sought and found the antidote for his political boredom and pain in the writing of fiction and, especially, in the sexualized escapades of Blackford Oakes, the fictional protagonist and hypermasculine Cold War hero who would first appear in the pages of 1976's *Saving the Queen*. Yet, like Buckley, Oakes did not cotton to contemporary feminist pronouncements that nonprocreative sex should involve feminine pleasure. Blackford Oakes instead became, for his inventor, a needed nationalist spectacle—a figure who offered Buckley, and American readers by extension, an antidote for the boredom and pain of sex and foreplay, on one hand, and for mid-1970s American intellectual cynicism of the values of the American fathers, on the other hand.

A true believer in the American creed of individual rights, Blackford Oakes embodied and updated the values of the nation's founding fathers—freedom, morality, limited government—that, we saw in the previous chapter, so inflamed cynics. Thus did Buckley intend for Oakes to replace Richard Nixon as a new American father. But it was not only Oakes's moral fortitude that qualified him for exalted paternal status: Blackford Oakes also radiated sex appeal. Indeed, like Herman Melville's Billy Budd before him, Oakes was "startlingly handsome"; his sex appeal crossed gender lines to make him both a "man's man and a woman's man." Even his KGB doppelgangers would admit that Oakes was a "handsome fox."[12] Yet unlike Billy Budd, whose innocence attracted recurring acts of sadist desire that forcibly expelled him from the *Rights of Man* and culminated in his metaphorical crucifixion, Blackford Oakes's sex appeal was at once instrumental and redemptive.[13] Channeling the authority of both Buckley's own biological father, on one hand, and the "certitudes" of the nation's founding fathers, on the other hand, Oakes compulsively revealed his manhood.[14] In so doing, he at once redeemed the American nation from Cold War critics and prepared the way for the coming Reagan Revolution in American politics that is the subject of the next chapter.

The Blackford Oakes novels are barely mentioned in standard biographical treatments of William F. Buckley Jr. They merit but two brief mentions in Lee Edwards's 2010 work, while John Judis's acclaimed 1988 work offers three pages on *Saving the Queen*, rehearsing the point that Blackford Oakes was modeled on Buckley himself and three more pages on the literary and aesthetic superiority of *Stained Glass* (the second Oakes novel). Such scant attention from his biographers is surprising, especially given the commercial and artistic success of the Oakes series as a whole and the first two novels in particular; *Stained Glass* won the American Book Award as the Best Suspense Novel of 1978 and *Saving the Queen* spent thirteen weeks on top of the *New York Times* best-seller list.[15]

Certainly Buckley himself thought of the Oakes novels as some of the more important accomplishments of his career. The series was, in the first place, an ongoing concern; Buckley produced ten Blackford Oakes novels between 1976 and 1994, with a final, eleventh tome appearing toward the end of his life (2005's *Last Call for Blackford Oakes*). Buckley affirmed the importance of the novels in his oeuvre, moreover, in countless interviews and even in his own literary memoir—2004's *Miles Gone By*, in which he included a biographical portrait of the fictional Oakes alongside the most important "people . . . [and] institutional presences in my life" (a list that included Whittaker Chambers, the conservative publishing magnate Henry Regnery, the *National Review*, and Buckley's long-running television show *Firing Line*).[16]

The Blackford Oakes novels are thus essential for any appraisal of the political and intellectual legacy of William F. Buckley Jr.—but not simply because of the commercial success that they enjoyed or the cherished place that they held in their creator's heart. Indeed, Buckley's political vision, I argue here, was most on display, and best articulated, in the Oakes novels. Few of Buckley's other writings—voluminous as they were—fixated so obsessively on what he took to be the distinguishing characteristics of the American nation and of its most virtuous and praiseworthy citizens. These characteristics, we shall see, are thoroughly sexualized and gendered: the virtuous American citizen (Oakes) was, in Buckley's prose, a hypermasculine, paternal hero who unambiguously preached and employed the rights of man. Thus was Blackford Oakes an icon, a "shining example," in his creator's words, of autonomous American citizenship; Oakes's paternal rights discourse, over the course of eleven novels, redeems nations and individuals alike.

And, yet, like all fathers, Blackford Oakes was first a son. Let us explore his maturation, first in the imagination of William F. Buckley Jr. and then in the fictional Cold War world that bears the marks of his distinctive, hypermasculine, rights-based nationalism.

"To Defend Free People from Being Enslaved"

William F. Buckley Jr. undertook fiction at the relatively advanced age of fifty, with the first Blackford Oakes novel, *Saving the Queen*, published in 1976, the year of Buckley's fifty-first birthday. Buckley had accepted an invitation from longtime friend and Doubleday Publishing editor in chief, Samuel Vaughn, to try his hand at fiction. Vaughn imagined a novel in the highly urbane style that had become Buckley's trademark. Buckley instead went popular culture, delivering a taut spy thriller that he drafted over the course of six weeks at a rented villa in the Swiss Alps. Vaughn, and most subsequent reviewers, were surprised by Buckley's genre choice. But the benefit of hindsight makes it clear that Buckley was well suited, both emotionally and intellectually, for the nationalist spy genre and, especially, for fictional immersion in a Cold War America that was increasingly defined by national security state prerogatives.

Buckley frequently discussed the conception of the Blackford Oakes novels. The immediate spur was his disgust over Sydney Pollack's 1975 film *Three Days of the Condor*. The movie stars Robert Redford as a CIA researcher who is unwittingly turned into a field agent when his entire office—except him, of course—is murdered. Audiences learn that Redford's character (Joseph Turner, aka "Condor") had stumbled on a clandestine CIA team ("a CIA within the CIA") that meant to initiate a covert invasion of unnamed Middle Eastern nations in order to secure future oil supplies for the United States. The slaughter of Condor's unsuspecting coworkers sets in motion a three-day chain of events that culminates in exposure of the CIA's nefarious plot in the pages of the *New York Times*.[17]

To be sure, the film drew from growing anxieties about actual CIA attempts to destabilize foreign regimes that were perceived as unfriendly to American interests, with the CIA's complicity in the then-recent (1973) coup of Salvador Allende's democratically elected regime in Chile the obvious real-world counterpart.[18] These anxieties were themselves products of a deeper suspicion of, and cynicism about, the nature of the American national security state itself—suspicions born in the Cold War, nuclear era of the early 1950s and accelerated by the conduct of American foreign policy in Southeast Asia and the secretive domestic politics of the Johnson and, especially, Nixon administrations. Hollywood movies in the 1970s, it turned out, offered particularly fertile venues for exploring these anxieties.

Indeed, *Three Days of the Condor* was released during the so-called Silver Age of Hollywood, during which a group of young, visionary directors who were trained in elite film schools—Francis Ford Coppola, Martin Scorcese, Terrence Malick, George Lucas, and Woody Allen, for example—broke the creative and labor stronghold that movie studios had long held on the movie industry. The most important and critically acclaimed Hollywood movies of the 1970s increasingly explored and criticized the seemingly pathological character of American political and social practices and the conventional cultural ideals that animated those practices. There was, suggested Malick's *Badlands* and *Days of Heaven*, a cultural rot at the core of Americana itself—a rot that created both the alienated, murderous figures at the center of Malick's films and the paranoid, conspiratorial figures on view in *Three Days of the Condor*.[19]

Blackford Oakes was an explicit reaction to this intellectual environment of suspicion and cynicism—the most worrying sign of which, for Buckley, was the growing sense that there was little difference between the clandestine operations of the Soviet security state (in the form of the KGB) and the American security state (in the form of the CIA).[20] Buckley worried that this conflation blotted out what he took to be the real and basic distinction between the two: the KGB acted in the name of world domination and repression, while the CIA acted, in sometimes admittedly unsavory ways, in the name of human freedom and individual rights. Reflecting on this theme in a 1989 interview, Buckley explained:

If there is a single lesson to be learned from the novels I've written, it is that there is a world of difference between *their* [the KGB] doing something and *our* [the CIA] doing something because the motives in both cases are entirely different. They want to maintain the slave state, we want to defend free people from being enslaved.[21]

Blackford Oakes, cast by Buckley as a CIA field agent, personified and dramatized the difference. The novels thus affirmed Buckley's conviction that the CIA was an agent of human freedom, liberty, and rights and that the Cold War, which Buckley viewed as the most important phenomenon of the twentieth century, was nothing less than a battle for the world's immortal soul.

Buckley's protagonist, accordingly, was a "shining perfection" who was endowed with the gifts of spontaneity, tact, self-confidence, wit, "easy intelligence," and belief that "this country [the United States] [was] the finest bloom of nationhood in all recorded time, worth the risk, which he so often took, of life and limb."[22] He was, recognized Buckley's fictional John F. Kennedy, "an interesting guy, cool, self-assured."[23] And all of these distinctively American traits appeared, crucially, in an irresistible, "startlingly handsome" body that was itself modeled on a most unlikely candidate, given Buckley's proclivities. Indeed, Blackford Oakes's real-world counterpart was that Hollywood icon whose screen roles of the 1970's—in *Jeremiah Johnson, The Way We Were, The Candidate, The Great Gatsby, The Sting,* and *All the President's Men*—gave voice in myriad ways to the American cynicism that Buckley found so offensive and whose own role in *Three Days of the Condor* served as Buckley's creative spur. "Oakes," Buckley told an interviewer in 1985, "is completely American . . . a Robert Redford." In fiction, Buckley subverted and transfigured Redford, turning him into a champion of the conventional American values that the actor's screen roles and later political activism had disparaged. This resignification was not painless; the fictional Redford would become the complete American his creator intended ("Blackford Oakes") only after suffering sadistic, Old World sexual humiliation and torture. The suffering of Billy Budd, Oakes's literary forerunner, transmogrified him into a Christ figure; Redford/Oakes's suffering transformed him into something else entirely: a "disgustingly handsome" CIA field agent—a paternal hero of the American security state who, Oakes assured his long-time paramour, Sally, was so "good-looking [that] people don't mind being killed by you."[24]

"`Courtesy of Great Britain, Sir'"

Blackford Oakes's good looks may have been inspired by those of Robert Redford. But his soul more closely resembled a different political icon who also had roots in Hollywood—a figure with whom Buckley was far more ideologically congenial. For Oakes, as did Buckley's close friend and political hero Ronald Reagan (the subject of Chapter 4), "felt and expressed the buoyancy of the American Republic."[25] Redford in body and Reagan in soul, Blackford Oakes was an index of conventional American masculinity. But his high distinction was only partially natural; like all American heroes, Oakes ascended to national virtue only after immersion in a natural and psychological wilderness and integration of the wilderness's distinctive techniques of self. In so doing, Oakes at once overcame the wilderness's extreme hardships—hardships both nationalist and sexually sadist in character—and became a new American man.[26]

The origin story of Blackford Oakes is contained in *Saving the Queen*, his first appearance. He is the son of a distant, unreliable father who is a test pilot and jet salesman and of a haughty mother who remarries a British aristocrat and leaves an adolescent Blackford in the United States as she enjoys her life of luxury abroad. She calls for her son, however, when he is fifteen years old. Blackford is to relocate to Britain, where he will attend Greyburn College, a famous preparatory school to which his new stepfather has secured him admission. At Greyburn, the young Oakes will be under the authority of the school's headmaster, Dr. Chase. As in the depictions of both Blackford's later time as an undergraduate student at Yale University and a new field agent in the CIA, Buckley called on his own life experiences as source material—for he had been sent, with two of his sisters, to attend a British preparatory school at the age of thirteen by his father.

Buckley's late-life account of his adolescent removal from the family compound in Sharon, Connecticut, is uncharacteristically heart-rending. According to that account, Buckley's father (William F. Buckley Sr.), who was traveling in Europe, sent the "dreadful news" home in a summer letter that William and two of his sisters (Jane and Trish) were to attend St. John's, Beaumont, preparatory school beginning that fall (1938). The paternal edict was "horrifying"; it "fractured the arcadian spirit of our summer." Life at "Great Elm" was, according to Buckley, "healthy and happy."[27] And although their parents (especially "Father") were frequently "absent" from home, the children had always looked forward to their father's letters—to his "directives touching on this or that subject, or references to a book Father had just read that we should know about, or read ourselves." Buckley writes that Father explained their coming enrollment at St. John's by noting that the younger Buckley children (William had nine siblings) lacked the educational refinement of their older siblings; indeed, Father complained that "'five years [had] gone by since he understood a 'single word' . . . uttered by any one of his children.'"[28]

What was the source of Buckley's dread? He was, in short, terrified of being caned. His older brother Jim had suffered such corporal punishment ("not once but t-w-i-c-e") during his time at Reading Preparatory School in Reading, England. Jim had been "called into the headmaster's study and told to bend over." And while Jim had been "swiped" only three times total (once during the first punishment, twice during the second punishment) and appeared to suffer no long-term emotional damage as a result of the canings, he was "for at least a year after the event regarded by his brothers and sisters as a mutilated object." Jim had on him, according to the estimation of his siblings, "the mark of Cain." The event, though Jim moved on from it easily, "disfigured" Buckley's impression of English schooling and filled him with anxiety over his coming time at St. John's.[29]

There are parallels and discontinuities in Buckley's depictions of how he and Oakes came to English boarding school. Oakes, for example, is summoned to the experience by his expatriate mother; Buckley, conversely, is at pains to explain to readers that his own mother (whom he eulogized as full of "warmth and diffidence and humor and faith") would never have subjected her children to such trauma. Oakes's father, like Buckley's own, was mostly absent from his son's life; but whereas Oakes lacks paternal influence altogether, Buckley's father, even though frequently absent physically, inundated his children with written "directives" from afar and so "was the unchallenged source of authority at home."[30] "No vertebrate," insisted Buckley, "had ever been known to defy . . . my father's orders."[31] And so there is another contrast between Oakes and his creator: whereas Oakes betrays no resentment of his father's neglectful parenting (as an adult, he even looks forward to spending time flying jets with him), Buckley's depictions of Father are ambivalent.

To be sure, Buckley lauds Father as a man of great achievement: a self-made Texan who practiced law in Mexico as a young man, gained the trust of American officials as a quasi-diplomat, "materially aided" the Mexican counterrevolution following the overthrow of Porfirio Díaz (whom Buckley regards, unpersuasively, as "benevolent"), and eventually accumulated great wealth as an oil speculator in Latin America. Buckley Jr. notes that Father was known outside the home for his "intelligence . . . wit . . . largeheartedness, and—always—the high principle, which brought him a singular eminence in the community." At home, "we only knew that the world revolved about him."[32] And yet the most notable attribute about Father's contribution to the Buckley household was his absence: "My father was missing from my own home four or five days a week."[33] Frequently traveling for both business and pleasure, Father's "unchallenged" authority at Great Elm was towering but spectral. But curiously, and against the available evidence, Buckley claims that Father was "there to fill [whatever] need" his children might have; "he would, by a word, bring us gently to earth."[34]

Absent and present at once, Father's authority (and Father himself) is in his son's prose, and in spite of the son's apparent intentions, the object of resentment. Implying that many of Father's travels that removed him from his children's lives were of a decidedly pleasurable bent, Buckley Jr. noted acidly that "my father was a retiring man who, however, saw no reason why his children needed to be retiring." Unlike Oakes, Buckley Jr. experienced the disembodied influence of an absent patriarch. While traveling the world, Father instituted and oversaw an intense educational regime that included tutoring in music, Latin, mathematics, and manners that otherwise besotted the "unmitigated pleasure" of living an aristocratic New England life during the throes of the Great Depression.[35] Later in life Buckley Jr. would take great pleasure in the piano, even occasionally playing classical music on stage with renowned symphonic musicians. He credits Father's unforgiving dictates for, among other things, instilling in him the understanding that "music is very serious business." But he acknowledges his lifelong ambivalence about Father—ambivalence that was never more pronounced than when confronted with Father's directive that his namesake attend an English boarding school that conjured Buckley Jr.'s deepest fear of having to "bend over" and experience the same sexualized trauma as had his brother Jim. "There were moments," equivocated Buckley Jr., "when we Hated Father, who was the most admirable man I ever knew."[36]

But Buckley had no such hesitation about embracing Father's political vision. No matter that this political vision was, like Father's parenting legacy, ambivalent; William F. Buckley Jr.'s full-throated embrace of it set the stage for his own articulation of the ambivalent, paternal rights discourse that is the hallmark of modern American conservatism. "My father's allegiances," wrote Buckley, "were in conflict":

On one hand, he himself had once been a revolutionary, or rather a counterrevolutionary, who, as a young man, undertook nothing less than the replacement of the order of things in all Mexico. On the other hand, he was the conservative who believed in law and order.[37]

At once defiant of and submissive to authority, Father's ambivalent politics were shared by his son, who, as we have seen, linked legitimate defiance to the "timeless" desires of the American fathers. Tethering his individual principles to the biological and metaphorical sanction of the fathers, Buckley Jr. believed himself "born inclined toward the service of my own opinions which, happily, tend to coincide with those of our Founding Fathers."[38]

Here, then, is the final, determinative contrast between Oakes and Buckley Jr. on the eve of their arrival in the Old World. Blackford Oakes has grown up without paternal influence or oversight; his characteristically American self-confidence and spunk are unharnessed by paternal discipline and the mature self-governance that it is supposed to produce.[39] Oakes instead exudes New World enthusiasm and egalitarianism. Buckley Jr., conversely, has learned the virtues of submission, without challenge, to the demands of paternal authority. He has "Hated" that authority at times, but he has come to understand it as central to the development of his own successful and full life. Indeed, by submitting to the "unchallenged" authority of both Father and the founding fathers, Buckley Jr. claims that he gained the mature character qualities, as well as the eventual approval, of his namesake. On his deathbed Father "registered in turn, joy, and indignation, and amusement, and sadness, as his wife read aloud to him from the latest issue of [Buckley Jr.'s magazine, the *National Review*]."[40] The adolescent Oakes lacks the mature self-discipline of his creator. Oakes will, as did Buckley Jr., eventually submit to paternal authority, and his submission will, after many years, act as the catalyst for his perfection as a mature, autonomous Cold War hero. But unlike Buckley Jr., the adolescent, rebellious Oakes is an "American brat," and so he experiences a paternal wrath unbound by respect for his burgeoning rights of man.

And so although both Buckley Jr. and Oakes arrived in England just prior to Germany's invasion in World War II, the author depicted his hero's experiences in English boarding school in a far different manner from how he depicted his own experiences. Both are terribly homesick on their arrival in the Old World, but Buckley writes that to his great surprise, he quickly took to the formality and order of St. John's and thrived.[41] Blackford Oakes, conversely, chafes, with that characteristically American, though immature, disdain for established authority, against the strictures of Greyburn College. Although his American lineage is held against him by many of his British instructors, at least a couple of them are enchanted by Oakes. "He is the strangest, most independent boy that I have ever known . . . and one of the most attractive," effuses Oakes's geography teacher.[42] But in an atmosphere of wartime anxiety and a felt need for discipline and resolve, Oakes—with his defiant character (he was "happiest when skating breezily along the edges of defiance"[43]) and, especially, the isolationist political orientation that he has learned from his unreliable father—draws the critical attention of both his Latin professor, Mr. Simon, and Greyburn's headmaster, Dr. Chase. Having previously insisted that "by all rights," Simon should allow him to learn Latin in the American, rather than the British, fashion, Oakes eventually goes too far.[44] Seeking to get a rise out of his docile, Old World classmates, Oakes is caught having sketched a vulgar picture of Simon on the instructor's own blackboard one day before Latin class.

Oakes's (and Buckley's) worst fear of attending English boarding school—that he will be forced to bend over and then caned with a birch rod—comes true, as he is sent for his punishment to Greyburn College's "inner sanctum": Dr. Chase's office. At this point, Buckley's prose turns highly graphic. Indeed, Buckley betrays an intimate knowledge of the conventions of corporal punishment in English boarding school, even though he frequently insisted that he had neither personally experienced such punishment nor had known anyone during his time at St. John's who had. Responding to an interviewer who asked if Buckley had himself been beaten as a student, his answer was at once definitive and ambivalent: "I was never caned, but I probably should have been."[45]

The corporal punishment that Oakes suffers at the hands of Dr. Chase is the pivotal moment in Oakes's origin story. Buckley had learned during his time at St. John's that convention held that only the most severe offenses were punished with the birch rod to the buttocks; less severe offenses were punished with strokes of a ferule (a flat wooden instrument) on the open hand. Buckley admitted to having been punished on multiple occasions with such hand strikes; they were "singularly painful experience[s]."[46]

Buckley further informs readers of both *Saving the Queen* and his later memoir (*Miles Gone By*) that the very worst of offenses would receive no more than six strokes of the birch rod on the buttocks. Thus, when a terrified Blackford Oakes is led into Dr. Chase's inner sanctum, forced to disrobe, held down by the wrists over a couch arm (by Anthony Trust—his later fast friend, covert CIA agent, and fellow survivor of Dr. Chase's sadism) with his buttocks exposed at a 45 degree angle, and thrashed not six but nine times by the headmaster, it is clear that Oakes has been the victim of an unusually cruel punishment—a punishment that Buckley inflects at every moment with analogies to sexual assault.[47] A victim of Chase's Old World sadism, Oakes is punished for his brash and defiant nature, for his very Americanness. "Dr. Chase, breathing heavily and drawing back his rod, red with Blackford's blood, said raspily: 'Courtesy of Great Britain, sir.'"[48]

Recall that Blackford Oakes is a "startlingly handsome" youth—a characterization that Buckley borrowed from Herman Melville's description of Billy Budd.[49] Budd, the "handsome sailor," was impressed onto a British naval ship in wartime, where he became victim of the master-at-arms, Claggart. Claggart's repressed desire for the innocent Billy leads eventually to both his and Billy's demise. Billy's departure from his previous post on a merchant marine ship named the *Rights of Man* prefaces his travails: "Goodbye to the Rights of Man!" Billy exclaims on beginning his fateful encounter with Claggart and his conflicted executioner, Captain Vere. Billy Budd responds to Claggart's tyranny with an instinctual, undisciplined violence that both kills Claggart and seals his own fate. Later, like an angel, Billy ascends toward the heavens, killed instantaneously by the hangman's knot.[50] Blackford Oakes, conversely, engages in repression: he immediately flees Greyburn College and, with American entry into World War II, returns to the United States.

Blackford Oakes carries his rage and Old World resentment with him: back to an American preparatory school, on to the front lines of World War II, and then to Yale for a degree in engineering. All the while his distinctively American traits—easy intelligence, wit, bravery, loyalty, self-confidence (which are now complemented by a hard-earned, paternally inflicted self-discipline)—grow apace. Already "startlingly handsome," "Blackie" grows irresistible, both a "man's man and a woman's man," as is attested to frequently by his college girlfriend, Sally. So overwhelming is Blackie's magnetism that even the alluring Sally—whom Buckley depicts as a naive Cold War liberal (she is a staunch supporter of Adlai Stevenson's politics)—falls under his spell. Sally is a brilliant, budding scholar who will go on over the course of the novels to gain her English PhD (specializing in the works of Jane Austen, that iconic chronicler of Old World aristocratic social and gender relations). She will eventually learn of Oakes's role with the CIA, but she disapproves of his politics and his frequent extended absences. And this is to say nothing of Oakes's serial philandering with international spies and diplomats (he even carries on a passionate nine-month affair with Catalina, an aide to Che Guevara, in 1985's *See You Later, Alligator*). Sally thus refuses to marry Oakes until late in the series.[51]

Explaining Blackie's infidelities, Buckley in 1996 invoked market pressures: "in my judgment when you write a novel post 1955 there's got to be a sexual element . . . the people expect it. . . . A book that doesn't have it is a book about which people, not even knowing what it is, tend to feel something's missing."[52] But earlier, in a 1985 interview, Buckley hinted at another reason for Blackie and Sally's failure to marry: "I can't have Oakes fooling around after he marries Sally, can I?"[53] Indeed, the very thought of finally betrothing the couple sent Buckley into authorial crisis. Thus, while Sally agrees to marry Blackie at some later, undetermined date in *See You Later, Alligator* (the sixth novel of the series), Buckley couldn't bring himself to complete the nuptials. So acutely did he feel the crisis (it was a "considerable problem [that] weighed considerably" on his mind[54]) that he, bizarrely, interrupted the chronology of the series as whole after *Alligator*. The events of *Alligator* take place immediately following the Bay of Pigs debacle in 1961; the following Oakes novel, 1986's *High Jinx*, transports the series back to 1954 *precisely* so that Blackie can continue to engage in sexual liaisons with exotic foreign spies without offending his creator's sensibilities about the sanctity of marriage.[55]

Oakes's sex life is clearly a very important (perhaps the most important) element of his identity as a paternally disciplined hero of the American security state. But why couldn't Buckley satisfy the supposed market demand for fornication by depicting Blackie and Sally's dalliances? Sally is, after all, described by Buckley as vivacious and endlessly interesting, both intellectually and physically, to Oakes: Why not engage in the timeless "attraction of opposites" trope and play up the sexual tension between a conservative, conventional American male and his liberal, professorial, feminist paramour?

The problem for Buckley was twofold. On one hand was the matter of his "terribly overdeveloped faculty against boredom."[56] "It's a terrible sin to bore people, and I'm easily bored myself. When I write, I do make an effort to please the reader."[57] Recall that Buckley's state of boredom was brought on easily, even among topics that one would assume would invigorate him: "I don't spend my time talking politics . . . because it's not the kind of thing that interests me that much"; being a CIA agent "bored me"; he wouldn't write for more than two or three hours a day because "the chances are you'll get bored with it"; even capitalism, which Buckley spent his career championing, was "boring."[58] Indeed, Buckley's analogy of the boredom induced by capitalism, in particular, was highly revealing. "It's like sex," he confided to Corey Robin. Presumably, then, Buckley thought that sex scenes between a husband and wife (even a husband and wife as otherwise fascinating as Blackie and Sally) would be seen, as he apparently saw them, as boring. Sex scenes between international spies, however, contained the promise of intrigue and danger. And to be sure, his depictions of sex in *Saving the Queen* between Blackie and Sally (which even a highly sympathetic interviewer called "perfunctory"[59])—in contrast to his salacious descriptions of an orgy with Parisian prostitutes in which Blackie participates and, as we will see, the decisive scene between Oakes and the queen of England—lends credence to such an interpretation.

But something more than aversion to the ennui of boredom is at work here. For, on the other hand, Buckley associated the writing process itself with pain. "I really don't like to write," Buckley confided to an interviewer in 1993; "It's terribly hard work."[60] Not just hard work: "writing is pain . . . it is to me. It should follow that the more painful the exercise is, the more quickly you want to get on with it." The writing process, Buckley opined, was like "execution" because "for years they've been trying to figure out how to execute a person more quickly, so that he feels less protracted pain." Rewriting, however, was something that Buckley "genuinely, genuinely enjoy[ed]." The "satisfaction" of writing, Buckley explained, was in "*having* written," not writing itself. "But that satisfaction is long after the *foreplay*." [61] To complete the analogy, writing is foreplay—it is painful; rewriting is penetration—it is highly enjoyable; having written is postcoital bliss—it is satisfying.

Why, then, was it crucial for Buckley to endow Oakes with a voracious sexual appetite that could not be adequately satisfied by Sally (or by any other monogamous partner, for that matter)? On one hand, Buckley was bored by conventional sexuality between husband and wife; it lacked the intrigue of sex between spies. It is perhaps not coincidental that Buckley himself married his lifelong spouse, Patricia, at the age of twenty-five years old and, by his own account, never took another sexual partner. Not considering himself a particularly adventurous person, Buckley perhaps imagined that the sort of adventure for which he intended Oakes required an all-consuming sex life that his creator did not possess.

But, on the other hand, sex between Blackie and Sally was, given Sally's characterization as a liberal feminist, unlikely to be particularly conventional after all. And this was exactly the problem. Buckley Jr. was deeply committed on moral, religious, and political grounds to the yoking of female sexuality to procreative purpose. He recoiled at injunctions offered by contemporary feminists, such as Gloria Steinem, that sex must be separated from conception and that, concomitantly, human sexuality might be about "mutuality" rather than "dominance and submission."[62] Sally would, in other words, likely join American feminists (whose numbers were burgeoning in the mid-1970s) in refusing the very perspective on female sexuality (women should have sex only to procreate) that her creator took as sacrosanct. Buckley Jr. had himself written a series of hyperventilating articles in the *National Review* on the subject, such as his 1968 account of a college student who lived with her (draft-evading) boyfriend off-campus in contravention of Barnard College rules. Decrying the "gluttonous" appetite for sex of a "pathetic little girl," Buckley Jr. raged against the "concubine": "There isn't anyone around who seems prepared to say to [this woman]: Look, it is wrong to do what you have done. Wrong because sexual promiscuity is an assault on an institution that is central to the survival of the hardiest Western ideal: the family."[63]

By 1997, Buckley had linked the exercise of such "unguarded sexual promiscuity" to its "fruit": "the besetting problem of illegitimacy . . . in which so many other concerns are subsumed." The problem of fatherlessness, according to Buckley, offered to American conservatism exactly the sort of "harnessing bias" that it had lost with the end of the Cold War and against which it could define itself as a meaningful political movement.[64] Buckley's concern with missing American fathers wasn't new; he had approved of the Moynihan Report's withering attack on the fatherless black family (if not of its solution of greater governmental support) in 1967 and throughout his career emphasized the pivotal role fathers played in the development of mature democratic citizens.[65] The problem, for Buckley, was not so much undisciplined male sexuality (which, he agreed with fellow conservative intellectual George Gilder, was the natural, if unfortunate, result of "male sexual rhythms"[66]) as it was the fidelity of unmarried women to the "Playboy philosophy" of having sex with unmarried men in the name of pleasure. When such encounters inevitably led to women being put "in the family way" by men who had no intention of being fathers, the result was children who experienced an elevated risk of ending up "in prison, on welfare, illiterate, and on drugs."[67]

In his portrayal of Oakes, however, Buckley was forced to compromise. Given his already cited concerns about the "market pressures" for sex, he couldn't very well portray Blackie as a dashing American sex symbol if his primary adult relationship was a celibate one. Matters were further complicated because Sally, given her characterization as a liberal feminist, was unlikely to accept the conventional, patriarchal tethering of her sexuality to the act of childbirth. She would not, accordingly, be content with simply being the "fuckee"; a liberated woman, Sally would undoubtedly demand satisfaction of her own during sex.[68] Sally would expect considerable foreplay from any partner (including Blackie), but given Buckley's phobias about female sexuality, this was more than he could depict in fiction. If, for Buckley, foreplay was like writing ("hard work" and "painful"), then writing about foreplay was intolerable.

Accordingly, fictional depictions of sexuality in which feminine pleasure were central aspects did not appeal to Buckley. It is thus on point that in none of Oakes's many sexual encounters (over the course of the eleven novels) is he depicted as offering sexual favors to his partners. Oakes is portrayed as an accomplished lover who invariably satisfies his partners, but his encounters consist always of nearly immediate penetration and rapid climax that, implausibly, leave his partners completely satisfied and in blissful states. The proof of Oakes's "distinctive" American masculinity lies not simply in his "startlingly handsome" features and bone-deep belief in the values and purposes of the founding fathers. Buckley's creation proves, again and again, that true American heroes (who "don't curtsy . . . even to the Queen of England"[69]) can bring beautiful women to climax without giving in to the feminist assault on conventional female sexuality. Like Oakes, they need not kneel before their partners and engage in the "hard work" and "pain" of foreplay in order to prove their mettle as lovers.

The point is clear: both his sex appeal and his actual, patriarchal sexual escapades are central elements of Oakes's identity as a heroic American spy. Even before his acceptance into the CIA, Oakes is already distracted, *while having sex with Sally*, by the possibilities: "Would his future duties require him to . . . seduce women regularly?"[70] It is, moreover, not too much to say that sex was one of Buckley's creative spurs (perhaps the primary creative spur) for writing the novels in the first place. Asked in a 1996 interview to name his favorite of the Oakes novels, Buckley made the link: "I think probably *Saving the Queen* is the most fun. Maybe because it's my first, maybe because the idea of seducing the Queen is kind of fun. . . . I guess I'm the proudest of that book."[71] Understand: Buckley's proudest moment as an author of fiction (a career that spanned thirty years and upward of twenty books) occurs when his protagonist sexually penetrates the (married) queen of England. And, indeed, the scene is freighted with meaning. For it is in this moment of conquest that Oakes both regains the rights of man that he had lost in sexualized humiliation in Dr. Chase's Old World inner sanctum and consolidates his identity as a mature American hero. As Buckley reflected in 1978, "There is something wonderfully American . . . about bedding down a British queen: a kind of arrant but loveable presumption."[72] Turning the queen of England into a fuckee, Oakes became a Casanova antidote for America's mid-1970s legitimation crisis.

"'Courtesy of the United States, Ma'am'"

Upon reaching his final semester as a Yale undergraduate, Blackford Oakes finds himself recruited by best friend, Anthony Trust, to a post with the CIA, which is now in full Cold War rivalry with its KGB counterpart. Oakes undergoes several months of covert training and is then assigned to a remarkably high-profile operation meant to discover the source of intelligence leaks to the Soviet Union regarding American progress on the development of the hydrogen bomb. The CIA has traced the leaks to an unlikely source: Windsor Castle and, in particular, the new, young, vivacious queen of England, Caroline. Thus Oakes's assignment is to penetrate the queen's "inner sanctum" to discover if Her Majesty is the communist sympathizer. Oakes discovers, in a predictably intimate way, that the communist mole is not the queen but rather her trusted cousin and British war hero, Peregrine Kirk. Oakes will eventually outwit Kirk, convincing him to commit suicide while piloting a jet fighter at an exhibition rather than expose his beloved cousin to ridicule and accusations of being a fellow traveler or, perhaps worse, a communist dupe.[73]

The plot of *Saving the Queen*, it turns out, is perfunctory Cold War intrigue. More: its jet fighter/suicide conclusion bears a strong resemblance to the conclusion of the movie *The Great Waldo Pepper*.[74] That movie was released to theaters a year before *Saving the Queen* was released to book sellers and starred—who else?—Robert Redford as its leading man. It's not the Cold War plot or its Hollywood ending, then, that deserves our attention. Focus instead on how Oakes goes about penetrating the queen's inner sanctums; his penetrations at once "save" the queen from infamy, release Oakes's repressed rage over Dr. Chase's earlier Old World sadism, and consecrate Oakes as a mature, rights-bearing icon of the American security state.

Blackford Oakes's CIA cover is to pose as an architectural engineer; his cover gains him entrance into London high society and, in short order, an invitation to a dinner party with Her Majesty at Buckingham Palace. At the party, Oakes's winning manner intrigues Queen Caroline; she finds herself immediately "greatly attracted" to him. For his part, Oakes regards Caroline as "a generator of power and sex"—as likely, he thinks, to order him shot as to seduce him.[75] Her Majesty invites Oakes to visit her residence at Windsor Castle at a later date in order to investigate its archives of blueprints of famous English buildings. His superiors are impressed with (even envious of) Oakes's successful entry into English high society. "My God, Oakes," exclaims a senior agent, "your instructions were to penetrate society, maybe the court. Not the Queen."[76]

But Oakes's successful reimmersion in English aristocratic society (this is his first time returning to England since Chase's thrashing of him) conjures acute psychological distress; his repressed Old World resentment returns unbound. Anthony Trust, who knows the secret source of Oakes's neurosis and has feared that it might surface,[77] attempts evasive action even before the dinner party: he arranges a date for Oakes with some of his favorite Parisian prostitutes, at which readers learn both of Oakes's massive "proportions" and of his distaste for anything resembling foreplay (in this case, a discussion of contemporary French politics with the headmistress).[78] Although Oakes enjoys his time in Paris, it does little to assuage his growing anxieties that his appearance in English high society will lead to the exposition of his humiliating past; he fears a repeat of the trauma that he has already experienced in the inner sanctums of Old World England.

And, indeed, his past is exposed on the first night of his visit to Windsor Castle by none other than Peregrine Kirk—the queen's beloved cousin, the Soviet mole, and, it turns out, a prefect at Greyburn College during Oakes's time there. "Our young American friend could not stand the rigors of a public school," Kirk explains to the other dinner guests. "He ran away in protest against a beating by Dr. Chase." Caroline asks Oakes if this is true; "Blackford . . . knew that a great deal would depend on his answer." Oakes adroitly deflects Kirk's accusation, insinuating that there was a great deal more to the story than Kirk knew, and the conversation moves elsewhere. Oakes's response is "greatly admired" by the queen, and the potential crisis is averted.[79]

But why does "a great deal depend on [Oakes's] answer"? Why would knowledge of Oakes's previous history in England imperil his mission on behalf of American national security? The answer lies in Oakes's fraught emotional state. Already edgy as a result of his return to England, Kirk's public exposition causes in Oakes, despite his outward calm, "a return of the rage he had never excreted. . . . Black's emotional resentment was bright again." Oakes had feared this moment:

It was less than the obsession it used to be, but Blackford knew that someday he would need to expunge it from his emotional system, though he could not guess how, or even to let his mind run over hypothetical means of taking condign, if asymmetrical, revenge. Perhaps he had no alternative than one of these days, after completing his present mission . . . [but to] walk into the inner sanctum, and [beat] the shit out of the august Dr. Chase.[80]

Kirk rekindled Oakes's long-repressed revenge fantasies; their return threatens to unhinge Blackford, to replace his mission on behalf of the American security state with a private mission of retribution.

And so Oakes, struggling to maintain his emotional stability, buries himself in the mission. He studies blueprints by day and attempts to discover the security leak by night. One day Caroline invites Oakes to ride horses on the castle grounds (an outing that Ronald Reagan would reprise with Queen Elizabeth II on a 1982 state visit). Following their spirited ride, the queen invites Oakes to a private dinner that evening. They barely make it through the first course before their mutual passions flare. The ensuing sex scene, which Buckley would later claim (unpersuasively) was simply the "obligatory sex scene" of spy novels, is freighted with symbolic, psychological, and political affect; it is anything but obligatory.[81]

Queen Caroline discreetly excuses herself from dinner, instructing Blackford to prepare his room for her coming arrival. Oakes showers, pours champagne, and bristles with excitement over the pending fornication. And then, suddenly, his mind turns to Dr. Chase, his schoolboy tormentor: "The piquancy was more than he could bear. Dr. Chase!" In the next moment Caroline has arrived; they drink a half-glass of champagne and, unable to contain themselves any longer, the queen leads Oakes to bed. With hardly any buildup (recall that Buckley considers foreplay both hard work and painful), Oakes enters the queen of England—at which point a "wild but irresistible thought struck him, fusing pleasure and elation—and satisfaction." Oakes, in the missionary position, shows "superhuman restraint" as he offers the queen the exact nine strokes that were the vehicle of his adolescent trauma.[82]

Inverting his history of Old World abuse and sexual humiliation, Oakes claims the dominant position. He is not forced to bend over and he does not kneel before the queen to pleasure her; Oakes is the fucker and Caroline his fuckee. And, as if by magic, his act of New World sexual domination purges Oakes's pent-up rage and resentment entirely. "And they collapsed into each other's arms in silence, with animated sobs coming from Caroline's throat. Blackford drew out, and in a voice kind, but gently stern and mocking, he whispered to her: 'Courtesy of the United States, ma'am." The ensuing pillow talk will reveal to Blackford, though not to Caroline, that Peregrine Kirk is the Soviet mole.[83]

Thus is Blackford Oakes's sexual conquest of the queen of England the critical moment in both the narrative trajectory of *Saving the Queen* and the constitution of his own character. In discovering that Caroline's own cousin is a Soviet mole, Blackford sets into motion the events that will save Caroline's reign from national security vulnerabilities and international humiliation. Oakes "s-c-r-e-w-s the queen," and, in so doing, he saves her from infamy.[84] In addition, Oakes's Lothario act preserves (albeit temporarily) America's hydrogen bomb secrets from prying Soviet eyes and ears; his sex is in the service of national security. But most important for the development of the Blackford Oakes character (and for the series as a whole), his sex in *Saving the Queen* rids him of the emotional trauma of his past. This trauma was, we know, the only thing that threatened Oakes's status as a Cold War hero; it pointed to a vulnerability and potential lack of discipline that could overshadow the otherwise sterling qualities of character, intellect, and physique that made him such an ideal candidate for CIA service. But Oakes's penetration of the queen of England's inner sanctum evacuates his adolescent vulnerability and rage (the rage "suddenly . . . just came . . . steaming out"[85]); it transforms him from the "man-boy" of Caroline's initial desires to the hypermasculine "shining perfection" of Buckley's own fantasies.

"I made Blackford Oakes such a shining perfection to irritate, infuriate the critics," Buckley claimed. And, like Oakes himself, "I scored!"

It is perhaps curious that a series of novels that were explicitly intended as Cold War interventions—meant, we have seen, to offer American readers a heroic account of the American security state to counterbalance the cynical ones—begins with a story in which Cold War imperatives are secondary (at best) to the continuing intrigues of the English monarchy. *Saving the Queen* is, at its lascivious heart, a novelistic treatment not of the then-contemporary Cold War between the United States and the Soviet Union but instead of the basic cultural and political themes that attended American independence from England. Buckley Jr. went back to the future in *Saving the Queen*; in order to create his perfect American hero— the one who would protect, in fiction, the American nation from Soviet subversion during the Cold War—Buckley would first subject Blackford Oakes to the exact victimization, humiliation, and loss of rights claimed by American patriots in the prelude to the Revolutionary War.

Accordingly, *Saving the Queen* mimics and updates the American founding mythology in order to point the way forward in the Cold War battle between the world's twentieth-century superpowers. Blackford Oakes begins his uniquely American journey in the Old World, where he is punished for his brash, egalitarian, and undisciplined manner. His rights of man cruelly violated by a sadistic father figure, Oakes is left a resentful, emotionally fraught "man-boy."[86] His journey to redemption, to the "complete American" of his creator's vision, requires that he return to the inner sanctums of Mother England to exact revenge. Having done so, Oakes's rights of man are vindicated, his Old World resentments forgotten; as is the American nation, Oakes is now prepared to step onto the world's stage and do battle with a distinctly New World enemy. William F. Buckley Jr. drew inspiration for Blackford Oakes from Billy Budd and Robert Redford. Budd's forced exile from the *Rights of Man* leads to his death; Redford/Oakes's forced exile from the rights of man leads him eventually to sexual conquest of the Old World, American heroism, and Cold War triumph. Let us now consider Oakes's journey from Old World victim to New World paternal hero—to his status as rights-bearing avatar of the coming Reagan Revolution.

"A Long Train of Abuses"

Americans, wrote Thomas Jefferson in 1776, had been the victims of "a long train of abuses & usurpations begun at a distinguished period" by King George; he had designed "to reduce [Americans] under absolute despotism." His was a "history of unremitting injuries & usurpations, among which appears no solitary fact to contradict the uniform tenor of the rest but all have in direct object the establishment of an absolute tyranny over these [American] states." The king and Parliament had, Jefferson insisted, reduced the inalienable rights of Americans to ash; having patiently suffered the abuses and provocations of the Crown, Americans were now duty-bound to "throw off such government." It was time for Americans to "dissolve the political bands which have connected them with [Great Britain], and to assume among the powers of the earth the separate & equal station" to which they were entitled.[87] For high principle, then—to reclaim their rights of man, which had been conspiratorially trampled underfoot—Americans would engage in armed insurrection.[88]

Jefferson's familiar origin story for American democracy, with its obsessive focus on international conspiracies against rights, was not unique among American patriots. His Declaration of Independence is, of course, the most famous version of America's countersubversive origins, but its sentiments were widely shared in the American colonies during the Revolutionary era.[89] Nor is the American "countersubversive imagination" that Jefferson articulated time bound; a constituent feature of the American mind, we have battled real and imagined conspiracies against our rights for time out of mind.[90]

But as in Blackford Oakes's origin story, America's founding was not simply a matter of high principle. Just as Oakes's Old World journey was propelled by erupting emotional trauma that imperiled his potential to become a complete, mature American, so too was the cause of American independence in turn motivated and threatened by emotional duress. As Burrows and Wallace's illuminating analysis of Revolutionary discourse makes clear, American patriots envisioned themselves in a relation of kinship with their British "brethren": they thought of themselves as the loyal, though increasingly abused, sons of Mother England. Not simply a political community, their common blood made Americans and Britons kin; the cause of American independence thus registered in the domain of anguished family drama. Americans imagined independence as an unfortunate but necessary separation of now mature sons from an increasingly overbearing Mother England and an indifferent, even vengeful brethren; Britons, for their part, imagined American patriotism as family betrayal.[91] Jefferson's original draft of the Declaration of Independence defends the conduct of Mother England's American sons, even as it hurls accusations against their British family:

[Britons] have been deaf to the voice of justice & consanguinity . . . [they] have given the last stab to agonizing affection, and manly spirit bids us to renounce forever these unfeeling brethren. We must endeavor to forget our former love for them, and hold them as we hold the rest of mankind, enemies in war, in peace friends. We might have been a free and a great people together; but a communication of grandeur & of freedom it seems is below their dignity. Be it so, since they will have it. We will tread it apart from them, and acquiesce in the necessity which denounces our eternal separation![92]

Fighting a conspiracy against their rights, on one hand, seeking recognition as mature coequals, on the other hand: the origin story of American democracy points to both high principle and prosaic family drama.

The origin story of Blackford Oakes, we have seen, also intersects Enlightenment principle with emotional trauma. Oakes's suffering at the hands of Dr. Chase—a sadistic, considered, nationalist assault on his rights of man—personifies and miniaturizes both the "long train of abuses" against rights and the vengeful parental wrath suffered by American patriots. "Admitting that we are children," asked John Adams, "have not children a right to complain when their parents are attempting to break their limbs, to administer poison, or to sell them to enemies for slaves[?]"[93] Chase's attack nationalizes and infantilizes the teenaged Oakes. A "cheeky American brat" with "bad manners," Oakes is forcibly disrobed ("Was there an unnecessary motion there?" Oakes wonders), held down over a couch arm, and brutalized by a "grim[ly] satisfy[ied]" Chase. The headmaster employs all of his "strength, wrath, and resentment" in delivering "foreign aid" to "one American at a time."[94]

American patriots responded to parental wrath by taking up arms; they risked familicide in order to establish their "separate and equal" status to Mother England. Blackford Oakes's path to maturity and the concomitant redemption of his rights—his path to becoming the "complete American" and "shining perfection" who will lead the Cold War American security state—was longer and more complicated. Perhaps even more emotionally scarred by parental violence than were the American patriots before him, Oakes needed to return to the site of his trauma and, once there, invert the sexualized aggression that generated in him the "rage" and "emotional resentment" that imperiled his American heroism. In bed, Oakes shows Queen Caroline he is no longer an American "man-boy"; he denies her foreplay but still gets her off by reprising the exact nine strokes that Chase had used on him. To do so required "superhuman restraint" on Oakes's part (a restraint that his adolescent self had not yet developed), but when the deed is done, he finds himself emotionally healed, a "complete American." Oakes proves to Caroline that America is no longer a "cheeky brat" but instead a "separate & equal" (even dominant) partner. Blackford Oakes fucked the queen of England, and in so doing, he retraced and updated the founding story of American democracy.

But Blackford Oakes accomplished even more. Tethering hypermasculine, sexual, and family politics to the redemption of American rights at home and abroad, Oakes prefaced, in fiction, another American conservative hero—one who was also frequently lionized in Buckley's prose and is the subject of the next chapter. Just four years after the publication of *Saving the Queen*, in which Blackford Oakes went back to the future to redeem both himself and the American nation from Old World tyranny, the Reagan Revolution commenced. Let us conclude.

Conclusion

William F. Buckley Jr. originally intended 1994's *A Very Private Plot* to be the tenth, and final, Blackford Oakes novel. The Cold War, the ostensible raison d'être for the Blackford Oakes series, was over. And with Oakes and Sally having finally married following the events of his previous installment (*Tucker's Last Stand*, set in the fictional 1965), Buckley was no longer able to satisfy market and private desires for his hero to engage in glamorous, dangerous, dominant sex with beautiful foreign spies and diplomats (indeed, there is not a single sex scene featuring Blackford Oakes in *A Very Private Plot*). Having lost both his ostensible and deeper motivation for the Blackford Oakes series, Buckley had at last grown bored with Oakes himself.[95] Buckley struggled to complete the book; he even required a visit to Switzerland from his long-time editor, Samuel Vaughn, to "check the book's progress and to encourage its author."[96] And although many chapters go by with no appearance whatsoever from Oakes, Buckley did manage to produce a book, even if its action was "sturdy" rather than "compelling" and even if it lacked the "dramatic intensity" and "antic invention" of the earliest novels, that held "small, but distinct pleasures."[97] Perhaps Buckley's interest was revived by his decision to portray in fiction his friend and political hero Ronald Reagan.

Set in 1995, *A Very Private Plot* features a now mostly retired Blackford Oakes and contains its action within a series of flashbacks to one final episode of Cold War intrigue: a 1985 presidential drama centered on whether to inform the new Soviet general secretary (Mikhail Gorbachev) of an assassination plot against him. The crucial decision, unlike in past novels, belongs not to Oakes but rather to Reagan. Blackford Oakes is rarely featured in the book (many chapters go by without an appearance by him), and it is Reagan himself who is the book's most consequential figure.

It was an obvious transference, for there were many similarities between the fictional Oakes and the real Reagan. Both figures endured fraught relationships with their fathers: Oakes's father was physically distant but still domineering; Reagan's father was an irredeemable alcoholic. Both were true believers in conventional American values: they "felt, and expressed, the buoyancy of the American Republic." Both were physically impressive; Oakes was "startlingly handsome" and Reagan flashed a "voluptuarian smile." Both were physically courageous; Oakes frequently risked his life on behalf of national security, and Reagan had, as a young man, frequently braved the dangerous currents of the Rock River as a lifeguard, saving at least one hundred people from drowning. And both Oakes and Reagan, of course, employed their considerable moral, physical, and intellectual gifts on behalf of American Cold War prerogative.

Here there was, though, a significant contrast between Oakes and Reagan: Oakes fought the Cold War in private, on battlefields and in bedrooms; Reagan was a "great public figure who moved mountains." The "political" hero of the Cold War, and so of the 1980s themselves, Reagan enjoyed a public renown that Oakes never did. Reagan was "larger-than-life"; Buckley never could convince Hollywood that Blackford Oakes was a viable cinema attraction.[98]

It is thus tempting to agree with Buckley's own assessment that Reagan was not just his friend but also his "tutor."[99] Buckley modeled Oakes after himself; he invested Oakes's origin story with his own life experiences. And like Oakes, Buckley's star—though considerable, especially in American conservative intellectual circles—never shone as brightly as did Reagan's. But to regard them as Reagan's inferiors is to sell Buckley and

Oakes short. Michael Rogin argued that Ronald Reagan learned, in part, how to be an American president by reprising the roles that he played as a Hollywood actor;[100] but Reagan learned Old World diplomacy not from Hollywood but from Blackford Oakes himself.

Six years after Oakes answered Queen Caroline's fateful invitation to visit her at Windsor Castle, Queen Elizabeth II invited Reagan to the residence. The president's acerbic and unpredictable advisor Michael Deaver made the queen wait nearly a month before responding to the invitation; the first lady needed time to consult her astrologer to ensure a favorable time for the visit. The wait was worth it. For when the Reagans finally did arrive in June 1982, Queen Elizabeth, like her fictional counterpart, found herself immediately drawn to her American visitor. As had Oakes and Caroline, the queen and the president rode horses, dined together, and toasted with affection both each other and the "common heritage" of their respective nations. The short visit left such a lasting impression on Queen Elizabeth that when he left office, she invited Reagan to Buckingham Palace and knighted him.[101]

But Americans no longer bowed down before the queen. Upon receiving his new title—"Ronald Reagan, G.C.B."—the ex-president, as a foreigner, had the choice of kneeling and being dubbed or of standing upright. Reagan stayed on his feet. He was "greatly honored" by the queen's attention, but like Oakes before him, Reagan did not do Her Majesty the pleasure of kneeling at her lap.[102]

4

"The Greatest Nation on Earth": Ronald Reagan, Fathers, and the Rights of Americans

[Jack] lifted me a foot in the air with the flat side of his boot. . . . Jack clobbered us . . . the licking I got for that . . . Jack's life [was] one of almost permanent anger and frustration.
—Ronald Reagan, Where's the Rest of Me?

Here for the first time the Founding Fathers—that little band of men so advanced beyond their time that the world has never seen their like since—evolved a government based on the idea that you and I have the God given right . . . to determine our own destiny.
—Ronald Reagan, "Encroaching Control"

No more appeasement. If it takes a bloodbath, let's get it over with.
—Ronald Reagan

Before he "delivered [us] from fear and loathing" and "remedied America of all self-doubt"[1]; before he "revived the confidence of Americans at a time when it was very low"[2]; and before he "changed the trajectory of America,"[3] Ronald Reagan endured the blows of an alcoholic, "permanent[ly] ang[ry] and frustrate[ed]" patriarch.[4] Before he stirred conservative audiences with invocations of the rights intended for Americans by the founding fathers, Reagan was an abused son. And, so, before he could offer to the American nation "his greatest contributions, [which] were psychological, amounting to nothing less than a reawakening of the American faith in common sense,"[5] the future president had personal demons to purge. His overcoming of those demons—his discarding of the political ideals of his biological father in favor of those of the founding fathers—made him an enduring icon of American conservative politics. His ghost continues "to hang heavily over" American conservatism.[6]

This chapter turns to Reagan's memoirs, speeches, letters, and radio broadcasts to show how he accomplished this feat of paternal substitution. In particular, we will see that Reagan habitually employed the same paternal rights discourse—the championing of both the authority of the nation's stern, responsible fathers and the spectral authority of the nation's founding fathers—in which William F. Buckley Jr. (and his fictional counterpart, Blackford Oakes) was fluent. As it did for Buckley, Reagan's use of the discourse replaced a personal history of paternal failure with a political history of paternal success. Yet as they also had for Buckley, Reagan's articulations served not merely as balm for his own emotional wounds. Instead, Reagan's paternal rights discourse also identified a series of enemies, both domestic and international, whose un-American activities required defensive, countersubversive measures. In so doing, that discourse escaped the confines of personal history; it reinforced for coming generations the "guiding assumptions and possibilities" of American conservatism.[7]

In particular, Reagan's paternal rights discourse demarcated the supposedly legitimate rights claims of America's "average" citizens from the supposedly illegitimate rights claims of its subversives—its "welfare queens," "wild animals," and "little criminals." The difference between the nation's valued citizens and its irresponsible others, Reagan held, was just the difference between autonomous, properly self-governing subjects who were the products of stable, patriarchal family units, on one hand, and heteronomous, undisciplined subjects who grew up without stern paternal influence, on the other hand. The rights claims of the nation's citizens thus stood, in Reagan's formulations, as barometers of both familial history and democratic character.

Ronald Reagan's paternal rights discourse was the unifying thread of his thirty-year political career; with it, he celebrated, attacked, persuaded, and governed American subjects. Conjoining submission to paternal authority with the mature and responsible practice of rights, Reagan's paternal rights discourse at once limited and authorized the exercise of governmental power. But the authority that it legitimized—the exercise of stern, paternal authority on subjects whose chaotic childhoods had ill prepared them for responsible democratic citizenship—was ultimately counterproductive to Reagan's goal of creating mature, autonomous citizens. Yet

Ronald Reagan's most audacious use of the paternal rights discourse—as the conceptual scaffolding upon which rested his conduct of the Contra war in Nicaragua—not only stoked rather than extinguished immaturity; it also exposed his presidency to scandal and near ruin.

It is by now conventional to recognize how, over the past generation, the culture wars that propel American politics and culture rely on a particular set of negative archetypes. There are the radical campus protesters, for example, who, encouraged by leftist professors, unfairly denounce America as cruel, racist, and sexist. There are the unrepentant violent criminals who are coddled by a misguided criminal justice system that dwells on the lowly socioeconomic background of criminals rather than the rights of their victims. And, internationally, there are the foreign radicals whose anticolonial, revolutionary activities threaten American interests and lives. These characters are the subject of widespread, general condemnation. But they excite the imaginations of modern American conservatives in particular. Their villainous heteronomy, indeed, contrasts with the autonomy of the nation's "average citizens"—those laudable figures whom Ronald Reagan celebrated as the "forgotten men and women in America . . . who [go] to work, [pay] their bills, [send] their kids to school and [make] this country run."[8] But as we will see, the nation's contemptible citizens were as much Ronald Reagan's people as were its heroic ones.

One's status as either a national hero or national villain turned, in Reagan's estimation, on how one exercised the right to freedom. For Reagan held that at the core of American identity was a distinctive and empowering, but ultimately ambivalent, charge—one that recalls the paradoxes inherent in conservatism's paternal rights discourse. America offered to citizens "the ultimate in individual freedom *consistent with law and order.*"[9] And Americans themselves were the arbiters of this "ordered liberty": "true freedom," Reagan wrote in 1971, "is the freedom of self-discipline—the freedom to choose within acceptable standards. Take that framework away and you lose freedom."[10] Autonomous self-creation, on one hand, the restraints of law and order, on the other hand: Reagan reconciled the competing prerogatives at the heart of his American dream by demanding that Americans discipline themselves.

The rewards of self-disciplined citizenship were substantial. Americans who exercised their rights in responsible, disciplined ways earned freedom from the overbearing influence of the American governmental "Leviathan";

they were free to unleash their "individual genius" and to "fly as high and as far as [their] own talent[s] and energ[ies] would take [them]."[11] But those who exercised their rights to individual freedom in irresponsible, subversive ways—in ways inconsistent with law and order—subjected themselves to the full force of Leviathan's might. Americans who refused to discipline themselves should, Reagan held, experience that discipline in the form of stern governmental authority; it was, accordingly, legitimate for American government to unleash the "law of the Father" on wayward subjects.

Reagan's abiding frustration with the state of American politics was precisely that so few Americans shared his equivocal vision of rights, freedom, self-discipline, and governmental authority. It was a normative vision, he and his fellows in the American conservative movement believed, that empowered Americans with the capacity to determine for themselves the character of their relationships with government. As such, it was a vision of American citizenship drawn from the aspirations of America's founding fathers. Yet Cold War–era America, Reagan agreed with his conservative allies, had rejected this paternal injunction in favor of supporting governmental action that rewarded rather than punished the deviant rights claims of undisciplined Americans.

Thus did Reagan and his conservative movement allies target irresponsible rights claims as both engines of social disorder and national decline and markers of family dysfunction. The misuse of rights registered in multiple domains at once: it flouted the desires of the founding fathers; it tarnished the legitimate, disciplined rights claims of America's "average," but increasingly "forgotten" citizens; and it testified to the eroded state of the American household, where paternal authority was frequently missing or otherwise emasculated. That the groups most prone to deviant rights claims were made up disproportionately of historically powerless and stigmatized people (the young, racial minorities, the poor, and women) only made matters worse. Not content with the governmental neutrality for which America's virtuous citizens asked, these people made excessive, "special" rights claims that enlisted the active help of government in the gratification of their unreasonable desires.[12] Reagan agreed with his friend and political ally William F. Buckley Jr.: the "only way," wrote Buckley in 1982, "to acquire any rights these days is to become a minority." Each was distraught that so few Americans agreed with the founding fathers that "a respect for the rights of minorities begins with a respect for the rights of majorities."[13]

Ronald Reagan, however, was not prone to despair. He neither acquiesced in his fellow Americans' abandonment of the founding fathers nor shirked his self-imposed responsibility to reignite popular belief in their vision of individual rights and self-discipline. "I think it's time," he intoned in 1964, that "we ask ourselves if we still know the freedoms that were intended for us by the founding fathers."[14] Reagan, accordingly, dedicated his life to animating American politics and culture with the distinctive paternal rights discourse that is the hallmark of modern American conservatism. And as did his conservative supporters and allies, the eventual president rested the revivification of the authority of the nation's founding fathers on the restoration of the supposedly waning authority of the nation's biological fathers. Yet, paradoxically, Reagan did so only by first overcoming the legacy of his own chaotic upbringing. An act of nationalistic transmogrification, Reagan's paternal rights discourse replaced the personal and political authority of his own biological father with the spectral authority of the founding fathers.

"A Restless Man, Burning with Ambition to Succeed"

Accounts of Ronald ("Dutch") Reagan's childhood consistently emphasize its instability, poverty, and rootlessness. They are consistent also in identifying Reagan's father, Jack, as the primary source of these maladies.[15] In this, though, the memoirists are simply following the fortieth president's lead. His own multiple accounts of his upbringing, beginning with 1965's *Where's the Rest of Me?*, detail Jack's many failings.

The father, his son eulogized, was "a restless man, burning with ambition to succeed."[16] But he lacked the commitment, the wherewithal, and, above all, the self-discipline to succeed. Indeed, the series of moves that the Reagan family endured during the first ten years of Dutch's life were brought on by Jack's delusions that prosperity was always just around the corner and the bouts of alcoholic self-sabotage that ruined the good career opportunities that he did enjoy.[17] Jack's frustrated ambitions and his "weakness" for alcohol led him to a condition of "almost permanent anger."[18] His benders would lead him to disappear for days on end and were the source of explosive arguments with Reagan's mother, Nelle. Alcoholism would eventually contribute to Jack's death in 1941, at the relatively young age of fifty-seven; it would act also as his son's entrée, at the age of eleven, into the world of adult responsibility.

Reagan relates the story of returning to the family home in Dixon, Illinois, one night after playing basketball. The Reagans had finally settled in Dixon; there Dutch would live until leaving for nearby Eureka College after graduating from high school. It was in Dixon where Dutch "really found myself—and discovered why Jack disappeared from home so often."[19] Returning home that night, the eleven-year-old encountered his father "flat on his back on the front porch and no one there to lend a hand but me. He was drunk, dead to the world." Dutch first equivocates, but then embraces adult responsibility:

I stood over [Jack] for a minute or two. I wanted to let myself in the house and go to bed and pretend he wasn't there. . . . But someplace along the line to each of us, I suppose, must come that first moment of accepting responsibility. If we don't accept it (and some don't), then we just grow older without quite growing up. I felt myself fill with grief for my father at the same time that I was feeling sorry for myself. Seeing his arms spread out as if he were crucified—as indeed he was . . . I bent over him, smelling the sharp odor of whiskey. . . . I got a fistful of his overcoat. Opening the door, I managed to drag him inside and get him to bed.[20]

The story inverts the conventional father/son dynamic. Jack's bodily surrender to a foreign agent (alcohol) at once confirms his heteronomy and sets the stage for Dutch's first act of autonomous agency.[21] The father's "weakness" renders him as helpless as a child even as it allows his son to grow into maturity. This theme—Dutch achieves personal and, eventually, political maturity by overcoming the character failings of his father—recurs throughout Reagan's self-narrative. But as we will see, discarding Jack created a paternal void—one that Dutch consistently filled with surrogate fathers both real and spectral.

Jack's "bouts with the dark demons in the bottle" inverted his relationship with his son, turning him into a helpless child who was "dead to the world."[22] But the lack of self-discipline that led Jack to alcoholism infantilized him in multiple ways. His volatility manifested, for example, as an explosive temper that, in Dutch's telling, led to periodic physical punishment of Dutch and his older brother, Neil ("Moon"). Indeed, the stories that Dutch tells of his childhood "Huck Finn–Tom Sawyer" days tend to end in his being beaten by his father.[23] There was the time when Jack decided that Dutch was insufficiently brutal to a classmate during a schoolyard fight and "lifted me a foot in the air with the flat side of his boot."[24] There was the time when adolescent Dutch and Moon were left alone at home in Chicago, got scared, and left to search for their parents without first blowing out a gas lamp: their mother, Nelle, "lost her temper and stood as a figure of righteous wrath while Jack clobbered us."[25] And there was the time when Dutch and his friend Monkey inadvertently blew a shotgun hole in the roof of Monkey's apartment: "the licking," recalls Dutch, "I got for that."[26]

It was not, though, the various beatings that Dutch endured that most fouled his childhood. His "worst experience as a boy . . . a thousand times worse" than the beatings was instead the result of another of Jack's childish get-rich schemes. Having purchased a sidecar of secondhand potatoes, Jack ordered Dutch and Moon to sort the good from the bad. "No one who has not sat in a stinking boxcar during hot summer days, gingerly gripping tubers that dissolve in the fingers with a dripping squish, emitting an odor worse than that of a decaying corpse, can possibly imagine the agony we suffered." Predictably Jack earned only "a little money" from the speculation.[27]

Yet in spite of Reagan's castigation of his father, he always acknowledged that Jack had some admirable character qualities. He was an ardent defender of "the rights of the individual and the workingman";[28] a staunch advocate for the rights of racial minorities (believing "literally that all men were created equal," Jack refused to take his sons to see D. W. Griffith's racist epic, *The Birth of a Nation*, and he once slept in his car rather than patronize an anti-Semitic hotel[29]); and a skilled raconteur (a trait that especially endeared him to his storytelling son[30]). Above all, Jack was a "sentimental Democrat"[31] who believed fervently in Franklin Roosevelt and his New Deal policies—never more so than when he secured a job with the Works Progress Administration in Dixon. These were aspects of his father that Reagan admired;[32] he would always recoil at accusations (particularly prominent during his presidential administration) that he was a racist or ignored the rights of ordinary citizens.[33] Similarly, Dutch would for many years maintain a hearty appreciation for Franklin Roosevelt, even modeling, in form if not in substance, his own 1970s' radio broadcasts after Roosevelt's "fireside chats."[34]

Yet for the most part, Dutch found Jack's personal and political legacy stifling. And he sought to overcome that legacy in two particular, mostly unconscious ways—each of which intersected in Reagan's veneration of American fathers ordinary and historical. First, as Anne Edwards (the definitive biographer of Reagan's pregubernatorial life) puts it: "There had always been an 'older' man to whom Dutch turned as a role model—a substitute for Jack whom he loved but did not want to emulate. . . . In later years, this list would grow with each new stage in his life."[35] Indeed, Reagan consistently told audiences of the influence that surrogate fathers had on the development of his "American life."

Some of those about whom Reagan rhapsodized were undoubtedly influential in his professional, personal, and political development: the stint in radio that paved his way to Hollywood was consistently nurtured by his boss, Peter MacArthur; during his Hollywood days with MGM, Reagan was a special favorite of Jack Warner; and his political conversion to conservatism was shaped indelibly by his close relationship with General Electric executive Lemuel Boulware.[36] But others of the surrogate fathers over whom Reagan swooned seemingly offered little more than an occasional word of encouragement, if that. Reagan, for example, lavishly credited the influence of Sid Altschuler (a wealthy Dixonite) for helping him break into the entertainment industry even though Altschuler lacked any contacts in that industry and offered only the most boilerplate of career advice.[37] Similarly, Reagan consistently held out his college football coach, Ralph McKinzie, as a man of great integrity who instilled in him considerable character qualities. Yet the record makes clear that McKinzie rarely gave Dutch a second thought during his four years at Eureka, initially refusing to play Reagan on tiny Eureka's *second* team, let alone its varsity team. Eventually McKinzie would welcome Dutch onto the varsity team and play the undersized Reagan on the offensive line, but by most accounts, "Coach Mac" was far more impressed with the football talents of Moon Reagan, who followed Dutch to Eureka.[38] No matter: both Altschuler and McKinzie received from Reagan the same effusive praise for their role in his development as did the more influential figures. All of them, Reagan consistently claimed, played vital roles in his discovery of "the rest of me."

The second way in which Reagan overcame Jack's legacy was political. While Reagan would always profess admiration for FDR's leadership style, he would eventually abandon the substance of FDR's politics— politics that Jack ardently supported . In contrast to the litany of real-life surrogates whom he employed to overcome Jack's personal legacy, Reagan relied primarily on the spectral influence of America's founding fathers to find his political self. Reagan's depiction of the fathers, we will see, emphasized their devotion to rights, especially the distinctive rights of

Americans to pursue the "the ultimate in individual liberty consistent with law and order."[39] At the core of Reagan's narrative of how he discovered the theretofore missing part of himself—his *political self*—was the paternal rights discourse that animates modern American conservatism.

By the time he was implanted in Hollywood, sweating out a living as an occasional A-list actor (Jack Warner never did see the future American president as leading-man material), Reagan was already reconsidering the basic principles of American New Deal politics—especially its apparent belief that dynamic governmental action was the answer to most of what plagued modern American society.[40] Elected president of the Screen Actors Guild (SAG) in the late 1940s, Reagan steered SAG away from the then-then prominent leftist labor union politics in the motion picture industry (exemplified by the influence of Longshore union boss Harry Bridges on the screen projectionist and set construction unions) and toward the anticommunist positions of his future employer General Electric.[41] Reagan served during this time as an FBI informant; he named communist-leaning figures in the motion picture industry, testified before the House Un-American Activities Committee, and engendered the lifelong animosity of those writers, actors, and directors who were blacklisted because of their alleged communist ties.[42] His Hollywood career floundering in the 1950s, Reagan was tabbed to host the new *General Electric Theater* television program—a position that ensured a steady income and exposed him to the staunchly probusiness, anticommunist economic and political philosophies of GE chairman Boulware (positions shared not by Jack Reagan, who died of factors related to alcoholism in the early 1940s, but by Reagan's new stepfather, the future first lady's patriarch, Loyal Davis).[43] By 1964, Reagan's transformation into a prototypical modern American conservative was complete: his televised thirty-minute speech on behalf of Barry Goldwater's inept presidential campaign was heralded by political reporter David Broder as the most explosive national political debut since William Jennings Bryan's Cross of Gold speech to the 1896 Democratic national convention.[44]

At the heart of Reagan's conservatism was the by-now familiar and paradoxical paternal rights discourse with which I am concerned. Later, as California governor doing battle with student protesters and as American president doing battle with the Sandinistas in Nicaragua, Reagan's invocation of paternal authority was literal: he would consistently blame the supposed leftist subversions of these (and other groups—street criminals, welfare recipients, university professors, licentious teenagers—all of the bêtes noires of modern American conservatism) on poor parenting and, in particular, on lack of stern paternal influence. But when speaking to a national audience, Reagan focused on the verities not of America's biological fathers—and certainly not those of Jack—but rather of its metaphorical, spiritual fathers:

Here for the first time the founding fathers—that little band of men so advanced beyond their time that the world has never seen their like since—evolved a government based on the idea that you and I have the God given right . . . to determine our own destiny.[45]

However, big government—in the guise of helping the less fortunate, of solving the social ills of the nation—had become a "leviathan"[46]: it confiscated revenue in the name of "progressive taxation"; it blanketed industry with unnecessary regulations; it saddled farmers with absurd crop and market quotas. In short, American government choked the productive life out of the nation's "average citizens." Ronald Reagan was no longer concerned with the political tenets of his biological father. Summarizing modern American conservatism's paradoxical obsession with rights and fathers, Reagan believed, instead, that it was time that "we ask ourselves if we still know the freedoms that were intended for us by the founding fathers."[47]

Thus was Reagan's ascension to "an American life" premised on overcoming the personal and political legacy of an unstable, heteronomous father. In thrall to foreign agents, Jack was compromised by both alcohol and "sentimental" partisanship. He was unable to provide Dutch with the paternal influence necessary for successful republican citizenship. But Reagan found paternal surrogates who compensated for Jack's failures. Indeed, by 1965, on the eve of his successful California gubernatorial campaign, Reagan proclaimed to the American people that with the help of these real and spectral surrogates, he had found the rest of himself. And in the paternal rights discourse that the founding fathers bequeathed to the American nation, Reagan was certain that he had found the key to successful democratic citizenship, especially for those Americans whose childhoods were tainted, as was his, by missing fathers.

§

The American dream that we have nursed for so long in this country and neglected so much lately is not that every man must be level with every other man. The American dream is that every man must be free to become whatever God intends that he should become. The restoration and the perpetuation of that dream is the greatest challenge confronting every one of us today.
—Ronald Reagan

A particular rendition of the American dream preoccupied Ronald Reagan. America, he held, was a nation uniquely dedicated to individual freedom. "America's strength," he claimed, lay in the way that "our system freed the individual genius of man," releasing "him to fly as high and as far as his own talent and energy would take him."[48] But the individual freedom that Reagan celebrated was circumscribed. "True freedom," he wrote in 1971, "is the freedom of self-discipline—the freedom to choose within acceptable standards. Take that framework away and you lose freedom."[49]

What of those who lacked the self-discipline to make good choices and police their own freedom? Then, as I explore later in this chapter, it was legitimate for American government to ensure that freedom remained "consistent with law and order," even to call out the "dogs of war" on the undisciplined when needed.[50] Virtuous Americans disciplined themselves and so were, by rights, shielded from overbearing governmental power; bad Americans, conversely, refused to exercise the discipline necessary to keep their freedom within "acceptable standards" and so brought down on themselves the full force of American law and order.

Embedded within the conditional freedom that Reagan linked to American purpose was a further understanding of the proper relationship between citizens and government. American government was not, he claimed, responsible for ensuring that "every man must be level with every other man," but rather that "every man must be free to become whatever God intends that he should become."[51] Here, then, was Reagan's American dream: government would not create and enforce artificial conditions of equal outcomes or results but instead create and enforce conditions of equal opportunity, whereby self-disciplined citizens could "fly as high and as far as [their] own talent[s] and energy[ies] would take [them]."[52]

Accordingly, Reagan consistently held that an individual's right to equal opportunity stood at the foundation of American freedom. The protection of this right was, moreover, government's primary responsibility.

Our nation is founded on a concern for the individual and his right to fulfillment. . . . We are equal before God and law . . . [and] let there be no misunderstanding about the right of man to achieve above the capacity of his fellows. [H]ere, to a degree unparalleled any place in the world, we unleashed the individual genius of man, recognized his inherent dignity, and rewarded him commensurate with his ability and achievement.[53]

This was all, Reagan held, in line with the desires of America's founding fathers, who had, after all, "evolved a government based on the idea that you and I have the God given right . . . to determine our own destiny."[54] But the dreams of the fathers were under attack. From the start of his political career, Reagan was convinced that the widespread violation by big government of the individual's right to equality of opportunity— the "right of man to achieve above the capacity of his fellows"—had led America to the brink. Reagan's public addresses were political jeremiads in which he detailed a coming slide into unfreedom unless the electorate took immediate action to reclaim its lost rights to equal opportunity.

Thus did Reagan link national decline to a voracious, irrational national government that flouted the desires of the founding fathers and committed itself instead to the perverted logic of equal outcomes and, by extension, personal license. In the hands of big government, ominous public policy trends abounded: tax policy was animated by the illegitimate, confiscatory principles of progressivism; property rights were dismissed as antithetical to the public interest; and overzealous intrusions into everyday life by "federal agents" deprived citizens of their Fourth Amendment rights to privacy.[55] Carrying the nation "a great distance from our founding fathers' vision of America," the purveyors of big government were in thrall to different fathers and their decidedly un-American creed: the "collectivist philosophy of nineteenth-century theorists like Rousseau, Fourier, and Marx."[56] America stood at the precipice: "Our natural, inalienable rights are now considered to be a dispensation from government, and freedom has never been so fragile, so close to slipping from our grasp as it is at this moment."[57]

In emphasizing how big government carried out wholesale violation of the rights of Americans, Reagan threw light on the misdeeds of the faceless "federal agents" who subverted the American dream of the founding fathers. But the products of their subversion were not faceless. Instead, governance practiced according to the reigning prerogatives of big government—with its inverted stances on rights, equality, and freedom—generated both heroes and villains. The heroes—the nation's "average citizens"—struggled against the political zeitgeist, employed their rights in a self-disciplined fashion, and proved their autonomy. In so doing, they at once honored America's founding fathers and, we will see, testified to the virtues of strong paternal authority at home. Conversely, the nation's villains employed their rights in undisciplined and childish ways that demanded that American government satisfy their wants and needs. Dishonoring the spectral fathers of the American household, their use of rights pointed to legacies of paternal dysfunction in their own homes—legacies that, unlike Reagan himself, they had not overcome.

Law, Rights, and the Perversion of the American Dream

The time has come to reclaim our inalienable rights to human dignity, self respect, [and] self reliance to once again be the kind of people who once made this nation great.
—Ronald Reagan

Reagan frequently valorized, as he did in a letter written in 1982, those "forgotten men and women in America . . . who [go] to work, [pay] their bills, [send] their kids to school and [make] this country run."[58] The celebration of such "average citizens" was a touchstone of Reagan's political vision:[59]

The average citizen is . . . willing to pay his fair share for schools and highways and welfare. . . . But, he expects every other citizen to pay his fair share too. He expects that money to be spent wisely and equitably for the common good and not for some special class or privilege.[60]

Reagan's fondness for farmers, small business owners, and home owners, for example, all derived from this understanding of who average citizens were and what it was about them that made their efforts virtuous. Average citizens were "simple souls," whose constant, ascetic self-exertion enacted the foundational American belief that "there just 'ain't no such thing as free lunch.'"[61] They believed in the dream of the American founding fathers: they "believe in this nation as a nation under God, and that our national purpose is to provide the ultimate in individual freedom consistent with law and order."[62] Average citizens, in sum, employed their rights to equal opportunity in self-disciplined fashions, flying as high as their talents would take them.

Virtuous though they were, America's average citizens found that their rights were under attack. Big government, remember, fostered that faulty logic of individual rights that held that Americans were guaranteed equal outcomes and conditions. This perversion of rights dishonored the fathers; it also wreaked havoc on the rights and interests of average citizens. Indeed, Reagan decried how the new vision of rights led to the conclusion that the hard working and virtuous were actually responsible for the problems that socially marginal Americans suffered.[63] The true cause of continuing marginalization and lack of opportunity, instead, was the misguided efforts of governmental planners, who believed that they could "solve all the problems of human misery through government and government planning."[64] But in so creating programs, procedures, and regulations for the elevation of the less fortunate, federal agents had overreached; they had violated the founding fathers' vision for American government: to "provide opportunity, not smother it; [to] foster productivity, not stifle it."[65] After all, "They . . . knew, those founding fathers, that outside of its legitimate functions, government does nothing as well or as economically as the private sector of the economy."[66]

While the equal outcomes version of rights did not lead to material improvements in the lives of the less fortunate, it did have some beneficiaries. The perversion of rights had led to a situation in which a series of undeserving people were gaining unfair advantages from big government. Worse, these advantages were gained at the expense of average citizens, whose rights and interests were sacrificed to big government's misguided attempts at equality: "Today, unfortunately, we see [our] freedom slowly vanishing on many fronts—all in the name of the common good—and stability sorely threatened by a political and social climate that acknowledges the rights of the individual, but not his responsibilities."[67]

Reagan castigated multiple groups of people who misused rights. His screeds against America's "welfare queens" are, on this score, both illustrative and infamous.[68] But it was the rights malfeasance of the students, and their allies in the professoriate, who protested America's college campuses in the late 1960s and early 1970s that aggrieved him the most.

These students, Reagan insisted, were the products of families marked by missing or otherwise ineffectual fathers. Their failures to find the paternal surrogates that Reagan had secured in his own life led them to exercise rights in ways that revealed, and confirmed, their heteronomy and irresponsibility. And their frequently criminal immaturity made them, eventually, the subjects of Governor Reagan's paternal wrath.

"Liberal Professors"

Professors should teach you how to think not necessarily what to think.
—Ronald Reagan

Ronald Reagan typically analogized the disruptive activities of the campus protesters with whom he clashed while governor of California to the violence committed by hardened criminals.[69] Each, he noted, displayed a lack of respect for law and the social standards that it prescribed; they practiced, instead, an unrestrained, undisciplined license. Even worse, both the campus protester and the violent criminal justified their disorderly conduct by resorting to a perverse logic of rights that suggested that such conduct was constitutionally protected activity. Moreover, in the employment of this illegitimate notion of rights, both student protesters and violent criminals were aided by the misguided sympathies of authority figures—cowardly administrators and, especially, liberal professors, on one hand; soft-hearted judges and incompetent parole boards, on the other. Just as violent crime prevented society from protecting the rights that guaranteed the freedom of average citizens, campus protesters (whom Reagan referred to, in private, as little monsters") interfered with the rights of the "silent majority" of college students, who wished only for the opportunities traditionally offered through higher education.[70] And, most important, the source of each group's lawlessness was found in the failure of American fathers.

Indeed, Reagan claimed that student protesters' childish attacks on campus life were caused by the failure of postwar American parents, especially fathers, to instill proper discipline at home. Moreover, the failure of the fathers at home was replicated on campus by cowardly administrators and "liberal professors."[71] But whereas university administrators were incompetent to perform the needed surrogate, en loco parentis responsibilities, liberal professors actually encouraged the protesters. The professors proclaimed that it was "no crime to break the law in the name of social protest" and acted, "in the name of academic freedom," as if "the campus was a sanctuary immune to the laws and rules that govern the rest of us."[72]

Reagan believed that the protesters should be "taken by the scruff of the neck and thrown off the campus—permanently."[73] But this sort of unbending response was not typically forthcoming from the university community. Administrators drew Reagan's ire for what he referred to as their cowardice and impotence. But he scorned the professors, who were both ideologically sympathetic to the radical goals of the protesters and provided intellectual cover for their lawlessness. Unstintingly critical of the free market and the values of the founding fathers because they did not produce equal outcomes, these professors derided American society as cruel, racist, and sexist. Such criticism, Reagan argued, amounted to an abuse of "academic freedom" by professors, whose tirades misshaped young, impressionable minds. In addition, Reagan believed that their supposedly un-American outbursts defeated the true goal of education: "society's attempt to enunciate certain ultimate values upon which individuals and hence society may safely build." Liberal professors trashed the dreams of the founding fathers and offered nothing in their stead; they failed to understand that universities were "institutions designed to impart sound discipline based on moral standards which will become self discipline in the individual student."[74]

The professors' definition of academic freedom was a large part of the problem. They limited academic freedom only to their rights to teach as they wished. Such an understanding ignored "the student's academic freedom and the right of parents to have some say as to what their children are learning," to say nothing of the academic freedom that should be enjoyed by taxpaying citizens who "finance the whole operation and have some beliefs about the kind of schooling they wish to make available with their contributions." Professors "should teach you how to think not necessarily what to think"; they should not "under the name of academic freedom . . . demand the right to indoctrinate."[75] Yet liberal professors taught that American society was unequal and thus corrupt; the professors then sent the most radical of their students out like a "virus . . . [to] infect the campus."[76] Indeed, these professors "looked kindly upon any effort to disrupt campus and community life."[77]

To be sure, liberal professors greatly contributed to campus unrest. But they were not the sources of the unrest. The problem, Reagan held, was that the professors had found easy targets; they had identified a group of young people who grew up without sufficient paternal authority and thus had never developed the character qualities of sacrifice and self-discipline that are vital for successful republican citizenship. Reagan grew up with emasculated paternal authority, but his biological and spectral surrogates eventually led him to "the rest of" himself, to personal and political maturity. Whereas Reagan's paternal surrogates were successful business and sports figures who preached the virtues of American capitalism and its system of interest group politics, the surrogates whom the students found were radical professors who trashed American institutions. Reagan replaced his father with Jack Warner and Lemuel Boulware; the students replaced theirs with Herbert Marcuse and Angela Davis.[78] Warner and Boulware reinforced Reagan's devotion to the founding fathers; Marcuse and Davis guided their students to the "collectivist philosophy of nineteenth-century theorists like Rousseau, Fourier, and Marx."[79] False idols, these real and spiritual fathers only further encouraged student protesters to disrespect the educational desires of the "silent majority" of their peers.

Indeed, Reagan was certain that the lawlessness of campus protesters caused great harm to the majority of the university's students. While the protesters were exceedingly disruptive, they were "admittedly only a few" of those enrolled in classes.[80] There existed on campus, Reagan noted, a "silent majority" of students. These students harbored legitimate grievances of their own, but they resisted the radical entreaties of the professors, refrained from lawlessness, and did their best to exploit the more traditional opportunities for learning and personal growth offered at institutions of higher education.[81] But the minority "subversive" element on campuses was so dedicated to disrupting the normal operations of the university that it was increasingly difficult for average, nonradical students to concentrate on their studies.

There were, in Reagan's view, significant parallels between the average citizens located on campus and those who were dispersed generally throughout the nation. Both groups were hard working, earnest, and well meaning; members of each group were the sorts of people whom Reagan championed as American heroes. And members of each group suffered the same indignities: the rights of each had been neglected amid the noisy protests of those who proclaimed that their rights (to equal outcomes specifically) trumped all other considerations.

Consider, for example, the figure of Alan Bakke, whose name graces the U.S. Supreme Court's landmark 1978 case dealing with the use of affirmative action policies in higher education.[82] Bakke was, for Reagan, iconic; he symbolized the campus version of the average citizen. Not an "impulsive troublemaker or sorehead," Bakke was a hard-working, disciplined American who had been harmed by the mistaken equation of individual rights with equal outcomes. After having been rejected twice for admission to University of California–Davis's medical school in spite of scoring higher on medical school entrance exams than had some admitted students who belonged to traditionally disadvantaged groups, Bakke claimed that the medical school's affirmative action program violated his constitutional rights. The problem, according to Reagan, was that UC–Davis's affirmative action program exceeded the founding fathers' visions of equal opportunity and instead endorsed the logic of equal outcomes:

I believe it is right that we have a program to ensure equal opportunity for those aspiring to the [medical] profession. But surely we can come up with something that doesn't result in the kind of injustice done to Alan Bakke.[83]

Alan Bakke symbolized the tarnished fates of good, responsible college students everywhere; he was a member of a "generation that is justifiably resentful of being fed into the knowledge factory with no regard to their individualism, their aspirations or their dreams."[84] Beset, on one hand, by campus radicals and liberal professors who spewed noxious accounts of individual rights and, on the other hand, by indifferent or cowardly university administrators, the average university student was lost, and not "even missed."[85]

The fate of average citizens on campus approximated the fate of those writ large in another way. Not simply isolated examples, the neglect they experienced undermined America's commitment to individual rights and thus dishonored the legacy of the founding fathers. Universities

were created, and are presently maintained, to insure perpetuation of a social structure—a nation, if you will. . . . Our nation is founded on a concern for the individual and his right to fulfillment, and this should be the preoccupation of our schools and colleges. The graduate should go forth, literally starting on a lifetime of learning and growing and creativity that will in turn bring growth and innovation to our society.[86]

The university was responsible for perpetuating respect for individual rights and, in so doing, priming the engines of national growth. The subversion of this mission by protesting students and liberal professors was thus a problem of national scope. America indulged the rights of campus protesters, ignored the rights of its hard-working, average college students, and so dishonored the legacy of the founding fathers at its own peril.[87] It was all, he revealed in his conduct of the "Battle of People's Park," too much for Governor Reagan to bear.

"Little Monsters"

When queried about the origins of the student protest that consumed California campuses during the 1960s, Ronald Reagan had, I have intimated, a ready response: it was the result of bad parenting. The problem was rooted, ironically, in the multiple successes of his own generation. Their virtuous exertions, which were enabled by consistent displays of self-discipline and the hard work that it made possible, had produced victory in World War II, clawed the nation out of economic depression, and propelled technical innovations that at once improved the quality of life for all Americans and generated the greatest sustained period of economic prosperity in the nation's history.[88]

And yet many in Reagan's generation had failed miserably in their parental duties. Eager to share the fruits of their considerable labors with their children, Reagan's generation had never asked their children to earn their privilege. "All too often," Reagan claimed, "because we had to earn, we wanted to give. Our motives have been laudable, but our judgment had been bad."[89] The unforeseen negative consequences of such generosity ran in multiple directions.

On one hand, not having to earn their privilege, a significant proportion of America's youth population had never learned the values of discipline, sacrifice, and hard work. Deprived of these values, young Americans were also deprived of the moral bases of virtuous American citizenship. Indeed, Reagan's generation had "shortchanged [young people] on responsibilities or the right to earn for [themselves]."[90] Accordingly, young people had been deprived of the means by which Americans gain maturity; their parents had failed to give them the tools to become truly adult.

On the other hand, having failed to teach the root virtues of American citizenship, Reagan's generation was incapable of imposing the firm, yet loving, parental authority with which unruly children are transformed into morally upright, responsible citizens: "'No' was either a dirty word or dropped from our vocabulary."[91] Such permissive parenting bred in children attitudes of disrespect for elders and other authority figures. The ordinary adolescent impulse to test boundaries and question authority thus went unchecked as children became young adults. Youth had "every right to ask the reason behind the mores and customs of what we refer to as civilization," but they had "no right and it makes no sense to reject the wisdom of the ages simply because it is rooted in the past." Only those people who were "sufficiently disciplined to know what the results" would be of such a rejection, only those who had "grown up as complete human beings," could be entrusted to make the choice.[92] And such self-discipline was an increasingly rare quality in America's youth population.

Indeed, Reagan was appalled at the degree to which university campuses in the 1960s and 1970s were overrun with "dirty and unshaven" hippies; these were people who proudly refused the practices of self-discipline that signified one's progression into adulthood.[93] Hippies were indecent in myriad ways: they disclaimed modest dress (they dressed "like Tarzan"); they grew their hair long (they had "hair like Jane"); they were unwashed (they smelled "like Cheetah"); and they participated in public, drug-fueled orgies ("on the dance floor girls strip to their waist(s) and some couples [find] intercourse more entertaining than dancing").[94] As if such barbarism wasn't bad enough, hippies were also displeased because universities weren't "sufficiently pleasant baby-sitting facilities."[95] And so they alternated between holding "raucous all night parties complete with bonfires and bongo drum serenades" and protesting university rules and regulations with "club and torch in hand."[96]

Accordingly, upon entering college, the learned incapacity for self-discipline borne of easy privilege combined with the nascent disrespectful attitudes toward authority borne of permissive parenting to make a recipe for disorder. This toxic combination led a segment of students to be particularly dismissive of laws (especially property laws) that were meant to uphold the patterns of privilege based on the traditional American virtues of self-discipline and hard work.[97] Although these patterns of privilege were inevitably unequal, the inequality itself was legitimate, because, after all, it was based on the dream of the founding fathers: "the right of man to achieve above the capacity of his fellows."[98] Such inequality, that is, was the product of self-discipline, hard work, and sacrifice; it reflected the "naturalness and rightness of a vertical structuring of society."[99] But these were exactly the values that protesting hippies mocked, dismissing as illegitimate the privileges that the values legitimized.

To be sure, Reagan consistently noted, inequality was unfortunate. It was reasonable to sympathize with those in poverty and also to seek ways to help impoverished people to succeed. But inequality, so long as it was the product of virtuous self-exertion, was natural and right; railing against such legitimate forms of inequality was akin to refusing to see the world as it really was. Protesting against such a natural fact was not only useless; it was an exercise in immaturity, a childish wail against the injustice of a world that does not match one's youthful idealism.

Yet parental failure had left student protesters unprepared to accept such hard truths. Instead, they were vulnerable to the unnatural, communist verities that ridiculed the vertical structuring of human life as inhumane.[100] Subject to the control of a "sophisticated, alien order," student protesters embraced the communist doctrines of their professors; they dismissed self-discipline and hard work, as well as the privileges that such practices generated, as exercises in racist and sexist domination.[101] Resistance to the regime of law and order that recognized the legitimacy of a vertical structuring of society was thus simultaneously a reflection of the protesters' defective moral training *and* an exercise in communist-inspired subversion. Parental incompetence eventuated in the subversion of American law and order as the familial pathologies that marked disorderly homes reappeared on college campuses.

Reagan's lurid 1966 campaign trail depiction of a student dance that took place on the Berkeley campus linked student protesters' immaturities and associated moral failings to the subversive threat. Indeed, the happenings at the dance—some of which were "so bad, so contrary to our standards of decent human behavior" that Reagan "could not recite them . . . in detail"—exemplified the degree to which parental failure had endangered America's traditional standards of morality and, in so doing, provided opportunities for communist subversion of American law and order:

Many of those attending [the dance] were clearly of high-school age. The hall was entirely dark except for the light from two movie screens. On these screens the nude torsos of men and women were portrayed from time to time in suggestive positions and movements. Three rock and roll bands played simultaneously. The smell of marijuana was thick throughout the hall. There were signs that some of those present had taken dope. There were indications of other happenings that cannot be mentioned here.

A "center of sexual misconduct," the Berkeley campus was suffused with a moral indecency that made it "a rallying point for Communists" who only too happily stoked the "rioting [and] anarchy . . . the assault [on] law" that destroyed the "primary purpose of the University: to educate our young people."[102]

How could such moral depravities, and the communist-inspired assaults on law and order that they encouraged, occur on the campus of a "great University"? "It happened," Reagan intoned, "because those responsible abdicated their responsibilities."[103] Here too was Reagan's explanation illustrative of his accounting of the larger problem of student resistance to law and order, which "began the first time that someone old enough to know better declared it was no crime to break the law in the name of social protest."[104] Indeed, the same parental permissiveness that created the "little monsters" whose moral immaturities at once fueled their sexual depravity and made them vulnerable to communist entreaties was reproduced on campus.[105] University administrators repeated the parental failures that allowed student protesters to demur mature and responsible citizenship.

Reagan was frustrated by the failure of university administrators to engage in the sorts of quick and harsh measures necessary to uphold law and order. Such administrators were, he held, typically cowed by student protesters and regularly gave in to a cascading series of unreasonable (immature) curriculum and admissions demands.[106] They did not do what was needed: "insist that those unwilling to abide by . . . rules and regulations . . . should get their education elsewhere."[107]

Here again the student protesters were failed by authority figures. The administrators knew the hard truths of the world. They knew that societies were naturally structured in vertical, not horizontal, ways; they knew that inequality, if often unfortunate, was an unavoidable feature of all human societies. And while they didn't thrill to the disorder practiced by the little monsters (as did the professors), they did little to combat that disorder; just as had the protesters' biological fathers, university administrators failed to impart the "sound discipline based on moral standards which will become self discipline in the individual student."[108]

Given this habitual lack of paternal authority—the multiple failures to exercise the tough love needed to wrench children out of immaturity and immorality and into a mature, reflective, autonomous state of citizenship—Reagan took it upon himself to bring the needed law and order to California's campuses. He had promised to do so, to public acclaim, during the 1966 gubernatorial campaign.[109] Reagan thus didn't hesitate when the opportunity presented itself in May 1969 at Berkeley's "People's Park."

By the mid-1960s, and owing to being the home for such flash-point events as the free and filthy speech movements, the campus at UC-Berkeley sat at the leading edge of the student protest that increasingly consumed American universities.[110] The events that gave rise to the "Battle of People's Park" began in 1967, when the university obtained, through the power of eminent domain, a parcel of land located near the campus. After demolishing the houses that sat on the land, the university allowed the space to sit uncleared of rubble and debris and unused for nearly two years. In April 1969, a coalition of students and "street people," with the support of local merchants, converted the parcel of land into a public park. An explicit challenge to the university's private property rights, the coalition claimed the land for the people of Berkeley and dubbed it the "People's Revolutionary Park."[111]

The following month, at the behest of Reagan himself, the university took the provocative action of hiring contractors to install a fence around the park in the early morning hours and reclaim the land. Incensed at what they considered to be the heavy-handed tactics of the university, the students protested and then marched to the park to confront the police officers who were guarding it. The confrontation soon turned violent, with a segment of the protesters battling Berkeley police in hand-to-hand combat. By the end of the day, hundreds of protesters had been arrested; scores of protesters and police officers had been seriously injured; one bystander (James Rector) lay fatally wounded by police fire; and Reagan had dispatched the National Guard to restore order. The military occupation of Berkeley that followed over the next month was characterized by curfews, harsh treatment of students by National Guard troops, and the occasional use of chemical weapons to break up student gatherings.[112]

Reagan was not especially troubled by the outbreak of violence at People's Park following his decision to call up the National Guard and, in his own words, "unleash the dogs of war."[113] He was satisfied that his unbending response was required in order to quell disorder; it was also the sort of resolve that was required writ large in order to combat the subversion of American law and order. His explanation of the People's Park incident bears scrutiny, as it presents the linkages among parental failure, immaturity, social disorder, and national subversion.

Reagan argued that, contrary to its moniker, the People's Park effort was instigated by well-known revolutionaries, none of whom were enrolled students. These subversives had refused the university's "repeated efforts to enter into dialogue" and duped "a number of legitimate citizens and some students" into converting the vacant lot into a park. The subversives' goal, in fact, was much less noble than they claimed: they did not intend to lead a "volunteer community project to pretty up an unused vacant lot" but rather to challenge "the right of private ownership in this country" as part of their ongoing attempts to establish a communist beachhead in Berkeley.

Railing against the right of private property—that aspect of law and order that most clearly affirmed the vertical structuring of society— marked the leaders of the People's Park movement in both their immaturity and subversive intent. Indeed, it was not so much a park that was sought but rather a "play-pen" in which subversives would be free to continue the debauched behavior that had characterized the People's Park prior to the university's reclamation:

The property . . . had already become something of a public nuisance. Nightly rallies, mass singing, shouted obscenities, bonfires throughout the night, and the gathering of unsavory characters had so frightened the housewives in the neighborhood that they wouldn't even walk down the street. . . . Part of the lush greenery that was planted . . . turned out to be marijuana. . . . The property was being used as a garbage dump and a toilet. . . . A 21-year old man [was] picked up for indecent exposure after the police found him sitting in the park, completely nude, in full view of the occupants and passers-by.[114]

With their playpen of communist iniquity at stake, the leaders of the People's Park movement responded to the university's reclamation with "sticks, bricks, and prepared jagged pieces of pipe and steel." "This was no spontaneous eruption," Reagan held: the subversive attack on law and order was well coordinated, well armed, and "out of control."[115] Given the situation, Reagan argued, he was duty-bound to militarize, and then occupy, Berkeley with the National Guard.

Reagan noted that protesters had found predictable allies in the liberal professoriate, whose members condemned the university, the authorities, and Reagan himself for instigating the People's Park confrontation. Such condemnation simply continued the paternal failure of the professors—those "supposedly reasonable mature adults." Further emboldened, the protectors issued a defiant thirteen-point manifesto in the aftermath of the violence. "Some of these points are very revealing," Reagan noted. The first two points that Reagan discussed fit his patricidal interpretation of student protest nicely:

• Young people leaving their parents will be welcome with full status as members of our community.

• We will turn the schools into training grounds for liberation.

Student protesters were thus not content with their own savage indecency and communist-inspired lawlessness; they sought to spread their disorder, "like a virus," to the entirety of the nation's youth.[116]

To prevent the cancer that was rotting out California campuses from metastasizing to the nation's youth writ large, it was necessary that authority figures follow Reagan's lead and "stand firm."[117] During his two terms as governor, Reagan encouraged, and thrilled to, stern responses to student protest. His favorite university administrator, S. I. Hayakawa of San Francisco State University, regularly offered just these sorts of responses.[118] Reagan made the point in a letter to a colleague in 1969: "I'm convinced we win when we defy the little monsters . . . after all, the Lord took a club to the money changers in the temple."[119] Or, as he put it less charitably in 1970 after members of the Ohio National Guard killed four student protesters at Kent State University: "No more appeasement. If it takes a bloodbath, let's get it over with."[120]

Reagan thus brought to the "cowardly little bums" the sort of stern, fatherly discipline of which they had been chronically deprived.[121] Yet it had not, by any reasonable account, worked. Rather than offering them tough love that would lead to self-discipline—rather than converting the immature little monsters into autonomous, "average citizens"—Reagan's paternal wrath had instead hardened their resolve. He escalated conflict with the students; they didn't back down. His exercise of paternal authority was counterproductive: it encouraged the allegedly immature and undisciplined behaviors that it sought to extinguish.

Worse, Reagan turned a dispute over municipal property into a violent conflict that left a bystander (not a protester at all) dead; it was, by any measure, a catastrophe. Yet Reagan did not, as American countersubversives typically have, internalize responsibility for his countersubversive violence.[122] One had to expect, said Reagan, that when youth rebelled against their fathers, people "will make mistakes on both sides."[123] After all, hadn't Dutch himself frequently seen the flat side of Jack's boot?

The catastrophe of People's Park didn't hurt Reagan politically. He was easily reelected to a second term as governor of California in 1970; he received generally positive reviews for his performance in office; he was unaffected by the Republican Party's involvement in Nixon's Watergate scandal; and he was disappointed but not deterred on losing the Republican Party's nomination for the 1976 presidential election.[124] Reagan spent the second half of the 1970s writing and recording syndicated radio presentations that further sharpened his own political vision and more deeply acquainted the American electorate with him.[125] His defeat of incumbent President Jimmy Carter in 1980 ushered in the Reagan Revolution in American politics.

The record suggests, accordingly, that Reagan moved on easily from the Battle of People's Park. Seemingly unaffected by the violence that he had instigated, it was not the last time that Reagan would yoke the misuse of rights to family dysfunction, heteronomy, political radicalism, and overwhelming paternal governmental authority. It was not, that is, the last time that he would interpolate subjects according to the paternal rights discourse that infuses modern American conservatism. Nor was it the last time that his use of the discourse would authorize the employment of paternal, but ultimately unproductive, governmental power against those whom it marked as children. Ronald Reagan had used conservatism's paternal rights discourse to help overcome the legacy of his own chaotic upbringing, to find "the rest of" himself, and, finally, to carve out a philosophy of governance; his facility with it vaulted him into the pantheon of American political heroes. And so by the time that he entered the White House, Reagan was fully devoted to the personal and political lessons that the discourse transmitted. It is ironic, then, but also revelatory of its paradoxical character and effects, that Reagan's most spectacular presidential use of the paternal rights discourse—against the Sandinista regime in Nicaragua—exposed his administration to scandal and near ruin.

Love and Death in Nicaragua

Ronald Reagan was obsessed with Nicaragua. There was no more pressing foreign policy issue during the first six years of his presidency.

His diaries were dominated by the issue,[126] it was the subject of twenty major presidential addresses, and his failure to garner substantial public and congressional support for the Contras who were fighting the Sandinista regime was the source of his greatest frustration as president.[127] The conflict between the Sandinista regime and the Contras was, in fact, a "great struggle"; it was "one of the greatest moral challenges in postwar history."[128]

At first blush, Reagan's understanding of the Nicaraguan conflict, in which an explicitly communist government battled an anticommunist guerrilla insurgency, offers a fairly straightforward instance of the anticommunism that had long animated Reagan's political vision. The conflict allowed Reagan to express the full repertoire of his standard anticommunist positions: he habitually castigated the Sandinista regime as a repressive, subversive force interested only in exporting revolution—and the chaos, disorder, and violence that it bred—throughout the hemisphere. Yet lurking in the background of Reagan's understanding was the same family drama that suffused his take on domestic subversives (and student protesters in particular). Indeed, the virus of communist subversion that the Sandinistas hoped to transmit was particularly horrifying because it threatened to "spread [the] poison" of lawlessness to the entire family of American nations that occupied the Western Hemisphere.[129]

As it had when applied to student protesters during his years as governor of California, Reagan's familicidal interpretation of the Nicaraguan conflict exerted constitutive force. By providing a conceptual terrain on which the Sandinistas were identified as an "outlaw" regime that threatened the extended American family, the terms in which Reagan made sense of the conflict encouraged him to support a series of actions meant to bring law and order to Nicaragua. But the stern paternal authority that Reagan visited upon the Sandinistas unnecessarily escalated conflict, authorized the commission of violence against innocent Nicaraguan citizens, and led his own administration to evade congressional prohibitions. Not an example of ordinary Cold War–era anticommunism, Reagan's conduct of the Contra war points instead to the tangled familial pathologies at the heart of modern American conservatism.

Indeed, when making the case for aggressive confrontation of the Sandinista regime, Reagan consistently, and explicitly, articulated family ties. These ties were, in part, a matter of geographic proximity. "Nicaragua," Reagan frequently reminded audiences, "is just as close to Miami,

San Antonio, San Diego, and Tucson as those cities are to Washington."[130] But it was not just that the nations of Central America were "our neighbors" and "very close and very important to us."[131] Our bonds with the nations of Central America were more intimate: "We have to remember that we're kin to each other"; we were, in fact, "all Americans—all of us from pole to pole in this Western hemisphere."[132] "We have" he said, "the same heritage as pioneers to these virtually undiscovered continents. . . . We worship from South Pole to North Pole the same God. . . . We are all Americans."[133]

While familial, the relationship between the United States and the nations of Central America was not fraternal; it was vertical, not horizontal. The American family, like all other good families, had its head. "Just as you work so your children will have a better future," Reagan intoned, "the United States must work so that the fledgling democracies of this hemisphere will have a better future." And as a successful child will eventually have the means to care for an aging parent, so too was the success of Central America vital "so that our own future can be more secure." In guiding Central American nations into mature democratic states as a parent guides a child into adulthood—in helping them to achieve "what we have achieved in this land—in freedom, in economic progress, in standard of living"—we thus secured our own golden years.[134]

The "irresponsible" prevarications of Sandinista Nicaragua, however, threatened familial bliss from within.[135] An "outlaw regime" (there was "no crime to which [they would] not stoop"), the Sandinistas flouted law and order in their pursuit of communist subversion:

The Sandinistas have revoked the civil liberties of the Nicaraguan people, depriving them of any legal right to speak, to publish, to assemble, or to worship freely. Independent newspapers have been shut down. There is no longer any independent labor movement in Nicaragua nor any right to strike.[136]

Just as the disorderly tendencies of unruly student protesters were exploited by domestic communists, so was Sandinista lawlessness cultivated by nefarious outside influence. Indeed, prior to coming to power in Nicaragua, the Sandinistas "were called to Havana, where Castro cynically instructed them in the ways of successful Communist insurrection." Having "listened and learned," the Sandinista regime sought a "communist stronghold on the North American continent—a green light to spread its poison throughout this free and increasingly democratic hemisphere."[137]

Announcing the Sandinista threat to the American family, Reagan supposed that "surely no issue is more important for peace in our own hemisphere, for the security of our frontiers, for the protection of our vital interests, than to achieve democracy in Nicaragua and to protect Nicaragua's democratic neighbors."[138]

The lawless subversion that the Sandinistas plotted was thus not simply the ordinary communist dream of dominating the world; it was an act of familicide. For, in addition to the usual acts of repression and denial of rights characteristic of communist, totalitarian regimes, the Sandinistas had betrayed their own brethren. On coming to power in 1979 after the abdication of the vile Somoza regime, the Sandinistas promised the Organization of American States (which had been instrumental in convincing Somoza to give up power) that they would hold free elections, observe democratic principles, and not use governing authority to enforce and spread the communism that had originally motivated them. But in spite of substantial financial support and goodwill from many in the American family (including, most prominently, the United States), Sandinista promises turned out to be "the same old" communist lies:

Just months after taking power, the Communists began doing what they'd planned all along—they ousted their critics . . . they tightened their military grip on the nation, and they censored the media in Nicaragua and suppressed free speech.[139]

Though the Sandinistas had "put on a façade of democracy . . . [it] was sheer deceit. . . . When the mask fell . . . the face of totalitarianism became visible to the world."[140] Permissive parenting, Reagan knew, had led to eventual social disorder at home. So too had American goodwill in the waning days of the Carter administration (especially the $75 million in economic assistance that Carter authorized to Nicaragua in spite of reservations about Sandinista support of communist insurgency in El Salvador) simply encouraged further Sandinista attempts to export lawless subversion throughout the hemisphere.[141]

Exposure of the Sandinistas' sinister goals revealed that just as student protest on university campuses sought to spread disorder "like a virus" to the American polity, Nicaraguan subversion aimed to go viral. The Sandinistas were "players in a drama whose aim is to spread communism throughout this hemisphere."[142] They sought "fratricidal bloodletting."[143] Indeed, the "cancer that is Nicaragua" was looking to "infect" the extended American family "through the export of subversion and violence," with the destruction of U.S. democracy itself as the end goal.[144] The Sandinistas would not stop until we "see them at the borders of Arizona and New Mexico."[145]

Confronted with a traitor in the extended American family—a duplicitous, untrustworthy son who spurned paternal and fraternal bonds, usurped the limits of law and order, and sought to seize absolute familial power for himself—Reagan urged Congress and the American people to adopt a stern response. And as the patriarch of the American family, it was up to the United States to lead the rebuke. Thus, in one of its first foreign policy initiatives, the Reagan administration in April 1981 cut off all economic aid to Nicaragua and conditioned the renewal of aid on the halting of Sandinista support for communist insurgency in El Salvador.[146] Having refused to curb their subversive inclinations, the Sandinistas were cut loose from US support, just like an unruly child who refuses the rules of the household is cast out from familial support. The termination of economic aid was thus an act of tough love, designed to encourage the Sandinistas to abandon their unruly, lawless ways and return to the embrace of the extended American family.

But the withdrawal of paternal support did not have its intended effect. Just as provoking confrontation at People's Park in Berkeley had emboldened student protesters, so too were the Sandinistas invigorated by the revocation of economic aid. Unrepentant, they intensified their already strong bonds with Cuba; accelerated their now successful attempts to garner financial support from the Soviet Union; and openly proclaimed their support of, and assistance for, communist insurgency in El Salvador and Honduras.[147] And just as Reagan's provocations laid the ground for coming violence in Berkeley, so too was the exercise of paternal authority against the Sandinistas a harbinger. Indeed, after its aid policy failed, the Reagan administration concluded that the Sandinista threat must be aggressively rolled back, not simply contained.

But Reagan charged that the Democratic Congress, because of the hesitance for aggressive intervention preached by its "irrational" leader Tip O'Neill, "kept pulling the rug out from under" Reagan.[148] With such prohibitive measures as 1984's Boland Amendment (which forbade the expenditure of funds on behalf of the Contras), the American family by 1986 was left vulnerable to the growing Sandinista cancer. Desperate to eradicate communist subversion and the lawlessness that it spread before it was too late, Reagan took to conflating the Sandinista threat with his own coming presidential mortality. Soon, Reagan reflected, he would no longer be able to exert the needed paternal authority: "I have only three years left to serve my country; three years to carry out the responsibilities that you entrusted to me; three years to work for peace. Could there be any greater tragedy than for us to sit back and permit this cancer to spread?"[149]

Yet Reagan realized that any direct attempts to contain the Sandinista threat would be constrained by the lingering "post-Vietnam syndrome" that affected the morale of the American public and made it wary of fighting communists in developing nations.[150] Indeed, in spite of some support for the option within his administration, Reagan never considered sending American military forces to Nicaragua.[151] Thus, Reagan saw the Contras—a coalition of disaffected revolutionaries, peasants, and indigenous people led by former members of Somoza's notorious National Guard and secretly organized and continuously funded and trained by the CIA—as an attractive alternative to the application of US force against the Sandinistas.[152]

The Contras were, according to Reagan, champions of democratic order in the face of Sandinista subversion. "All they want," Reagan said of the Contras, "all they're fighting for is to return to the principles of the revolution that overthrew Somoza—free elections, human rights, free press, all of those things."[153] Because they were "trying to restore the democratic promises made during the revolution," the Contras were "patriots who fight for freedom."[154] The Contras, that is, sought to bring legal principles to an "outlaw" regime; with US military support, they would quash the "chaos and anarchy" with which the Sandinista regime threatened the Western Hemisphere.[155] Surrogates for the direct exercise of American paternal power, these "brave Nicaraguan freedom fighters" were, accordingly, fathers in training; already "the moral equivalent of our founding fathers," US military support would allow the Contras to replace the communist disorder practiced by the Sandinistas with the dreams of America's founding fathers.[156] Indeed, Reagan identified with the Contras' paternal mission: they "are against . . . Communist [subversion] . . . and so [this] makes me a Contra too."[157]

Yet Reagan was never able to garner more than lukewarm congressional and public support for the Contras. His inability to convince a skeptical Congress and American public that the Contras were, in fact, reincarnations of the founding fathers was at once Reagan's (self-diagnosed) greatest failure and a lingering source of incomprehension. Engaged in a "life and death struggle" for the extended American family's liberty and for the US place as its patriarch, the Contras were forced by congressional obstinacy and public wariness to go to war against "helicopters piloted by Cubans with Band-Aids and mosquito nets"; it was a "disgrace."[158] Still Reagan exhorted: "Will we give the Nicaraguan democratic resistance [the Contras] the means to recapture their betrayed revolution, or will we turn our backs and ignore the malignancy in Managua until it spreads and becomes a mortal threat to the entire New World?"[159]

Although Reagan sourced the widespread skepticism of the Contras in the combination of post-Vietnam wariness and a "very sophisticated disinformation campaign that completely bamboozled many," the harsher truth was that the Contras were simply not believable in the exalted role in which Reagan cast them.[160] Numerous dispassionate reports and exposés revealed that the Contras were as likely to brutalize, torture, and murder Nicaraguans as they were to defend them against the supposedly lawless assaults of the Sandinistas.[161] Substantial evidence of Contra drug running was produced.[162] But Reagan habitually claimed to the American people that these "so-called" Contra atrocities were actually the duplicitous handiwork of the Sandinistas, who were attempting to deceive international opinion and cast themselves as the true humanitarians:[163]

The truth is, there are atrocities going on in Nicaragua, but they're largely the work of the institutionalized cruelty of the Sandinista government. This cruelty is the natural expression of a Communist government, a cruelty that flows naturally from the heart of totalitarianism. The truth is Somoza was bad, but so many of the people of Nicaragua know the Sandinistas are infinitely worse.[164]

Even when confronted with unassailable, undeniable evidence of Contra atrocities, Reagan insisted that they were representative of neither Contra practice writ large nor of the moral character—the paternal virtues—of Contras. Instead, such occasional atrocities were the unfortunate consequence of battling the savage communist enemy. Here again Reagan harked back to his experience battling student protesters on California campuses: "Once the dogs of war are unleashed, you must expect that things will happen, and people being human will make mistakes on both sides."[165] Anyway, the occasional Contra mistake, borne of paternal zealousness in the cause of American rights, paled in comparison to the organized reign of terror practiced by Sandinistas both on the Nicaraguan population and on the extended American family.[166]

Reagan was so exercised by the Sandinista threat that he and his administration consistently evaded congressional prohibitions on US support for the Contras.[167] For example, 1984's Boland Amendment was undermined through the administration's solicitation (complete with personal cajoling from Reagan himself) of Contra aid from such nations as Saudi Arabia.[168] And the 1986 congressional refusal to release military aid to the Contras set the stage for the Iran-Contra scandal, in which the proceeds from covert arms sales to Iran were transferred to the Contras. While the scheme was the brainchild of renegade administration officials (National Security Council aide Oliver North and National Security Advisor John Poindexter, in particular) and most likely proceeded without Reagan's knowledge, the dedication that it displayed to the Contra effort was consistent with Reagan's conviction that the Contras must be supported "body and soul."[169] Reagan, concludes one of his most authoritative biographers, "thought that helping the Contras was 'the right thing to do.' He had no interest whatever in the legal restrictions that Congress . . . had imposed on him and on the executive branch."[170]

Having led him to unnecessarily escalate conflict with the Sandinista regime, Reagan's paternal embrace of American power led him also to back a murderous, exterminatory guerrilla insurgency—one for which he was willing to evade congressional restrictions and prohibitions. Such evasion was necessary if the Contras were to be allowed to "stand firm" against the Sandinistas, if they were to be allowed to "unleash the dogs of war" and bring the necessary paternal discipline to an unruly, "outlaw" regime. That the exercise of paternal authority by the American president might require the evasion of congressional restrictions was of no concern to Reagan. His conduct of the Contra war thus updated and internationalized the formulation of a fellow acolyte of modern American conservatism's paternal rights discourse. "When the President does it," claimed Richard Nixon, "that means that it is not illegal."[171]

Conclusion

Reagan's conduct of the Contra war reflected in multiple ways his earlier experience of bringing law and order to the unruly hippies who populated California's university campuses. Convinced that the denial of legitimate forms of inequality marked one as immature and so invited communist indoctrination, Reagan's countersubversive inclinations suggested that the egalitarian politics practiced by both student protesters and the Sandinistas required a stern, paternal response in order to prevent the disorder that they threatened from spreading throughout the American family. Although law and order could not be directly given to the Sandinistas (as it was to student protesters at the Battle of People's Park a generation earlier), Reagan could direct his surrogates—the Contras—to teach Sandinistas the hard truths of vertical inequality that communist doctrine refused. As such, he could offer the unruly children within the extended American family the tough love that conservatives prescribed as necessary for mature, adult practice and that Reagan had personally offered to student protesters.

Second, Reagan understood that paternal discipline—while always necessary for the production of autonomous citizens—was sometimes resisted and, accordingly, it might be necessary, as he had at Berkeley, to take "a club to the money changers in the temple."[172] In such a case, more than the Band-Aids and mosquito nets offered to the Contras by the permissive Democratic Congress were needed. The stern hand of the father, which was akin to unleashing the "dogs of war" on unrepentant children, was thus an ever-present possibility.

But Reagan's conduct of the Contra war extended paternal violence abroad. In so doing, it affirmed the traditional understanding that American foreign policy required an assertive imperialism that brought the blessings of American liberty and the training with which to effectively practice it to the world's immature, nonwhite peoples.[173] Channeling the basic logic of the Monroe Doctrine, Reagan meant to ensure that the United States supported and protected the fledgling, immature democracies that dotted Central America just as a loving father supports and protects his children until they are capable of standing on their own as adults.

Yet the family drama within which Reagan played out the Contra war reveals, finally, a deep irony. In attempting to bring fatherly discipline to the treacherous bad sons within the extended American family, the Reagan administration consistently exceeded the limits that Congress had placed on Contra aid. Such evasion set into motion the events of Iran-Contra, a scandal that exposed Reagan's presidency to congressional investigation and oversight. Consumed by anxieties about bad parenting and the need for paternal influence, the paternal rights discourse at the heart of modern American conservatism encouraged perhaps its most important figure to pursue a course of action in Nicaragua that eventuated in his own subordination to an "irrational," permissive Democratic Congress that refused to "stand firm" against the lawless Sandinista regime. Finally deprived of his capacity to exert paternal authority, President Reagan was, ironically, returned to the sort of dysfunctional family unit that Dutch had spent his entire adult life trying to flee.

Coda

Ronald Reagan never got over his inability to convince the American public and Congress of the dire threat that the Sandinista regime presented to the extended American family. Nor could he accept his failure to persuade the nation that the Contras were its founding fathers reincarnate. Reagan self-diagnosed these as the biggest failures of his presidency; they haunted him well after he left the Oval Office. By 1990, he confided to Richard Nixon, Reagan realized that he had previously underestimated the Sandinista "disinformation program" that he believed was responsible for his failure to persuade. Indeed, Reagan was still "surprised at the effectiveness" of the program, which continued to fool countless members of Congress, disinterested journalists, and even members of the American public. "They must have outside help," Reagan concluded.

America's fortieth president made the point to the nation's disgraced thirty-seventh president with a personal story: "One day a slick paper magazine turned up on my desk in the Oval Office. It was cover-to-cover propaganda [for the Sandinistas] and contained a card telling readers how to use it to provide a subscription for their senator or congressman." But, as it turned out, support for the Sandinista subversion of the American family was an inside job. In a literal return of the repressed, it was the little monsters whom Reagan had subjected to paternal law and order a generation earlier who were responsible. "The magazine," Reagan noted, "was published in Berkeley, California."[174]

Postscript

Ronald Reagan's presidential administration had not yet begun in December 1980, when San Francisco hosted a conference for young black conservatives. But members of Reagan's transition team noticed a *Washington Post* article that praised the conference's breakout star, Clarence Thomas; they promptly offered him the position of assistant secretary for civil rights in Reagan's Department of Education.[175] It was a fitting appointment. Clarence Thomas, like William F. Buckley Jr. and Reagan before him, had overcome a legacy of paternal failure on his path to American conservatism. He too had found succor in paternal surrogates real and spectral. Thomas was fluent in conservatism's paternal rights discourse.

But unlike Buckley and Reagan, Thomas struggles with the paradoxes of that discourse. At once American conservatism's greatest living success story and a testament to the incoherence of its animating creed— its simultaneous embrace of the undying influence of the fathers and the autonomy of the sons—Clarence Thomas is, in the unintentionally damning words of fellow black conservative Shelby Steele, an "archetype."[176] Chapter 5 explores his struggles.

5

All the Rage: Clarence Thomas, Daddy, and the Tragedy of Rights

The story of Clarence Thomas is really the story of the American Dream.
—Senator Jack Danforth

I am a strict law and order man.
—Clarence Thomas

Modern American conservatives revere US Supreme Court Justice Clarence Thomas. He is, according to the *Weekly Standard*, the "leading conservative in America today." The *American Spectator* agrees that Thomas is the "most eloquent, most consistent conservative leader in the country." The *National Review* esteems him "a model Justice . . . the best on the [Supreme] Court." More than just an iconic conservative, Thomas, according to *National Review* editor Rich Lowry, is "an extraordinary man." Conservative law professor Henry Mark Holzer credits him as a "fine human being, doting father, loving husband, patriotic American, and brave man." Rush Limbaugh hails Thomas as a "national treasure," while 2012 Republican Party presidential candidate Herman Cain affirmed that the justice was the best then serving on the Supreme Court and was "one of my models."[1]

How are we to understand the ascent of a formal legal figure to the status of national hero in the conservative imagination? What is it about Clarence Thomas that makes him, like William F. Buckley Jr. and Ronald Reagan before him, so compelling to American conservatives? What makes Thomas, as in R. Emmett Tyrrel Jr.'s estimation, the "most noble public figure in American life today"?[2]

We will see, first, that the personal and political narrative that Clarence Thomas espouses articulates with conservative renderings of the virtuous, autonomous American citizen. This citizen, we have seen, embodies the values of mature self-discipline.[3] Clarence Thomas—whose self-narrative depicts an extraordinary rise from appalling life circumstances that were inflected with race and class-based dynamics, in addition to significant family dysfunction—is thus an icon. Indeed, conservative columnist Rod Dreher depicts Thomas as an embodiment of the American dream: his life story is "so profoundly moving, and so profoundly true to this nation's ideals, that every American father" should tell it to his children.[4] Thomas, according to fellow black conservative Shelby Steele, is "the freest black man in America." Having overcome what the justice calls the "frailties" of life, Steele sees in Thomas "an almost heroic individualism—an individualism that is quite beyond the old framework of race."[5]

But Thomas's "heroic individualism," which is also the foundation of his Supreme Court jurisprudence, points at once to personal repression[6] and nationalistic aspiration. His jurisprudence, supposedly freed from the strictures of identity, speaks to "a characteristically American . . . respect for individual self-reliance and individual choice." Thomas's legal narrative is thus said to be sourced in a personal overcoming that itself points to a larger national triumph; his jurisprudence, concludes conservative legal scholar John Yoo, is "forged in the crucible of a truly American story."[7] Cleansed of the stain of personal and racial history, Clarence Thomas's "originalist" jurisprudence enters the corpus of American tradition while its author enters the same conservative pantheon of American heroes that houses Buckley Jr. and Reagan. Thomas, accordingly, is not simply "the most interesting Justice to sit on the Supreme Court in a generation" or only "a model Justice . . . the best on the [Supreme] Court"; he is also the "single greatest living American office-holder."[8]

This point of departure is not original. As Jane Flax argued, both Thomas and his admirers emphasize how the justice's personal history—which is presented as an overcoming of manifold structural inequalities through the practices of self-discipline and skepticism of government—validates the myth of American individualism and the autonomous subject that underlies that myth.[9] Critics, of course, excoriate Thomas on precisely this score. They argue that the governmental sponsorship and assistance that he has received, even as he refuses it for others, makes Thomas shortsighted and cold-hearted at best and hypocritical, self-hating, and racially conflicted at worst.[10] Clarence Thomas is not, his critics maintain, the isolated, autonomous individual that self and conservative appraisal makes him out to be.

But the "reality" of Clarence Thomas's life story—the narrative that he tells about himself—is ultimately beside the point. To understand how and why Clarence Thomas's life story, a narrative in which law and rights are deeply imbricated, signifies both to himself and to others requires us to move beyond felt inconsistencies—beyond the familiar, hoary opposition of "subjective" narrative to "objective" truth. For the appeal, the resonance and the power of the narrative of Clarence Thomas lie not in the realm of empirical fact but in the realm of mythical vision. Clarence Thomas's American heroism, I argue, points not only to the dictates of articulated conservative ideology and conscious national ideals; it also lays bare the paternal desires and fears that animate modern American conservatism.

In particular, I argue that the intellectual Right's canonization of Clarence Thomas speaks to the same distinctive elements of modern American conservatism that have been the subjects of this book: rage at and rejection of maternal, feminine influence; an associated longing for paternal authority and the self-disciplined, autonomous subjectivity that it is believed to produce; and the promotion of law, which is figured as the "law of the father," as the primary means by which to achieve order and repress the chaos associated with the maternal realm. The personal, political, and legal narrative articulated by Clarence Thomas affirms that familial anxiety is the ideological catalyst of modern conservative politics. And it confirms that conservatism's paternal rights discourse is simultaneously the conduit through which that anxiety is expressed and the prescription for how it ought to be treated.

Accordingly, to treat Clarence Thomas as a conservative icon is not simply to document his celebration in conservative intellectual circles. It is instead to interpret that celebration as communal ritual. Thomas's own "heroic" story of elevation over the pathologies of race, class, and family thus points to specific desires in his supporters; his paternal rights discourse rescues the American nation, and the privileged places occupied in it by those autonomous citizens whom conservatives champion, from the subversive assaults of those undisciplined, heteronomous citizens who, unlike Thomas, are said to succumb to life's frailties.

But the lessons of Thomas's paternal rights discourse are more ambiguous than either he or his conservative supporters recognize. On one hand, the justice's self-presentation continually emphasizes how child-hood submission to the sort of stern paternal authority that he himself experienced produces autonomous, rights-bearing citizens who are capable of governing their selves, and the nation, in virtuous and responsible ways. Thomas thus unsurprisingly conceives of his elevation to the US Supreme Court in the same way as do his conservative supporters: as the culmination of a life lived according to the paternal lessons of self-discipline that were harshly inflicted on him by his maternal grandfather.

But even here, at the professional pinnacle of his life, the justice insists that he is not autonomous, not free to make the independent, mature judgments that are supposed to be the fruits of a lifetime of virtuous self-discipline. Thomas proclaims instead that his judicial self-discipline requires that he once again submit to a paternal will that obliterates his individuality, renders moot the virtuous self-governance that he has spent his life cultivating, and turns him into a personality-less, judicial automaton. Once suppressed by the heavy, punishing hand of a harsh grandfather, Thomas's autonomy, insofar as he envisions himself as a judicial "originalist," is now voluntarily discarded in the name of fidelity to the spectral desires of the founding fathers. Accordingly, when Thomas claims, as he often does, that serving on the Supreme Court feels like being "home," he offers a telling, if ambiguous and ironic, proclamation: unquestioning submission to stern paternal authority—which, as we have seen throughout, is represented in modern American conservatism as productive of self-governing, autonomous citizens—generates citizens whose commitments to self-discipline lead them to voluntarily abdicate the mature autonomy thought to be central to the possibility of self-governance itself.

Previous chapters have explored the paternal rights discourse that came to suffuse American conservatism in the post–World War II and late Cold War eras. These were the eras in which Clarence Thomas came to self-identify as a conservative. Thomas, we will see, readily identified with the discourse's themes of absent fathers, pernicious mothers, and the importance that family dynamics played in the formulation of disciplined and/or deviant American citizens. Indeed, in his current role as a Supreme Court justice, Thomas is an exponent of that distinctive paternal rights discourse—a discourse that sees rights as guarantors of both limited government and social order. And just as the previous chapter established that Ronald Reagan was willing to let loose the forces of "law and order," which he referred to as the "dogs of war," on the immature and undisciplined American selves who refused this understanding[11], so too does Thomas affirm the stern paternal role of government where literal and metaphoric paternal influence fails.[12]

Accordingly, the familial fears and desires transmitted by the paternal rights discourse—fears and desires that animate, regenerate, and trouble modern American conservatism—materialize in the figure of Clarence Thomas. Such fears and desires are indeed at the very heart of the considerable appeal that the justice holds for American conservatives. Thus, as were William F. Buckley Jr. and Ronald Reagan before him, Clarence Thomas is an index of conservative obsession over the place of fathers and rights in the contemporary American polity.

It is unsurprising, then, that Clarence Thomas suffuses his self-narrative—told in his autobiography, numerous public speeches, and multiple interviews—with the search for stable, paternal influence and the concomitant achievement of self-discipline and autonomous citizenship. The attainment of self-discipline, Thomas intimates, involves overcoming both literal maternal dependence and the avatars traditionally associated with the maternal realm. Thomas also presents this overcoming as vital for the practice of good citizenship writ large. Indeed, Thomas's prescription for autonomous citizenship involves the continuous overcoming of chaotic, passionate, dependent, and ultimately maternal influences—influences that punctuate the scheming of both actual women (such as that practiced by some members of Clarence Thomas's own family and, later, by Anita Hill and her feminist "enablers") and governmental planners.

Before proceeding, I wish to acknowledge those who argue, with significant cause, that Thomas's self-narrative is riddled with half-truths and evasions.[13] At issue here is not simply the charge, noted earlier, that Thomas has personally benefited from many of the governmental programs that he routinely disparages and, as Supreme Court justice, denies to others. Instead, there is a more persistent, more troubling accusation that Thomas is a serial prevaricator who manipulates the facts of his life in order to fit a prefabricated, conventional tale of American success. If this claim is accurate, and certainly there are sufficient discrepancies between Thomas's self-narrative and most dispassionate accounts of his life to lend the claim credence, isn't Clarence Thomas rendered an unreliable, even cynical reporter of his own life? Wouldn't an analysis of Thomas's role in American life thus properly be an act of expository truth telling?

Perhaps. But my analysis here means to put such concerns about the justice's veracity beside the point—or, rather, the (real) possibility that Thomas self-consciously wrenches the story of his life into a template that both he and his supporters find persuasive makes that template *itself* the point. What is it about Thomas's self-narrative that is so appealing to him and his conservative supporters? To which widely shared, though half-conscious, desires and fears does that self-narrative appeal? My purpose is thus not to gainsay Thomas's story of self. Such a project has been done repeatedly.[14] Instead, in the same way that previous chapters have taken seriously the autobiographical accounts of Buckley Jr. and Reagan, I here take seriously the justice's own account of his life. In so doing, the mythic power of Thomas's self-narrative—which itself relies on and reinforces the conventional, familial understandings of American law and politics with which this book is concerned—is revealed.[15]

A Grandfather's Son

Clarence Thomas was born in Pinpoint, Georgia—an "unforgiving," tiny coastal hamlet southeast of Savannah—in 1948. His mother, Leola ("Pigeon"), had previously given birth to a daughter, Emma Mae, in 1946 and, later, to another son, Myers Lee, in 1949. Pigeon and the biological father of her three children, M. C. Thomas, divorced in 1950. M. C. promptly moved to Philadelphia, abandoning his children.

Clarence's first recollection of his biological father is a brief meeting with him that took place at Pigeon's apartment in Savannah when he was nine years old. M. C. promised to send Clarence and Myers "a pair of Elgin watches with flexible bands, which were popular at the time." The watches never arrived. "My father," writes Thomas, "had broken the only promise that he ever made to us."[16]

But in spite of paternal rejection and brutal poverty (the Thomas residence in Pinpoint lacked electricity, heat, and running water), Thomas describes life in Pinpoint as "idyllic."[17] He refers to skipping oyster shells on the water, fishing, and hunting for fiddler crabs on the beach. Significantly, Thomas depicts Pinpoint, an isolated peninsula inhabited primarily by the descendants of slaves, as mercifully free of overt racial prejudice. All of this changed in 1954 when Clarence was six years old; his brother, Myers, and a cousin accidently burned down their Pinpoint house while playing with matches. Clarence and Myers subsequently moved with

Pigeon to Savannah, where Pigeon worked as a housekeeper for a white family.

Savannah, writes Thomas, "was hell. Overnight I moved from the comparative safety and cleanliness of rural poverty to the foulest kind of urban squalor." Thomas's depiction of life in Savannah is notable. First, Savannah is depicted entirely negatively, as a place of absence: absence of heat ("without the prospect of warmth"); of food ("Never before had I known the nagging, chronic hunger that plagued me in Savannah"); of money ("We couldn't afford sugar"); of friends ("I was alone, a stranger in an unfamiliar, ugly world"); of intellectual stimulation ("My lessons [at school] were slow moving and repetitive"); of hope ("Pigeon always came home tired and drained. It was as though her job sapped all the hope out of her"); and, significantly, of self and, especially, bodily control. It is, in this last respect, worth quoting Thomas at length:

The only running water in our building was downstairs in the kitchen, where several layers of old linoleum were all that separated us from the ground. The toilet was outdoors in the muddy backyard. The metal bowl was cracked and rusty and the wooden seat was rotten. I'll never forget the sickening stench of the raw sewage that seeped and sometimes poured from the broken sewer line. Pigeon preferred to use a chamber pot, and one of my . . . chores was to take it outside and empty it in the toilet. One day I tripped and tumbled all the way down the stairs, landing in a heap at the bottom. The brimming pot followed, drenching me in stale urine.

Absence; despair; the stench of human waste; spilled bodily fluids: these are the haunting images that Thomas associates with his family's arrival in Savannah.[18]

Second, it is significant that Thomas explicitly blames his absent father for the circumstances into which his family had sunk. M. C. "did nothing—and I mean nothing—to help us. A court had ordered him to pay child support to Pigeon, but he ignored it." But Thomas also depicts his fate in terms of Pigeon's incapacities. An unskilled worker, she was forced to take "a full-time job that paid only ten dollars a week" and left her "unable to take care of two energetic young boys."[19] In addition, there were maternal failures that Clarence alone suffered. The family's only bed was shared by Pigeon and the smaller Myers, "leaving me to sleep on a chair. It was too small, even for a six-year-old."[20] And it was his mother's refusal to use the outhouse that ultimately resulted in the indignity of Thomas being covered in human waste.

These passages at once highlight Pigeon's inability to create a stable home and set up Thomas's discussion of what was clearly the most important event in his youth: Pigeon taking Clarence and Myers to live permanently with her parents, who also lived in Savannah, but in a new cinder-block house with hardwood floors and, significantly, "an indoor bathroom." Thomas writes that he doesn't "know the whole story of Pigeon's decision" to transfer parental responsibility of her sons to her father and stepmother. But he suggests that Pigeon's punishing work schedule and her "refusal to go on welfare" eventually led her to ask her father for help raising her children.[21] But Thomas's autobiography is discreet, for he has previously told a significantly different and more damning account.

As related in Peyton Thomas's (no relation to Clarence) sympathetic biography: "Leola found another man. He made it clear, according to Clarence's later account, that he 'didn't want children from the previous marriage around.'" Clarence, writes Peyton Thomas, "would always speak of this event with great bitterness."[22] Although his autobiography presents Thomas's move to his grandparents' house as the result of a difficult decision made by an overwhelmed but loving mother, his more private versions of the event present his mother as neglectful in her parental responsibilities, willing to abandon her children in pursuit of sexual union.[23]

Thomas's ambivalence toward his mother, and her abandonment of him, appears in sharp relief when he depicts the new living arrangements with his grandparents. "In all my life," writes Thomas, "I've never made a longer journey" than the two-and-a-half-block walk from his mother's apartment to his grandparents' "spotless white house." Thomas's grandparents, Myers "Daddy" Anderson and Christine "Aunt Tina" Anderson, were successful entrepreneurs who ran a business that delivered wood, coal, ice, and fuel oil to local homes. Frugal and hard working, the Andersons had built their own home; it "had two bedrooms, one bathroom, separate living and dining rooms, a den, and a kitchen." The house "wasn't all that large, but to us it looked as big as a palace." Compared to living with his mother and the "filthy outdoor toilet" that occupied the backyard of her tenement apartment, life with Daddy and Aunt Tina was a "life of luxury." The young Clarence had "never seen a house . . . with an indoor porcelain toilet that worked. I flushed it as often as I could in my first months [there]."[24]

The terms in which Thomas depicts the differences between living with his mother and living with his grandparents are stark and evocative.

It is notable that what most strikes Thomas about living with his grand-parents is the ability to dispose of bodily contents cleanly and efficiently. No longer would the stench of human waste and the touch of his mother's urine on his skin dominate his existence. Life with his mother, in which bodily control (which Erik Erickson described as the first and most important stage in the attainment of self-discipline[25]) was often precarious, was replaced by a "life of luxury" in which Thomas was free to discipline his body without worry. Self-control was now both possible and rewarded.

The change in physical circumstances was, according to Thomas, indicative of the change that he and Myers experienced in parenting styles. Previously left for hours on end without parental oversight ("our mother had allowed us to come and go as we pleased"), it "soon became clear that [Daddy] meant to control every aspect of our lives. . . . There would be no more carefree days spent wandering through the marshes hunting for fiddler crabs, no more roaming the streets instead of going to school." Clarence and Myers lived according to their grandfather's "unbending rules"; failure to obey resulted in punishment that was "swift, sure, and painful." Daddy's violent physical punishments "were far from infrequent."[26] "My grandfather imposed a rule that seemed pretty harsh: If you don't work, you don't eat. And he meant it."[27] Abruptly leaving behind a permissive maternal parenting style for a domineering and violent paternal one, the Thomas brothers experienced what Lakoff describes as the "stern father" model of parenting.[28]

Yet, like both the modern conservatives whom Lakoff analyzes and those iconic conservatives who are the subject of this book, Thomas argues that paternal domination was just what he and Myers needed. It taught them the material importance of self-discipline and hard work. Daddy Anderson's house was, accordingly, an "island of safety" amid a neighborhood replete with vice.

We often saw drunks (some of whom were relatives of ours) roving up and down our own block, often in packs, looking for a drink . . . One morning [I] had to step over the body of a man passed out on the sidewalk. Vomit and spittle flowed from the corner of his mouth, forming a puddle near his head.

Daddy, conversely, "put his faith in his own unaided effort—the one factor in life that he could control—and he taught Myers and me to do the same."[29] The "greatest man" that Thomas has "ever known," Daddy raised Clarence and Myers "with discipline because [he] understood that if [he] did not, we would perish."[30]

Thomas's articulation of the differences between life with Pigeon and life with Daddy—stern (frequently violent) paternal authority that instills self-discipline and paves the way to modest, earned luxury, on one hand, and paternal absence and maternal neglect that fosters license and sloth and thus leads either to material or moral poverty, on the other hand— evoke the exact family/nation nexus that defines modern American conservatism. Had he continued on the path he was on when living with his mother, Thomas is sure that he would have ended up a "statistic," either dead or in jail, like so many of his peers.[31] And, indeed, Thomas reports that he threw himself into his studies, which occurred in austere, ascetic settings: the local public library and in Catholic school, where Daddy's brand of stern discipline was mimicked by the nuns.[32]

Still, Thomas makes clear that he frequently resisted Daddy's harshness, initially through acts of what might be called "everyday resistance"[33] and, later, through the wholesale rejection of Daddy's faith in self-discipline and hard work. This latter rejection occurred following Daddy's disavowal of Thomas on learning that Clarence had dropped out of Immaculate Conception Seminary in 1968 after experiencing a racially charged incident that shook his faith in the Catholic Church. Daddy (a devout Catholic who had thus far financed Clarence's religious education) kicked Clarence out of his house and initiated a chilly relationship, refusing, for example, to attend Clarence's wedding to his first wife, Kathy, in 1971.

Daddy's rejection devastated Thomas: "Where could I go? What would I do? Was it really possible that the man on whom I had always counted was going to turn his back on me?" With no job, no money, and with his first act of adult independence resulting in paternal rejection, Thomas was forced to move back in with Pigeon ("reversing the journey" that he made as a child[34]) and take a menial summer job at a racially hostile paper company in Savannah. A pattern was now clear in Clarence Thomas's life, one that would continue until he joined the Reagan administration: his biological and metaphorical fathers eventually rejected him, forcing him to return to his mother's care, where he was deprived of the paternal authority critical for generating the self-discipline that was necessary to overcome life's "frailties" (themselves exacerbated by racial discrimination) and become autonomous.

Increasingly despondent over Daddy's rejection, the contemporaneous assassinations of Martin Luther King Jr. and Robert Kennedy and the racist practices to which he was daily subjected, Thomas's reengulf-ment in the maternal sphere coincided with his giving in to the "rage that threatened to burn though the mask of meekness and submission behind which [Southern blacks] hid our true feelings." He enrolled in the College of the Holy Cross, embraced the nascent black power movement, "tore off the beliefs that I had learned from Daddy," and became "an angry black man."[35] "I was," Thomas told a 1998 audience, "being consumed by the circumstances in which I found myself." Rejecting Daddy's influence, Thomas "felt the deep chronic agony of anomie and alienation." In despair he found purpose: he was "empowered by the anger" and engaged in a series of confrontational protests in and around Holy Cross.

But Thomas soon grew frightened of his rage, which, although "intoxicating to wear . . . on one's shoulder," was "ultimately destructive."

I knew that unless I contained the anger within me I would suffer the fates of Bigger Thomas and Cross Damon. . . . It was clear to me that the road to destruction was paved with anger, resentment, and rage. But where were we to go?[36]

Thomas's answer to his personal crisis was to return to his roots, to return "home" to Daddy's lessons. Indeed, after graduating from Yale Law School in the mid-1970s and accepting a job with Jack Danforth (the future US senator from Missouri and new father figure), Thomas returned to Daddy Anderson's paternal prescription for personal salvation and suc-cess (though not to Daddy himself; they remained estranged). And in the books of black conservative economist Thomas Sowell, which he "soaked up . . . [like they were] glass[es] of water [being poured] on the desert," Thomas found an intellectual base for the lessons of self-discipline and self-reliance that he had learned from his grandfather.[37]

A speech that Thomas delivered on Father's Day in 1984 confirmed his growing confidence in the enduring value of stern paternal author-ity. In it, Thomas implied that the products of paternal authority radi-ated in two directions at once: it instilled the character qualities necessary for autonomous citizenship even as it provided the resources necessary for resisting the seductive allure of "indolence or pleasure," which was embodied for Thomas, revealingly, by a mother on welfare who ignores the needs of her children so that she can watch soap operas. Thomas first waxed eloquently about fathers:

What is a father, a grandfather? He is a setter of standards. He is a maker of dreams. He is a demander of hard work, of the best his child can do. He is an answerer of questions, who is not ashamed to say he doesn't know. He is a setter of direction, who helps put the first steps on the way. He is the lion of children's safety and he is the sheep of their peace. He provides and protects and he loves and he gives and he is wise because he has lived in a world where he must be wise to survive. His is the hand that gives discipline. His is the hand that helps heal. He is tough when necessity demands toughness. He is gentle when life demands love. He is the setter of rules, because he knows the "why" of those rules. He is the teller of truth because he can always be trusted. He is patient when circumstances demand patience and understanding, and when all else seems to have failed, he is a mender of life's broken pieces. He is always there to be turned to and is turned to because he is strong. Father is a word, in all its translations, honored by every people on earth. It means the founder, the originator, the leader. We address our Lord as our father. . . . It is a title, not a hereditary title, but a title that must be earned and re-earned. It is a title of love.

Contrast this glowing, omniscient father with the "absentee fathers," like his own, who "by their own selfishness and immaturity ruin the young lives of their children." Rather than instilling the self-discipline in their children that will lead to mature, autonomous citizenship, those who, as he noted in a later speech, "procreate with pleasure and retreat from the responsibilities of the babies [they] produce"[38] end up breeding "poverty by breeding those they do not love and cannot or will not support." Contrast the idealized father also with the neglectful, indolent mother: "I want to tell her to turn off *Dallas* [and] *Dynasty* . . . when her own child needs help with his or her homework."[39]

Even apart from his condemnation of welfare mothers, Thomas leaves little obvious room or purpose for maternal influence. Father is "the founder, the originator, the leader," but also "a title of love," "gentle," "understanding," "patient." When mothers appear at all, they are either overwhelmed "teenage mothers" or the licentious welfare mothers who draw Thomas's ire. All-encompassing and ever-present fathers; absent, silent, or neglectful mothers: the speech reveals Thomas's conceptions of both a well-ordered home and, by extension, a well-ordered polity.[40]

But as it happened, Thomas found that living the self-disciplined, virtuous life bequeathed to him by his grandfather was difficult. Prior to his second (and current) marriage in the late 1980s, Thomas forthrightly reveals that his life was filled with financial struggle, marital unhappiness, functional alcoholism, personal despair, and suicidal thoughts. In early 1981, just before going to work for the Reagan administration at the Department of Education, Thomas left his first wife and temporarily abandoned his son. "It was the worst thing I've done in my life," he laments.[41]

Professionally, though, Thomas was thriving. A sympathetic portrayal of Thomas (who had recently spoken at a San Francisco conference of black conservatives) that appeared in the *Washington Post* and was penned by journalist, and future friend, Juan Williams[42] gained the attention of high-ranking officials in the Reagan administration, who offered Thomas the position of assistant secretary for civil rights in the Department of Education. Thomas was ambivalent. While he was excited by the prospect of working for an administration whose professed conservative political vision was so close to the one that he had come to hold, Thomas was uncomfortable with the content of Williams's article (in which Thomas criticized his own sister for her alleged welfare dependence[43]) and troubled by the suspicion that his was a symbolic appointment in an administration already perceived as hostile to black interests. "What other reason" could there be for his appointments, Thomas asked an interviewer in 1987, "besides the fact that I was black?"[44] Indeed, "I had no background in th[e] area [of civil rights policy], and was sure I'd been singled out solely because I was black, which I found demeaning." After speaking with a friend, however, Thomas decided to accept the post, confident that he had "a moral obligation to see if I could put some of my ideas into action."[45]

But Thomas never resolved his ambivalences. Especially galling was the persistent sense that high-ranking officials saw him as a token figure whose input was unwelcome.[46] The lack of respect accorded to Thomas was most in evidence, he writes, on issues involving the administration's approach to black civil rights. Not that the Reagan administration was, in this respect, out of step with prevailing orthodoxy, for "conservatives don't exactly break their necks to tell blacks that they're welcome."[47] Yet "the aggressive, tone-deaf manner in which the administration made some of its early civil-rights decisions," none more infamous than the administration's support of Bob Jones University's attempts to restore the tax-exempt status that it had lost as a result of its racially discriminatory campus policies, both alienated Thomas personally and ensured that "most blacks would never take [the administration's] goodwill seriously." The administration's approach in the Bob Jones University case "shocked" Thomas:[48]

I came close to resigning from the Department of Education over the Bob Jones case. The only reason that I stayed on was because I still believed in the Reagan administration's commitment to limiting the role of the federal government in the lives of blacks (and everyone else). . . . [But] I no longer hoped to have any positive impact on race relations or on black attitudes toward the administration.[49]

Moreover, Thomas freely conceded that "there [were] a lot of racists in the Administration." His concession reinforced the fatalistic vision of race relations that he outlined for his friend and journalist Juan Williams: "[Thomas] does not, deep down, share the Reagan Administration's professed belief in a 'colorblind' society, because he believes that such a society probably cannot be achieved . . . there is nothing that a black man can do to be accepted by whites." "Which group," Thomas asked, "always winds up with the least? Which group always seems to get the hell kicked out of it? Blacks, and maybe American Indians." Thomas's deep pessimism over American race relations led him to dismiss all governmental attempts to remedy structural patterns of racial inequality as the schemes of liberals who didn't actually have the interests of ordinary black people at heart. The best thing that government could do for black people, Thomas consistently held, was leave them alone—to "stop stopping us."[50]

Thomas thus explicitly refused the rights consciousness endorsed by many in the black civil rights establishment. This consciousness forwarded that untoward "proliferation of rights"[51] that Buckley Jr. and Reagan (among other prominent conservatives) had earlier tied to radical youth and black militants. Such new rights demanded governmental programs to enforce "group" rights to equal outcomes rather than the conventional "individual" rights to equal opportunities.[52] This supposedly perverse rights consciousness was at once fraught with practical difficulties and subversive of the American nation. On one hand, it pit group against group and so "buil[t] up racial conflict"—a conflict that, given his race fatalism, Thomas was convinced that blacks would lose. Ironically, group rights did not actually work in the interests of black people. "Blacks are out here raising Cain for group rights," Thomas averred, "and the ones who benefit the most, I think, would probably be white females," since affirmative action policies, for example, rarely proved of assistance to the black underclass.[53] The concept of group rights, championed by those who "claim to be so warm toward minorities," thus turns out to be "quite pernicious."[54]

Impotent to accomplish its stated goal of equal outcomes, this mistaken conception of rights instead undermined the moral foundations of the American nation. It amounted to an attack on the "notion of individual rights [with] notions of 'group rights' and 'social man' and all sorts of principles justifying economic redistribution." It was "an attack on freedom and rights [that] had to be accompanied by their redefinition": "Before, a right meant the freedom to *do* something; now a right has come to mean, at least in some, unfortunately growing circles, the legal claim to *receive and demand* something. . . . [It is] a short road from rights to . . . entitlements."[55] A recipe for entitlements, the attack on "individual rights" revealed contempt for the "qualities [of] self-discipline [and] self-respect" that were practiced and taught by Daddy Anderson and which Thomas believed to animate virtuous American citizenship.[56]

Yet Clarence Thomas is not Pollyannaish about the possibility of black self-help; he freely admits that racism dominates every vector of American society and that it makes black success much more difficult. But the notion of group rights, which he declares to be morally offensive and ineffective in practice, is a cruel "mirage of promises, visions and dreams."[57] The province of the "idealistic professions: journalists, lawyers, and professors," the group rights conception degrades individual effort and the self-discipline that it evinces. It thus attacks the "conditions of freedom." Accordingly, as Thomas told graduates of Savannah State College in 1985, the perversion of rights must be resisted, for in the "mean, callous world out there that is still very much filled with discrimination," blacks must rely on their own "unaided effort"—effort borne of exactly the sort of stern discipline that Daddy Anderson practiced with his grandchildren:[58] "It was necessary to be . . . self-sufficient and, hence, protected from the effects of bigotry. To my grandfather, self-sufficiency in an otherwise hostile world was freedom."[59]

In spite of his open frustration with the Reagan administration (though never with Reagan himself),[60] Thomas's ascent within both the administration and larger conservative circles continued apace. By 1982 Thomas had been confirmed as the new chairperson of the Equal Employment Opportunity Commission, a post in which he served until the end of the Reagan administration. During his time at the EEOC, Thomas was both celebrated by conservatives and pilloried by liberals for concentrating the agency's efforts on remedying individual cases of employment discrimination and ignoring historical patterns of employment inequality. And then, finally, Thomas was nominated for a pair of high-profile judgeships by President George H. W. Bush: first the prestigious DC Court of Appeals in 1989 and, then, the US Supreme Court following Thurgood Marshall's retirement in 1991.

Thomas professes characteristic ambivalence in his reactions to the possibility of these judgeships. Although he had frequently told acquaintances and friends of his ambition to serve on the Supreme Court prior to his nomination,[61] Thomas writes in his memoir that he thought of himself as too young and inexperienced to serve on the bench: "I couldn't see myself as a judge," he notes.[62] Even more troubling was the ever-present concern that his eventual nomination to the Supreme Court was based not on merit but rather on the color of his skin—a concern that would take on greater weight when Thomas heard Bush's unconvincing declaration that Thomas was "the best qualified [nominee for the Supreme Court] at this time." "Even I had my doubts about so extravagant a claim," writes Thomas. After all, accusations that his personal success was due to racial paternalism constituted "the soft underbelly of my career."[63] Thus, although he "was sure that he could do the job [of Supreme Court justice]," there "was no way I could really know what the President and his aides had been thinking when they picked me."[64]

Creating even more hesitation about accepting the nominations to the federal bench, according to Thomas, was the realization that the hearings before the Senate Judiciary Committee would again expose him, as they had Robert Bork previously, to the liberal critics with whom he had publicly battled while at the EEOC. "Was I prepared to run the risk of being put through a similar ordeal [as had Bork]—especially since I wasn't sure I wanted to be a judge in the first place?" Ultimately Thomas accepted his nomination to the Court of Appeals and survived the "long, unpleasant process" that was his (nevertheless uncontroversial) appearance before the Senate Judiciary Committee and the subsequent Senate vote.[65]

Although Thomas discovered, to his surprise, that he "liked the job" of being an appellate judge, he was "relieved" when the rumors that Bush would nominate him to replace the retiring William Brennan for the US Supreme Court turned out to be wrong, since "I'd only just arrived at the court of appeals and was still learning how to be a judge." Conversely, Thomas "felt sick" upon learning through back channels that he would be Bush's next nominee to the High Court. Thus, when news of Thurgood Marshall's impending retirement was announced in spring 1991 and Bush staffers began speaking with Thomas about a potential nomination, Thomas "felt as though I was losing control of my life." And then, a few days later, when Bush formally asked Thomas to accept the nomination to the US Supreme Court: "Events were overtaking me, and once again

I had the impression that somebody else had seized control of my life."[66] Thomas's loss of control was literal: he felt "trapped and bewildered"; he "had trouble getting out of [the] chair" in which he had been sitting when speaking to Bush; his "hands were trembling." Prefiguring the "long, hard ordeal" that he was certain would be his nomination process, Thomas quickly learned that the black civil rights establishment would oppose his nomination: his "heart sank."[67] Just as he had walked past drunken family members who had lost bodily control because of their submission to an alien force, so too did Thomas's body succumb to external command: "'Yes, Mr. President,' I heard myself reflexively saying. It felt as though someone else were doing the talking for me."[68]

Loss of bodily control—of autonomy—when confronted with circumstances that fail to yield to his "unaided effort" characterizes Thomas's adult life. At Daddy Anderson's funeral, "I started to weep shamelessly and uncontrollably, something I'd never done in public. . . . I wept beyond tears, slipping into the barren, rhythmic heaves of a body seeking something more." Personal and professional despair led him, during the summer of 1983, to contemplate suicide; it "[drove] me to my knees." Thomas's "paranoia" over how "some of his opponents would try to kill" him left him, on the morning of his nomination hearings before the Senate Judiciary Committee, "half-frozen with fear. My stomach heaved and my legs felt like they were carved out of wood." After each day of the hearings, he was "tired, tormented, and anxious."

And, then, the nadir: Anita Hill's allegations of Thomas's sexual harassment, which confirmed that the "phalanx of smart, well-heeled interest groups that were working hand in hand with the media and the powerful politicians who opposed my nomination . . . were out to kill me." "Now I knew who 'the man' was. He'd come at last to kill me, and I had looked upon his hateful, leering face as he slipped the noose of lies around my neck." Thus at the "mercy of people who would do whatever they could to hurt me . . . to [taste] my blood," the ensuing, infamous Hill-Thomas hearings made Thomas "wild-eyed and desperate . . . half crazed with fear"; thrust him into "a dark, cramped hell devoid of hope"; and, finally, left him "curled up in a fetal position" on his bed, "hyperventilating . . . [my] heart pounding in my chest."[69]

The repeated loss of bodily control underlines just how precarious was Thomas's achievement of autonomy, and the self-discipline that fueled it. Thomas's depictions, accordingly, evoke childhood memories of instability, absence, and despair; they put him in "hell," just as the Savannah household dominated by maternal influence and devoid of paternal authority was "hell." Thomas's loss of bodily control, memorably depicted as a return to the fetal position, thus points to maternal reengulfment and the concomitant loss of the disciplined, autonomous self that he first began to realize under the harsh tutelage of Daddy Anderson. Thomas was emasculated by the Hill allegations, left, according to his second and current wife, Virginia, "shrinking hour by hour into less of a man."[70]

Nor does Thomas depict the agony of loss of self-control and the metaphorical return to the maternal sphere as a matter of happenstance. Thomas instead presents himself on these occasions as the victim of feminine malice, through the active scheming of either real women (his mother; his sister who accepts the "pablum of welfare"[71] and thus embarrasses his own self-disciplined efforts; Anita Hill, who was the "weapon of choice" for his pro-abortion, feminist enemies[72]) or of forces committed to the "new intolerance" and its maternal values of dependence, entitlement, comfort, and license (the civil rights establishment, liberal planners, intellectuals, journalists[73]). In these instances, Thomas despairs as the self-discipline that he drew from paternal authority is overwhelmed by the mounting chaos of subversive maternal forces.

And, crucially, these subversive forces were armed with the perverse conception that envisions rights as group-based, legal entitlements to perfect social equality. It is a conception of rights that stands in contrast to the vision of individual rights that "informed the world of our founders" and was especially prominent in the political thought of James Madison, the "father of our Constitution."[74] But while one could learn the proper understanding of rights by studying the founding fathers and the "great books" that they authored, such a study "cannot take the place of [proper] rearing [and] a decent upbringing." National virtue thus began at home, in the strong influence of stern fathers, of "real [men]" like Daddy Anderson:[75] "In my grandfather's view, a man had a right and an obligation to produce. . . . Why don't we see more people actively pursuing the . . . rights which he exercised?"[76]

Celebration of stern paternal authority; horror over maternal reengulfment; competing conceptions of rights that articulate these themes: Clarence Thomas's personal narrative and the political vision that he draws from it meshes neatly with modern conservative renderings of the American nation. But Thomas's narrative is especially appealing to American conservatives, as are the narratives of Buckley Jr. and Reagan, because it is a *legal* narrative. Indeed, his jurisprudence, which tethers conservatism's paternal desires and fears to the mythic images that constitute modern legal practice, transforms Clarence Thomas into a conservative hero.

The myth of modernity, writes Peter Fitzpatrick, is that we have overcome and grown out of myth itself.[77] Modernity, according to this "anti-mythology,"[78] thus disavows any mythological foundations, emphasizing instead its supposedly rational, reasonable character; origins are found in enlightened, empirical grounds. Myth, superstition, irrationality: such "premodern" forces are consigned to an earlier, immature time and space.

Law, argues Fitzpatrick, exercises functions that are at once practical and symbolic in this modernist intellectual configuration. The achievement of law—the universal commands of the sovereign—marks the beginning of truly modern times; it orders societies not according to superstition, passion, and tradition but instead according to rational dictate. Particularity is overcome in the name of general application; law enacts the rational via universalistic process. The coming of law marks in both practice and symbol the dawning of modern times.[79]

What does a society run according to such "law and order," or order because of law, claim for itself? It claims a government that acts reasonably, through law, for the general benefit. It disavows fidelity to particular interests and so disavows the use of governmental action in the name of the partial, the superstitious, the passionate, the irrational (Thomas's "frailties" of life). Law and order is at once the metaphoric overcoming of the tyranny of irrationality and the practical means by which such irrationality, and the disorder that it produces, is removed from, and kept at the borders of, legitimate social practice.

But such a conviction—and the manifold individual and social actions and institutional configurations that are built atop it—never fully represses the mythological foundations that law disavows. Law does not avoid particularity; it incorporates in myriad ways the irrationalities and passions that motivate individuals and collectives. Law, notes Fitzpatrick, "is effective because of its correspondence to a transcendental myth or origin."[80] Law thus relies on unreason—myth, passion, "frailty"—in order to make it intelligible; superstitions and origin stories animate, and leave their traces in, particularly legal configurations, including institutional legacies and popular and scholarly narratives about law.[81] Accordingly, what makes modern law distinctive is not the mythological elements that animate it but the consistent repression and disavowal of these elements.

Popular ideals of and attachments to law thus emphasize the impartiality and rationality to which the legal order aspires. They emphasize, for example, that laws have a general meaning that is distinct from human interpretation. Clarence Thomas affirms that "the law is not a matter of purely personal opinion. The law is a distinct, independent discipline, with certain principles and modes of analysis that yield what we can discern to be correct and incorrect answers to certain problems."[82] Such an irrefutable meaning can be discovered by the practitioners who put aside their own partialities—their political, moral preferences—and attend faithfully to the legal text. The personality-less, judicial automaton—the deraced, unsexed, robed judge—is thus the hero of modernist fantasies of law. This judicial figure receives the impartial laws of the sovereign and discovers, articulates, and applies that impartiality to factually similar situations. The ideal judge is dominated, willingly, by the legal text; the judge's individuality is obliterated in the name of reason and impartiality. The judicial act is a literal self-sacrifice, and the judge is nothing more than an oracle—a relay transmitter for the impartial, universal law of the sovereign.[83]

That we know that such images—of law, of legal institutions, of judges—are wildly divorced from verifiable legal practice does little to harm the persuasiveness of the images; they remain the standards by which the democratic legitimacy of American law is established. But as Peter Goodrich argues, there is an additional characteristic of the mythology of modern law: the universal commands of the sovereign have been typically depicted as *paternal* orders.[84] The laws that emanate from modern sovereigns are thus figured as "laws of the father," and compliance or resistance to these laws is analogized to filial obedience or betrayal. Violation of law thus provokes either paternal mercy or, more commonly, paternal wrath. Such representations of the paternal sovereign incorporate an explicitly familial logic that turns citizens into children and the body politic into a national family.[85]

How do these considerations shed light on conservative reverence for Clarence Thomas? How does fixation on the supposedly rational, paternal character of modern law elevate Thomas into a conservative American hero?

Recall Thomas's ambivalence about the place of rights in contemporary America. It is, as we have seen throughout this book, an ambivalence that is widely shared by modern conservatives, who characteristically denounce the supposed abuses of law and rights perpetrated by the nation's subversive populations. Deviant behavior is thus measured against a particular standard: American subversives employ law to secure group-based, "special" rights from government. They rely on the misguided sympathy and cloying paternalism of governmental officials and cultural elites in order to realize (equal) outcomes that are incommensurate with their efforts or merits.[86]

And rather than rebuking such efforts, government and even legal institutions, conservatives argue, tend to kowtow to these extravagant, undeserved claims. They act, that is, as indulgent parents who allow their children to run amok, without stern guidance and lacking the self-discipline that such guidance is said to instill. Parental failure, we have seen, is literal, as subversives are frequently depicted as having been raised without stern paternal influence. And so where biological paternal influence lacks or falters, it must be found in "law and order"—in an unforgiving criminal justice system that is led by the neutral, personality-less judge who delivers the general and universal commands of the paternal sovereign.[87] It is thus unsurprising that Clarence Thomas, a prominent exponent of the mythology of modern law and its paternal roots, offers himself up as a "strict law-and-order man."[88]

It is through law, and especially through their paternal rights discourse, that modern American conservatives transmit the countersubversive practices needed to protect the American nation. The mythology of modern law thus provides the arena for Clarence Thomas's transformation from frail, maternally dominated subject to a mature "law-and-order *man.*" Yet becoming such a man—becoming the ideal modern judge who willingly forfeits his autonomous judgment to the paternal demands of the legal text and, in the process, confirms his heroic character to American conservatives—involves Thomas in a paradoxical act of self-sacrifice about which he is deeply ambivalent. The next section traces his sacrifice.

The Judge

When deciding cases, a judge's race, sex, and religion are not relevant.
A judge must push these factors to one side, in order to render a fair,
reasoned judgment on the meaning of law. A judge must attempt to
keep at bay those passions, interests, and emotions that beset every
frail human being. . . . When interpreting the Constitution and stat-
utes, judges should seek the original understanding of the provision's
text. . . . [B]y tethering their analysis to the understanding of those who
drafted and ratified the text, modern judges are prevented from substi-
tuting their own preferences for the Constitution.
—Clarence Thomas

I have come here today . . . to assert my right to think for myself, to
refuse to have my ideas assigned to me as though I was an intellectual
slave because I'm black. I've come to state that I'm a man, free to think
for myself and do as I please. I've come to assert that I'm a judge and I
will not be consigned the unquestioned opinions of others.
—Clarence Thomas

[The Supreme Court] is a wonderful place.
—Clarence Thomas

There's not much that entices about the job [of being a Supreme Court
Justice]. There's no money in it, no privacy, no big houses, and from an
ego standpoint, it does nothing for me. . . . I wouldn't say I like it.
—Clarence Thomas

Clarence Thomas is a decidedly ambivalent Supreme Court justice.
On one hand, he envisions his position as the fruit of his victory in the
bruising, emasculating process that constituted his confirmation. The
role of a justice is one, moreover, that Thomas sees himself as well suited
to fill. A domain of the head rather than the heart, law is an enterprise
that is naturally attractive to a figure such as Clarence Thomas, who
has consistently portrayed his own success, as well as the broader goal
of citizenly virtue, as the triumph of rational, disciplined will over the
sentimental, debilitating attachments of life's frailties: race, class, and
family. His work as a justice, according to Thomas, requires exactly this
sort of triumph on a small scale. Justices must bracket off their sympathies to particular litigants and causes, no matter how much their heart

implores them to help, and consider only the impersonal requirements of law, as revealed in both the legal text and the desires of the founding fathers. Judging is thus a daily exercise in the triumph of the ego over the id; the Supreme Court is not the place for "emotional outbursts" or "temper tantrum[s]."[89]

Yet the triumph of the head over the heart, of logic over sentiment, also requires self-sacrifice and constant paternal domination. The substitution of paternal desire for judicial individuality makes the work of a Supreme Court justice, according to Thomas, a thorough-going process of repression and self-annihilation.[90] Thomas's ideal judge is never released from tutelage, never trusted to make a truly mature, individual assessment—for to do so is, by definition, to stray from the paternal demands of the legal text. Judging, which is at first blush the culmination of Thomas's lifelong yearning for escape from the sentimentality and immaturity he associates with the maternal realm, turns out to be just another moment in his personal history of paternal disappointment. Paradoxically, Thomas's judicial self-discipline keeps him in an arrested state of childhood; it prevents him from fulfilling his desire, as revealed in one of the epigraphs to this section, to be "a man" and "think for" himself. Accordingly, while the role of Supreme Court justice is the fulfillment of Thomas's deepest longings, it is a role that he cannot fully embrace. His renderings of the judicial life, found in both his judicial philosophy and his depictions of the life of a Supreme Court justice, are thus animated with resentment and regret over the loss of the autonomous self that submission to the legal text and, especially, the desires of the founding fathers entails.

"There are some cases," Clarence Thomas told a 2009 audience, "that will drive you to your knees."[91] These cases are not the intellectually tough cases, but rather the ones that test a justice's discipline, the ones in which a justice is tempted to step out of the role of impartial judge and instead embrace the role of policy advocate:

There are some opinions—a class of opinions—where something inside you as a human being says, "Boy, I really need to do something. I really would want to do something. This just isn't right." But you have no authority to do anything. That's when discipline is required. . . . That class of cases is the hardest. . . . That when you have no authority, no capacity, no ability to help somebody who needs help—to right a wrong that you just in your heart, you know is a wrong, but you have no authority to do anything about it. It is that class of case that really keeps you up at night and makes you agonize.[92]

Indeed, the legitimacy of the judicial project writ large hinges on the judge's capacity to successfully navigate the "hard case" and to ward off the "temptation" to do what "your heart really wants to do." It is there, Thomas avers, where "you see whether or not you are a judge, or you're lawless."[93]

Thomas consistently notes that adherence to the original intent (which he sometimes refers to as the "original understanding" or, simply, the philosophy of "originalism"[94]) of the legal text is necessary for the exercise of judicial self-discipline. Indeed, "There are two ways to decide a case. You can try to determine what the Constitution says, and what the framers were trying to say; that's originalism. Or you can make it up."[95] Channeling the desires of the founding fathers protects judicial impartiality, and thus law, from multiple threats to its integrity, from "lawlessness." On one hand, it allows for judges to be "impartial referees who defend constitutional principles from attempts by particular interests (or even the people as a whole) to overwhelm them."[96] On the other hand, fidelity to the fathers allows judges themselves to "make a firewall between our personal opinions and the law."[97] Accordingly, Thomas's "judicial philosophy is to try to discern the intent of the framers in constitutional cases, and in statutory cases, the intent of the legislature and to try to keep my personal views out of it completely, as best I can."[98] "What else am I supposed to do," he asked an audience in 2011, "use a Ouija board, chicken bones?"[99]

Yet when taken as seriously as Thomas insists, submission to the founding, paternal will that is embodied in the legal text requires that he voluntarily "strip" himself of all of the virtuous character qualities that he has spent his life gaining. Although Thomas insists that he is "a man" and that, accordingly, he has the "right to think for" himself,[100] his conception of the judicial role demands paternal domination: "the job is important, it's not about me."[101] "My role," Thomas told Rush Limbaugh in 2007, "is to interpret the Constitution, when it's a constitutional case. It's to interpret a statute. It is not to impose my policy views or my personal views on [the Constitution] or on [the] laws."[102]

Thomas sometimes invokes his opinions in two particular cases to illustrate the self-sacrifice that being a good judge requires. Although he personally found the Texas antisodomy statute that was invalidated in the landmark *Lawrence v. Texas* case to be an "uncommonly silly" use of "valuable law enforcement resources," for example, Thomas found no constitutional right to privacy with which to discard the law. "As a member of this Court," he intoned, "I am not empowered to help petitioners and others similarly situated."[103] Yet in spite of his confidence in the rightness of judicial self-restraint, Thomas admits to being personally stung by the harsh criticism that accompanied his dissent in the 1992 case of *Hudson v. McMillian.* His opinion argued that the shackling and beating of a Georgia prisoner by prison guards did not violate the Eighth Amendment's prohibition of cruel and unusual punishment. Thomas argued that the beating may well have been criminal in nature, but that it did not rise to the level of a constitutional violation.[104] Still, some critics accused Thomas of being insensitive to the victim and, worse, of tacitly condoning the brutal conduct of the guards.[105] These critics, maintained Thomas, did not appreciate the self-disciplining responsibilities of a judge; their attacks on his personal character were the products either of "illitera[cy] or . . . malice."[106]

Thomas's ambivalence over the judicial role, and the self-sacrifice that he believes that it requires, appears also in his contrasting depictions of life as a Supreme Court justice. Consider, for example, a 2001 formulation that is typical of Thomas's depiction of the personal burdens of being a justice:

There's no money in this [serving on the Supreme Court]. There's a total loss of anonymity. My hair in 10 short years has gone from black to gray, what's left of it. There is no place, I think, in the job that I do for ego. . . . No, it's not a matter of ego.[107]

Having prematurely aged his body, annihilated his private life, and left his ego neglected, Thomas's time on the Supreme Court and the suppression of his self to the desires of the founding fathers, he insists, has not been personally enriching. It has been, instead, an unyielding act of civic sacrifice and public service. Thomas confessed to a 2007 audience, "I like sports. I like to drive a motor home. But I wouldn't say that I like [serving on the Court]."[108] It is thus unsurprising that Thomas frequently speaks of how much he enjoys spending his summer vacations, when the Court is in recess, taking long trips across the nation in his motor home with his wife, Virginia. During these trips, Thomas rejoices in meeting "the common people," who, unlike the people who live and work within the Washington, DC, beltway, "are doing things, [they] actually believe in their country, [and] actually want it to work."[109]

But not all Washington insiders are cut from the same corrupt timber. Indeed, Thomas's characteristic ambivalence about life on the Supreme Court is fueled by his recognition that "unlike the unfortunate practice or custom in Washington and in much of the country, the Court is a model of civility,"[110] a "wonderful place." Thomas consistently affirms that he has "never [before] had the occasion to be a part of an institution that is so civil, so respectful, and so dedicated to doing its best as [is] the Court."[111] It is a place made up of self-disciplined adults who "control [themselves]" and "don't throw temper tantrums" in the Court's "inner sanctum."[112]

But as I have been arguing, Thomas's own depictions suggest that he is far more ambivalent about such judicial "self-control" than he lets on. To be sure, Thomas argues that judicial self-discipline at once affirms the justices' statuses as mature adults who can control their selves and so avoid the sorts of childish "emotional outbursts" that mark beltway politics. And as we have seen, such self-discipline is also the hallmark of modernist fantasies of judging—fantasies that Thomas voices with his regular gestures to the supreme acts of will that are required in order to subordinate one's personal wishes to the originalist, paternal desires that suffuse legal texts.

Yet the subordination of self involved in judicial self-discipline amounts to a disavowal of all of those hard-earned character qualities—independent judgment, wisdom, sagacity—that mature, disciplined behavior is supposed to foster. Paradoxically, the self-discipline that convinces Thomas of the legitimacy of the judicial role writ large and his own place on the Supreme Court undermines the "right to think for [him]self" that he has spent his entire life cultivating. Accordingly, when Thomas states, "I'm a judge and I will not be consigned the unquestioned opinions of others," he embroils himself in a fateful contradiction of his own making.[113] His judicial self-discipline, and especially the fidelity to the originalist desires of the founding fathers that it enables, means that precisely because Thomas is a judge, he *will* be consigned the unquestioned opinions of others. Accordingly, Thomas's ascension to the Supreme Court, at first blush the culmination of a lifelong desire for the autonomy from external control that paternally induced self-discipline is alleged to produce, turns out to be a cruel mirage. Unlike the open road that he frequently dreams of traversing, a life of law as experienced by service on the Supreme Court does not offer escape from pernicious external control.

But there is a crucial distinction between the forms of external control that Thomas depicts his life as an overcoming of and the control exerted by the legal text. Whereas his prejustice failures of self entailed the loss of self-control to an overbearing maternal influence and concomitant reengulfment in maternal spheres, his domination by the legal text is a purely paternal affair that requires, rather than overcomes, his self-control. Judicial self-discipline thus turns out to be a straitjacket: to refuse it is to indulge in personal fantasies of law and so to engage in immature, emotional identifications with particular litigants and causes; to exercise it is to submit to unquestioned paternal desire. Either way, Thomas is trapped in the childlike state of dependence with which he has been at war for his entire life.

Conclusion

> The life history of a historical figure . . . in all its uniqueness and yet
> also in its conflictedness and failures, must be seen, for better and for
> worse, as prototypical for [its] time.
> —Erik Erikson

It is telling that Clarence Thomas has come to depict his contemporary life, and especially his tenure on the US Supreme Court, as a return "home."[114] Thomas is not speaking of a literal geographic place, for he is typically unwilling to visit his childhood homes in Pinpoint and Savannah, having been regularly absent from both important civic events and ceremonies held in his own honor.[115] Thomas instead means that his current station in life is a return to the values and life lessons that characterized his upbringing with Daddy Anderson and Aunt Tina. Thomas, as we have seen, portrays the professional and personal successes that he has enjoyed as the fruits of the self-discipline and resulting autonomous citizenship that Daddy's stern paternal discipline instilled in him. Conversely, all of Thomas's confessed life and professional failures are attributed to his periodic failures to live a sufficiently disciplined and autonomous life. In such moments, Thomas has given in to self-doubt, rage, and hubris: the lack of self-discipline and self-control that characterizes these times, Thomas claims, has returned him to the same "hell" that marked his early childhood years of instability, poverty, anxiety, and, critically, maternal oversight. It is, accordingly, possible to interpret Clarence Thomas's self-narrative as a story of the ever-present conflict between contrasting visions of "home": a paternal, stern, uncompromising, and frequently violent yet somehow stable home, on one hand; a maternal, permissive, undisciplined, frequently neglectful, and always unstable home, on the other hand. Clearly, then, in describing himself as content in both his professional and personal life and in depicting such contentedness as being "home," Thomas means to convey a hard-earned, final overcoming of maternal influence.

As I have argued, this vision of personal and professional success—in which stern paternal authority defeats overbearing though permissive and frequently absent maternal authority—is consistently offered by Thomas as a general prescription for American success. In so offering, Thomas joins his voice to that of American conservatism writ large: the strength of the American nation, it insists, depends on the literal generation of paternally disciplined selves and the autonomous citizenship that these selves will practice. Autonomous citizenship is thus depicted in modern American conservatism as a masculinist overcoming of literal and metaphoric feminine influence.

This family drama, I have argued throughout this book, registers especially in conservative discourses on law and rights. On one hand, conservatives denounce supposedly unreasonable uses of law and rights—such as those claims of "group rights" that are associated with the desire for equal outcomes and thus pervert the legitimate claims of "equal rights" associated with the possibility of equal opportunities—as the childish outbursts of undisciplined and chaotic individuals. Indeed, in conservative parlance, it is exactly such abuses of law and rights that mark subjects as immature and unreasonable, as lacking the character qualities that good, stern parenting should have instilled. On the other hand, conservatives tend to champion the use of "law and order" on these same deviant subjects. The progeny of missing paternal authority, such subjects are said to be the proper recipients of the harsh "laws of the father" that are meted out by an increasingly punitive American criminal justice system. Thus, when Clarence Thomas declares himself a neutral, personality-less judge whose own maturity is evident in his ascetic acts of judicial self-discipline, he at once announces himself as a "strict law and order man" and sings to the conservative choir.

But as I have also argued, the judicial self-discipline that Thomas claims is the key to his jurisprudence makes clear that his association of the US Supreme Court with his own paternal home (neither, he explains, countenances "temper tantrums") is far more ambivalent than Thomas lets on. And this ambivalence points, finally, to the self-deception and futility at the center of the autonomous subjectivity that both Thomas and his conservative champions claim is essential for the practice of virtuous American citizenship. On one hand, Thomas consistently portrays his "original understanding" jurisprudence as a daily triumph of the masculinist values of detachment, rationality, and self-abnegation over the childish and feminine values of sentimentality, emotion, and self-indulgence. Being a good justice, Thomas claims, requires favoring the head over the heart, the mind over the body. Such discipline and rationality are, moreover, conventionally taken to be the hallmark attributes of an autonomous citizen, a citizen who can govern his or her own self and, so, can be safely empowered with the authority to govern other selves. But, on the other hand, Thomas's judicial self-discipline, and the "originalism" that it enables, requires always, in the last instant, not the mature and autonomous judgment befitting a modern, disciplined individual but instead the willing subjugation of such judgment to the desires of others.

The law, accordingly, is not an arena within which the autonomy and independence for which Clarence Thomas has always longed can be legitimately expressed. It is, instead, a place of self-obliteration in which the lack of agency that Thomas experienced in different forms in both the maternal and paternal homes is reprised. Being a Supreme Court justice, in Clarence Thomas's account, ensures that he will never escape the dependence whose overcoming is the dream of the conservative, indeed modern, vision of autonomy. Whereas "home" once signified Daddy Anderson's overwhelming influence, it now signifies the overwhelming influence of the founding fathers, whose domination of Clarence Thomas is, he claims, no less real for being spectral in nature. Thomas's quest for autonomy thus not only stigmatizes and demonizes the many valuable qualities that he and his conservative allies consign to the supposed trash heap of the maternal sphere; it also, paradoxically, "binds [them] to socially-recognized forms of self-limitation," such as, prominently, the obsession with stern paternal authority.[116]

Yet we should conclude by acknowledging, in spite of its paradoxical quality, the transformative nature of modern American conservatism's paternal rights discourse, especially as it is evidenced in the self-narrative of one of its most prominent heroes. Indeed, Clarence Thomas's self-narrative—riddled with the personal, political, and legal resonances that I have canvassed here—elevates him, in the conservative political vision, from the profane to the sacred. Clarence Thomas, the son, on one hand, of a harsh grandfather and, on the other hand, of the vaunted American ethos of masculine self-discipline and its unrealizable, futile goal of autonomous citizenship, is a conservative icon.

Leave, then, the final word to fellow black conservative Shelby Steele. But understand Steele's analysis not as the personal praise that it is meant to be, but instead as synoptic of personal and national tragedy. Clarence Thomas, writes Steele, is "now an archetype [that] will inspire others."[117]

Coda—Daddy's Head

When Clarence Thomas's Supreme Court nomination was confirmed by the US Senate in fall 1991 the new justice's wife, Virginia, presented him with a bronze bust of Daddy Anderson's head. Thomas immediately installed it in his judicial chambers, on a bookshelf overlooking his desk. In its imposing, disembodied presence, Daddy's head recalls the stone colossal heads made by the Olmec people of ancient Mesoamerica that were exhibited at San Francisco's de Young art museum in spring 2011. The colossal heads visited the city just over thirty years after Clarence Thomas had attended the San Francisco conference of young black conservatives that launched his national political career. But this geographical overlap notwithstanding, the colossal heads and Daddy's head share little in common. Whereas the meanings that the colossal heads held for the Olmec people are impenetrable to contemporary observers, the meaning that Daddy's head holds for Clarence Thomas is clear. Memorializing the confusion between paternal and professional homes that distinguishes Thomas's judicial life, Daddy's head admonishes the justice, his "grandfather's son" still, not to "whine" or "complain."[118]

6

A Nightmare Walking: The Haunting of Modern American Conservatism

Something that I feared, somehow is now endeared to me.
—Harry Revel and Mack Gordon

You are all my children now!
—Freddy Krueger

It is no longer the case, as it was a decade ago, that law and society scholars neglect the law use of American conservatives. Indeed, much valuable scholarship on conservative legal mobilizations has recently appeared. Some of this scholarship—such as that produced by Steven Teles, Anne Southworth, and Amanda Hollis-Brusky—illuminates what Charles Epp referred to as the "support structures" for conservatism's formal legal claims. These scholars find that conservative cause lawyers, in particular, followed the earlier, more left-leaning public interest litigation model: they built and participated in institutions such as the Federalist Society and the Pacific Legal Foundation—bases from which they initiated litigation and promoted conservative judicial candidates for local, state, and national courts.[1]

Other scholars have complemented this focus on conservatism's formal legal strategies by exploring the rights discourse that animates these formal claims. My own 2008 book took some initial steps in this direction, arguing that rights discourse is a foundational aspect of the "countersubversive" identity that both infuses modern American conservatism and has been so on display in this book.[2] Joshua Wilson's 2013 text on antiabortion protesters went further, arguing that the protesters gained sustenance and strength from their rights claims, even if those claims ultimately locked them into a vision of state authority that grated uncomfortably against their religious commitments.[3] Similarly, Joseph Mello's recent scholarship on conservative campaigns against same-sex marriage reinforced both the centrality of rights discourse to those campaigns and emphasized that it was more effective as a catalyst for establishing an insurgent conservative identity than it was for winning cases in court.[4]

This book belongs to the burgeoning law and society scholarship on modern American conservatism, but it has different emphases and accent points. For one, whereas the existing scholarship, including my own, approaches conservatism's rights talk from the "bottom up," via the law use of citizen-activists, this book has, similar to the support structure scholarship, interrogated the rights discourse of prominent conservative leaders. Unlike the support structure work, however, I have been concerned with the political effects of conservatism's culturally resonant discourses of rights and family—with its paternal rights discourse. Moreover, and perhaps most distinctive, I have interpreted the paternal rights discourse of American conservatism's most prominent figures with an eye toward tethering that discourse's effects at once to conservative movement politics and the personal histories of its proponents. I have sought, accordingly, to show how American conservatism's paternal rights discourse intersects political and personal ambition—how it articulates in the domains of both the conscious and instrumental and the semiconscious and emotional.

In this concluding chapter, I explore exactly this intersection by elevating a theme that has so far been just out of reach. Recall that I have pursued two primary arguments here. First, the paternal rights discourse that distinguishes modern American conservatism at once constitutes national heroes and enemies; it identifies and orients action against supposedly heteronomous, immature, and subversive people and, in so doing, gilds the fractious tendencies at American conservatism's core by giving its most devoted practitioners something to believe in. Yet, second, that unifying discourse works as an ambivalent and paradoxical creed for the movement as a whole. As we saw most clearly in the case of Clarence Thomas, it introduces continuing instability by demanding both self-governance and undying fidelity to the timeless desires of fathers real and spectral. Its paternal rights discourse, accordingly, distinguishes, unifies, propels, and troubles modern American conservatism.

But what does this troubling mean for American conservatives themselves? Why, even in the face of its ultimately paradoxical and ambivalent effects, do they so desire this particular figure: father? To which deep-seated needs does conservatism's undying paternal desire point? What does it mean that modern American conservatism is haunted by the rights claims of the fathers?

Of Fatherhood and Democratic Desire

Start with Bing Crosby. Singer, actor, and all-around entertainer, Crosby was a titan of American popular culture both before and after World War II. He was also, it turns out, a dedicated conservative who helped with the initial funding of William F. Buckley Jr.'s the *National Review*—that vehicle for Buckley's ambition of providing American conservatism with intellectual coherence and respectability.[5] It is unsurprising, then, that Buckley's sustained mediation on the character of American conservatism—the essay that begins this book and yoked paternal rights discourse to conservative purpose—was titled after a song that Harry Revel and Mack Gordon wrote for the 1933 Hollywood movie *Sitting Pretty* but was popularized and most associated with Bing Crosby. "Did You Ever See a Dream Walking?" was the title of Buckley's 1970 edited collection of representative conservative writings and his introductory essay. The song is not referenced in any way in the body of the essay. Can we interpret the meanings that the song's lyrics held for Buckley in light of his essay's exposition of the paternal rights discourse that infuses American conservatism?

Something very strange and mystic
happened to me
Something realistic and as weird as can be
Something that I feared, somehow is now
endeared to me
And what a funny feeling, odd and yet
so true
Did a thing like this ever happen to you?
Did you ever see a dream walking? Well, I
did[6]

The song's lyrics refer, at first blush, to romantic love and, in the parlance of Leslie Fiedler, to a sentimental reconciliation of the modal terror of American masculinity: adult, mature relationships. "It is maturity above all things," wrote Fiedler, "that the American writer fears, and marriage seems to him its essential sign."[7] The song thus works against national tradition, pointing to acceptance of the "weird" but "realistic" thing that the singer "feared" but to which he is now "somehow endeared." The singer, also against national type, is no longer interested in exchanging adult responsibility for (homoerotic) wilderness adventure with his racial double.[8] Instead, the singer's "walking dream" is mature, domestic contentedness.

But does Buckley's invocation of the song's title do similar interpretive work? In a sense, yes. To be sure, the virtuous American citizen whom Buckley, Reagan, and Thomas all champion is, we have seen throughout, depicted as a self-governing subject whose autonomy can be trusted and, in fact, guaranteed as a matter of right precisely because that subject displays self-discipline—precisely, that is, because that subject has reached a state of maturity. The crucial moment in the achievement of this maturity, each of the three conservative heroes insists, is the experience of having grown up in a family environment characterized by strong paternal and weak, submissive maternal authority. Only in such environments do children experience the discipline that is the seedbed of the character qualities of sacrifice, hard work, generosity, forbearance, and thrift. Strong fathers are thus crucial to the development of the self-disciplined, mature, and autonomous citizens who both thrive in advanced capitalist societies and are the bulwarks of republican government itself; republican democracies can have limits on the power of government only because such democracies are inhabited by citizens capable of limiting themselves. Paternal authority thus sits, we have seen, at the root of democratic possibility itself. So in part we can understand Buckley's invocation of the "dream walking" in the same way as the lyric writer, Gordon, presumably intended: as an acceptance of the "realistic" and "so true" responsibilities of mature, adult life and, in particular, of mature, self-disciplined, rights-laden citizenship.

And yet this message—that stern paternal authority is the essential moment in the constitution of eventually autonomous, disciplined, properly rights-bearing citizens—is, as also in Gordon's lyric, "very strange." It is odd not only because of the paradox between an apparently unending submission to paternal authority (whether real or spectral) and the injunction to be self-governing and autonomous. It's not just the message that involves us in paradox; it's also the messengers. Indeed, each of the three iconic conservatives who sit at the center of this book's analysis—Buckley

Jr., Ronald Reagan, and Clarence Thomas—experienced childhoods characterized by overwhelming paternal influence. But rather than the stable childhoods that generate the autonomous, self-governing citizens of conservative lore, the evidence presented here indicates that their childhoods were instead characterized by instability, chaos, and, above all, fear—fear, primarily, of paternal influence.

Reconsider, then, the lyrics to "Did You Ever See a Dream Walking?": "Something that I feared, somehow is now endeared to me." Doesn't the song speak of both submission and repression? How else are we to interpret the "very strange" phenomenon of conservatism's iconic figures—people who experienced frequently absent, distant, or abusive fathers—demanding not only literal submission to paternal authority at home but continuing submission to the spectral authority of the nation's metaphoric fathers—its "founding fathers"? Isn't the figure of father so cathected with emotional energy that it conjures, as in the song, both desire and fear, both longing and dread? And don't we deny the dread and the fear in the paternal injunction of American conservatism only at the cost of ignoring what is plainly in front of our faces? Doesn't the paternal rights discourse that distinguishes, propels, and destabilizes American conservatism and its foremost spokespersons point not only to Bing Crosby and the sweetness of "walking dreams" but also, on one hand, to the hell of childhood vulnerability and, on the other hand, to the truth of Karl Marx's understanding that "the tradition of all dead generations weighs like a nightmare on the brains of the living"?[9] Isn't modern American conservatism's paternal rights discourse also an exercise in the return of the repressed, wrathful American father?

To speak of longing, fear, and repression is, of course, to leave the relatively firm ground of articulated conservative doctrine about rights and to enter the more inchoate terrain of conservative *desire* about rights. It is to consider, in Colin Dayan's words, how "legal rituals give flesh to past narratives and new life to the residue of old codes."[10] I thus conclude this book by interrogating at least some of the prevailing "ideologies, fantasies, and unconscious desires that support legal discourse from underneath."[11]

In order to do so, I will draw on Julia Kristeva's concept of "melancholia,"[12] as it is applied to contemporary America by political theorist Mary Caputi. Indeed, conservatism's paternal rights discourse is an exercise in melancholia because it speaks to a bone-deep desire for order, stability, and coherence in a world that appears to the afflicted as unstable, out-of-control—a living hell of proliferating, over-determined meanings. It is a world that has forgotten "the intuitive wisdom of the founders" (Buckley); that has denied, in Reagan's words, that "here in this land for the first time it was decided that man is born with certain God given rights"; a world that, according to Thomas, has forfeited the vision of individual rights that "informed the world of our founders" and was especially prominent in the political thought of James Madison: the "father of our Constitution." Isn't it time, Reagan demanded of audiences, that "we ask ourselves if we still know the freedoms that were intended for us by the founding fathers"? And so the melancholic conjures a past—a nostalgic, imagined past in which reigned, according to Buckley, "the art of state-craft . . . [and] . . . the meaning of the spirit of the West," the wisdom of the founding fathers —fathers, claimed Buckley, who were more like "supermen" than they were corporeal beings.

Not exclusive to modern American conservatism, this longing for stability, for an end to what William Connolly calls the "homesickness" of the human condition, is a hallmark of modern living. Modern times, Connolly argues, are defined by the widespread loss of belief in transcendent purpose (in "myth") and, accordingly, by an eruption of nihilism. But this nihilism, and the felt loss of meaning that accompanies it (of Kristeva's "melancholia"), is so upsetting that it has been the subject of an astonishing range of ameliorative attempts.[13] Hence the feverish devotion to those human projects that attempt to establish the sorts of "antimyths" that Fitzpatrick locates at the heart of modernity: projects of science, reason, and the state, for example, with which human life might be organized and infused with the noncontingent foundations that existed before (to paraphrase Nietzsche) humans killed off God.[14]

Thus did modern legal theorists find the antidote to nihilism in positive state law and, in particular, in what Robert Cover called the "jurispathic" powers of judges to kill off alternative, equally compelling legal interpretations; positive law was the "solution to the problem of too much law."[15] But modern American conservatism takes a different approach; it seeks to ward off the melancholia of modern times with an alchemy of modern and premodern enchantments. The paternal rights discourse voiced by American conservatives takes the American nation back to the future; it adorns the revived, again omniscient authority of America's biological and metaphorical fathers with the symbols of the modern state's legitimacy: law and rights. Modern American conservatism fights homesickness with paradox: in the paternal demand for rights.

Indeed, "[American] conservatism," writes Caputi, "seeks to regain control over the meaning that has . . . been destabilized. It seeks to reaffirm a 'clear sense of what it means to be an American' and thus to parry the painful indeterminacies of our nation's floundering, globalizing, multicultural identity."[16] The melancholic longs for "control: self-controlled individuals, controlled families and neighborhoods, controlled conversations. . . . It is the control that emanates from the fact that our culture's definitions are stable and intact, for we are, in this [state] . . . at home in the spiritual space where we belong."[17] The object of desire—the "ancient mooring" (Buckley) to which American conservatism anchors—is Father himself: the desire, again in Caputi's words, "induces a shift . . . away from an organic, maternal world order toward one more aligned with paternal demands and the chastising superego."[18] And this remedial Father of American conservatism originates, notes Caputi, at the nation's "Founding."[19] The founding fathers are, accordingly, American conservatism's desired, mythical objects; they will purportedly be the stabilizing "antecedent [meaning] amid an otherwise overwhelming sense of disarray."[20]

Thus does the "reconnection" that American conservatives seek with stern paternal authority "become highly charged, fraught with special significance . . . the very idea of a past in which life knew more correspondence and more embedded meaning appears desirable."[21] So it is, to paraphrase political theorist Kennan Ferguson, that "the emotional intensity of [conservative] political life is dependent on families."[22] But as with all other modern attempts to forestall nihilism, it turns out that the melancholic's desire is "impossible." "Hence in melancholia we see the doubled gesture of reaching forward and backward, of projecting the past onto the future and of moving forward in order to regain the past."[23] The desire for the stable object is impossible and magical because the object (Father) is oversaturated with meaning; it is itself a floating signifier that is purposed and repurposed according to the endless demands of desire rather than to the rigors of logic or intellectual coherence.

Always just out of reach, its mythical biological and spectral fathers haunt American conservative politics and its foremost spokespersons. Investing those politics and those persons with both emotional heat and desperate longing, the desired fathers are avenging spirits meant to enforce conventional American values on disorderly populations. But for the central icons of American conservatism who have been the subjects of this book, the experience of overwhelming, wrathful paternal force was not metaphorical, and so their paternal rights discourse at once conjures the supposed sources of democratic stability and the actual sources of their childhood instability. Their paternal rights discourse, accordingly, is an exercise in ambivalent reconciliation: an articulation of something that they feared but to which they are now endeared.

Daddy Can't Help You Now

I have argued throughout this book that the paternal rights discourse endemic to modern American conservatism works in a variety of cultural and, so, political ways: it at once distinguishes, catalyzes, unifies, and troubles both the movement and its foremost icons. Exploration of this last element—the discourse's haunting, ultimately ambivalent place in American conservatism—brings the book home. We have seen how some central icons of modern American conservatism—William F. Buckley Jr., Ronald Reagan, and Clarence Thomas—repressed the wrathful and unstable fathers of their personal histories and how, in narrative, they replaced them with both prosaic figures reminiscent of Fred MacMurray's gentle but stern patriarch from *Father Knows Best* and with America's magical founding fathers. We have also seen how each of these icons has yearned for and employed such imagined fathers—how their rights discourse, that is, has been employed in the pursuit and justification of harsh discipline for those people upon whom conservatism projects the repressed chaos and heteronomy of modern times. Stern discipline is recommended, we have seen, for women seeking greater bodily and sexual autonomy; for children and youth seeking respect and fairness; for anticolonial insurgents abroad; for racial and sexual minorities seeking to make good on the promises of American citizenship that are encoded within the rights that the founding fathers themselves bequeathed to us. American conservatism imagines them, emblems of subversion all, as irresponsible and undisciplined, in need of the paternal "law and order" of the American state.

But the wrathful, unstable father—the William F. Buckley Seniors, the Jack Reagans, the Daddy Andersons—returns, I have been arguing, to haunt the modern American conservative imagination itself. Indeed, the fathers of American conservatism's "walking dream[s]" resemble not only Fred MacMurray but also a far more menacing patriarchal figment of the contemporary American imagination (a figment even more dreadful than MacMurray's own duplicitous, murderous insurance agent from the film noir classic *Double Indemnity*). Indeed, Jane Caputi persuasively argues that contemporary American popular culture complements the mythologizing of the "old founding fathers" with celebrations of its "new founding fathers." Similarly valued as eradicators of the proliferating meanings that so trouble modern American conservatism (none more so than the multiple meanings of rights), it is, shockingly, male serial killers who assume the paternal role in contemporary times. The male serial killer, writes Caputi, "is actually the 'cop,' the enforcer of such foundational values as male supremacy, violent masculinity, egocentrism, consumerism, excess, and the erotic joys of domination"[24]—the values exactly that are said to be under attack from the rights claims of America's undisciplined, heteronomous citizens.

Caputi analyzes the celebration of American male serial killers real and fictional, but she finds Freddy Krueger, the terrifying antagonist of the *A Nightmare on Elm Street* movie franchise, to be "far more interesting" than the others. Collapsing the distinction between the nation's good and bad fathers, Freddy is "Ward Cleaver [from *Leave It to Beaver*] unrepressed, running amok, wielding a cleaver. He is the incestuous/alcoholic/abusive/murderous father, hidden behind the placid facade of Elm Street, U.S.A."[25] Caputi is right to tilt her analysis to fiction and, in particular, to the desires and fears that surface in the nation's popular culture texts. I here follow Caputi's lead in form and in substance, for "the assumptions underlying our legal discourse . . . derive powerful support from the ideas and ideals pronounced in our cultural texts and practices,"[26] and there are few better or more memorable embodiments of the ambivalent paternal desires at the core of modern American conservatism than Freddy Krueger.

Caputi's illuminating analysis is confined to Freddy's first appearance. *A Nightmare on Elm Street* from 1984 sees Freddy murder his victims in their nightmares; his full horror isn't realized until 1985's *A Nightmare on Elm Street 2*. For it was in the sequel that Freddy Krueger escaped the nightmares of his victims, took over a human body, and materialized in real life.[27]

To be sure, Freddy (as in his first appearance) terrorizes the subversives of the American conservative imagination: he tortures and murders the gay high school physical education teacher Coach Strickland (who frequents S&M bars in the evenings and forces rebellious students to "assume the position" as punishment—he means the plank position); Freddy guts a "bad," sexually promiscuous high school girl on the school bus; after taking over the body of the movie's putative protagonist (Jesse), Freddy savagely murders Jesse's best friend, Grady (on whom Jesse has a homoerotic crush—we are introduced to Grady when he depantses Jesse on the softball field at school and exclaims that Jesse has a "nice ass"); and he menaces and kills a series of drunken, sexually active male teenagers at a high school pool party.

But Freddy is most sadistic in his harassment of Jesse—a paternally disciplined, sexually ambiguous "good boy" whose family has recently moved to 1428 Elm Street in Springwood, Ohio. Jesse is, indeed, an all-American good boy: he loves baseball and is a good athlete, as evidenced by the tennis and running trophies that adorn his room. An early scene indicates his Ward Cleaver–like father prohibiting Jesse from visiting the girl-next-door Lisa until he unpacks his room. Jesse utters nary a protest at the paternal injunction. Paternally disciplined, Jesse is, moreover, chaste. Awash in a pubescent sea of iniquity, Grady can't understand why Jesse doesn't "mount" Lisa "every night." Jesse appears, in other words, as exactly the sort of budding, autonomous citizen whom conservatism's paternal rights discourse finds worthy of rights.

But Jesse's sexuality is in crisis. When alone, he dances suggestively (gyrating his pelvis and simulating masturbation with a drumstick) to disco music ("you're my candy man," purrs the female vocalist); his nighttime reading is Jack Kerouac's ode to ambiguous, closeted sexuality, *On the Road*; in one of Jesse's initial nightmares (just as Freddy is beginning to terrorize him), we see the candle in his room melted into a phallic shape, the dripping wax a clear allusion to leaking semen; while about to sexually consummate his budding relationship with Lisa, Jesse hallucinates a lizard tongue shooting out of his mouth, panics, and runs to the bedroom of Grady (who is sleeping in the nude). Awakening from a nightmare Jesse wanders out of the house in the middle of the night and eventually winds up at "Don's Place"—one of the S&M bars that the PE teacher Strickland frequents. Thus, according to the countersubversive imagination that was analyzed by Michael Rogin and which sits, we have seen, at the heart of modern American conservatism, Jesse, although a paternally disciplined "good boy," possesses the apparent weakness, heteronomy, and lack of masculine character to make him an easy target for the nefarious Freddy

Figure 1. Freddy comes out. *A Nightmare on Elm Street, 2.*

Krueger.[28] Freddy will, with little difficulty, invade Jesse's dreams, bring him to the brink of psychic breakdown, and ultimately burst from Jesse's innards like the grotesque extraterrestrial that bursts out of John Hurt's chest in 1979's *Alien* (see Figure 1). "Daddy can't help you now!" exclaims Freddy, and Freddy/Jesse embark on a murderous spree that leaves dead a multitude of people, including, prominently, the apparent objects of Jesse's closeted desires (Coach Strickland, Grady, a bevy of licentious high school boys—but not, significantly, Lisa, Jesse's apparent love interest).

The movie points, ironically, to the failure of fathers. Freddy's victims, in the moments before their terror, invariably call for help from their fathers, who are incompetent or unable to help. Lisa's father is particularly impotent; he is filmed topless, his grotesque breasts sagging over his protruding belly. Later he attempts to shoot Freddy/Jesse with a shotgun and badly misses from a short distance; Lisa then prevents him from taking another shot, fearful that he will hit and kill Jesse (who is still inside Freddy). Jesse's own father—initially reminiscent of the stern but loving patriarch of conservative lore—becomes increasingly shrill and useless as the movie proceeds, eventually chalking up Jesse's deteriorating psychic condition, and the father's total inability to help, to drug abuse.

Thus does the movie testify to the paradoxical inability of stern fathers to mold the secure, self-disciplined, autonomous, self-governing citizens of American conservative dreams—the very same paradox that courses through conservatism's paternal rights discourse. Jesse's father can do nothing to assuage, or even understand, his son's anxieties over his sexuality—anxieties that, the movie suggests, make Jesse the easy (perhaps even willing) target of Freddy's malevolence; Grady's father is helpless to respond to his son's terrified calls in the moments before his gruesome murder; Coach Strickland, a surrogate father figure who engages in harsh discipline with his student wards ("assume the position!"), ends up whipped and murdered in the gym showers by Freddy/Jesse, his lifeless, naked body held upright by jump ropes that are tied to the shower heads. Subversive and heteronomous, the movie's licentious adolescents—who drink, smoke, and fornicate while the fathers are absent—are exposed, finally, to Freddy's omniscient paternal wrath: "You are all my children now!" he exclaims prior to his pool party murder spree (see Figure 2).

Freddy thus emerges as the vengeful, wrathful father who at once haunts and excites the American conservative imagination. In the space between Jesse's hidden desires for self-determination (which register here in the domain of sexuality) and his longing for the paternal authority that his biological father can no longer provide emerges Freddy himself. Unbound by sentiment, Freddy Krueger delivers the "law of the father" to the heteronomous objects of Jesse's repressed fantasies.

It is fitting, then, that at the conclusion of *A Nightmare on Elm Street 2*—where, as is conventional for the slasher-film genre, it is revealed that Freddy has somehow survived his apparent death in the penultimate scene—a particular song plays over the ending credits. Summarizing both the film's and modern American conservatism's ambivalence over undying paternal authority, we hear Bing Crosby singing "Did You Ever See a Dream Walking?"

Conclusion: Reagan, the Dog

Freddy Krueger, we have seen, was neither the first nor the last iconic American conservative to detect family dysfunction in subversive politics. Nor was he alone in prescribing that subversion be countered with rejuvenated paternal wrath. Indeed, prominent American conservatives continue to link vexing social and political problems to family matters, and they continue to recommend that subversives receive the harsh law of the father.

Consider, for example, 2016 Republican presidential candidate Rand Paul, who explained that the violence that marred the April 2015 Black

Figure 2. "You are all my children now!" *A Nightmare on Elm Street, 2.*

Lives Matter protests against police brutality in Baltimore had nothing to do with the nation's fraught and continuing history of racism; the episodes of "thuggery and thievery" were, instead, the result of "the breakdown of the family, the lack of fathers, the lack of a moral code in our society."[29] Fellow presidential candidate Ted Cruz agreed, but he focused less on the "root causes" of the violence and more on the psychic damage that it did to American families: "no man, woman, or child should fear for his or her safety in America—not in their schools, not in their neighborhoods, not in their cities—but today families are scared."[30] Their competitor, New Jersey governor Chris Christie, concurred with Cruz that American government must defend families and, in so doing, "perform its central functions and purposes: to preserve the peace, protect the people, and serve justice"; Christie sent one hundred New Jersey state troopers to help keep Baltimore families safe.[31] These candidates sought to reframe the violence as a product of absent fathers rather than as a corollary of the nation's ongoing legacy of racism; it wasn't just "a racial thing," according to Paul.[32] Donald Trump, on the other hand, clearly evoked the connective tissue that links undisciplined children to national threat: casting President Barack Obama as a weak father, Trump tweeted that "our great African American President hasn't exactly had a positive impact on the thugs who are so happily and openly destroying Baltimore!"[33] Having already diagnosed them as products of paternal lack, Trump encouraged supporters of his own 2016 presidential campaign to "knock the hell out of" peaceful Black Lives Matter protesters at campaign rallies.[34]

Family dysfunction linked to heteronomous subjectivity linked to national subversion linked to countersubversive paternal response: in evoking and articulating this discursive chain, contemporary American conservatives paint by numbers. Recall, for example, Governor Ronald Reagan's justification for calling out the California National Guard on peaceful student protesters: "Once the dogs of war are unleashed, you must expect that things will happen." Or his response a year later, in response to the Ohio National Guard's 1970 killing of four peaceful protesters at Kent State University: "If it's to be a bloodbath, let it be now. Appeasement in not the answer."[35]

Similarly, William F. Buckley Jr., who considered treason an act of "patricide," defended the countersubversive brutalities of Chilean dictator Augusto Pinochet long after disinterested observers had well judged his psychopathic tendencies.[36] The determinative question, Buckley was still asking as late as 2000, was "whether his victims were casualties of a revolution." After all, "when insurgents assert power, there is almost always carnage."[37] Nor did Buckley rest his defense of American capital punishment, as is conventional, on its supposed deterrent effects; "irrespective of the deterrent factor . . . we are supposed to be a self-governing society," and sometimes a crime is so offensive (such as patricide) that "we just want to kill [the criminal], and quite right."[38] Thus did Blackford Oakes—the "complete American" of Buckley's fantasies—make a career out of vanquishing America's enemies, both in and out of the bedroom.

Clarence Thomas is not so cavalier in his yoking of self-governance to paternal authority. Unlike Reagan and Buckley, he is tormented by the "hard cases"; he is haunted by beliefs that "I really need to do something" and that injustice "just isn't right."[39] But, still, Thomas insists that "as a member of the Court, I am not empowered" to help, for example, heteronomous victims of state persecution such as tortured prisoners and sexual minorities.[40] As much as he would like to be the autonomous citizen of conservative lore, Thomas finds that he cannot escape the paternal gaze—a gaze that is, for him, symbolized by the bronze bust of Daddy Anderson's head that overlooks his judicial desk.

It is appropriate, then, that while American conservatives tend to admire and identify with Thomas's struggles, they instead deify Reagan and Buckley. Otherworldly figures whose cocksure articulations of the paternal rights discourse pointed to the complete eclipse of their own flawed biological fathers with America's superheroic founding fathers, Reagan and Buckley are themselves now the impossible objects of conservative desire. "Reagan's ghost," offers conservative activist Linda Chavez, "hangs heavily" over American conservatism;[41] national Republican candidates bustle to present themselves as a "new Reagan;"[42] it is rumored that Reagan's ghost haunts his former residence, Rancho del Cielo.[43] Meanwhile, Buckley's cleansing of American conservatism of its extremist, paranoiac elements—his employment of the paternal rights discourse in order to make conservatism "intellectually respectable and politically palatable"—is, according to prominent conservative George Will, the benchmark by which "counterfeit" conservatives are identified and illegitimized.[44] Fast friends in real life, Reagan and Buckley are tethered to one another in eternity, themselves the new founding fathers who haunt modern American conservatism.

But as Buckley himself knew, it is undoubtedly Reagan's spectral star that shines the brightest. So present, in fact, is the ghost of Ronald Reagan for American conservatives that, when confronted with a spirited campaign for governor of Florida in 2010, Republican candidate Rick Scott made headlines by adopting a rescue dog, a light-colored labrador retriever. He asked for Facebook friends to help him name it. "Reagan," they decided.

Dogs, white dogs in particular, according to Colin Dayan, are frequently understood to be manifestations of the spirit world:

In all parts of the world and throughout history, [dogs] are cast . . . as gatekeepers to the realms of the dead, whether understood as the religious or the legal recesses of punishment. . . . In the meeting of the actual and the imaginary, ghosts and dogs bear down on the world of social relations.[45]

Reagan the dog invigorated Scott's campaign, which was further bolstered by the support of Tea Party activists and his unbending opposition to the Affordable Care Act (aka Obamacare). Obamacare was, Scott held, just the sort of un-American governmental regulation that was "so old that Thomas Jefferson listed this problem among his charges against the King of England in the Declaration of Independence."[46] Reagan the dog may thus have been the gatekeeper to Scott's paternal rights discourse, linking Scott's prosaic opposition to Obamacare to the timeless desires of the founding fathers. But Reagan the dog turned out, like all avenging fathers, to be an ambivalent figure in the governor's tenure. Indeed, after reporters for the *Tampa Bay Times* realized, in 2013, that Reagan the dog had not been seen for some time, it came to light that Scott had given him back to the boarding kennel from whence he came. Reagan the dog—Scott's mythical link to the "legal recesses of punishment," to the rights claims of the founding fathers—had introduced chaos in the gubernatorial mansion; he "barked like crazy" and, like the strong American fathers who preceded him, "scared the living daylights" out of everyone.[47]

Notes

Chapter 1

1. John B. Judis, *William F. Buckley, Jr.: Patron Saint of the Conservatives* (New York: Simon & Schuster, 1988).

2. William F. Buckley Jr., "Did You Ever See a Dream Walking?" in *Did You Ever See a Dream Walking? American Conservative Thought in the Twentieth Century*, ed. William F. Buckley Jr. (New York: Bobbs-Merrill, 1970), xv.

3. William F. Buckley Jr., "Our Mission Statement," *National Review*, November 19, 1955, 1.

4. Buckley, Jr., "Did You Ever," xvi.

5. Ibid., xviii.

6. Ibid., xix–xxxii.

7. Ibid., xxxviii.

8. Ibid., xxxviii–xxxix.

9. Buckley, Jr., "Our Mission Statement," 1.

10. See, generally and for example, Stuart A. Scheingold, *The Politics of Rights: Lawyers, Public Policy, and Political Change,* 2nd ed. (Ann Arbor: University of Michigan Press, 2004); Michael W. McCann, *Rights at Work: Pay Equity Reform and the Politics of Legal Mobilization* (Chicago: University of Chicago Press, 1994); Paul A. Passavant, *No Escape: Freedom of Speech and the Paradox of Rights* (New York: New York University Press, 2002); Patricia J. Williams, *The Alchemy of Race and Rights: Diary of a Law Professor* (Cambridge, MA: Harvard University Press, 1991). See also Mary Ann Glendon, *Rights Talk: The Impoverishment of Political Discourse* (New York: Free Press, 1991).

11. Claire E. Rasmussen, *The Autonomous Animal: Self-Governance and the Modern Subject* (Minneapolis: University of Minnesota Press, 2011); Jeffrey R. Dudas, Jon-Goldberg Hiller, and Michael W. McCann, "The Past, Present, and Future of Rights Scholarship," in *The Handbook of Law and Society*, ed. Austin Sarat and Patricia Ewick (New York: Wiley-Blackwell, 2015), 367–381.

12. There is a considerable scholarship establishing this point. Enduring works include Scheingold, *The Politics of Rights*; McCann, *Rights at Work*; and Williams, *The Alchemy of Race and Rights*. See also Elizabeth Schneider, "The Dialectic of Rights and Politics: Perspectives from the Women's Movement," *New York University Law Review* 61, no. 4 (1986): 589–652; Francesca Polletta, "The Structural Context of Novel Rights Claims: Southern Civil Rights Organizing, 1961–1966," *Law and Society Review* 34, no. 2 (2000):

367–406; Didi Herman, *Rights of Passage: Struggles for Lesbian and Gay Legal Equality* (Toronto: University of Toronto Press, 1994); David M. Engel and Frank W. Munger, *Rights of Inclusion: Law and Identity in the Life Stories of Americans with Disabilities* (Chicago: University of Chicago Press, 2003); and Felicia A. Kornbluh, *The Battle for Welfare Rights: Politics and Poverty in Modern America* (Philadelphia: University of Pennsylvania Press, 2007).

13. Peter Fitzpatrick, *The Mythology of Modern Law* (London: Routledge, 1992), 9. See also John L. Comaroff and Jean Comaroff, *Of Revelation and Revolution: The Dialectics of Modernity on a South African Frontier,* vol. 2 (Chicago: University of Chicago Press, 1997), 365–404; and Eve Darian-Smith, *Religion, Race, Rights: Landmarks in the History of Modern Anglo-American Law* (Oxford: Hart Publishing, 2010).

14. Patricia Ewick and Susan S. Silbey, *The Common Place of Law: Stories from Everyday Life* (Chicago: University of Chicago Press, 1998).

15. I borrow the phrase *empire's children*, even as I expand its application to include all of those peoples who have been subjugated by prevailing Anglo American orthodoxies, from Saada. Emmanuelle Saada, *Empire's Children: Race, Filiation, and Citizenship in the French Colonies,* trans. Arthur Goldhammer (Chicago: University of Chicago Press, 2012).

16. McCann, *Rights at Work*, 272–276.

17. See, generally, Charles Taylor, "Interpretation and the Sciences of Man," *Review of Metaphysics* 25, no. 1 (1971): 3–51.

18. "The interpretive approach," write Rabinow and Sullivan, "emphatically refutes the claim that one can somehow reduce the complex world of signification to the products of . . . self-consciousness." Paul Rabinow and William M. Sullivan, "The Interpretive Turn: A Second Look," in *Interpretive Social Science: A Second Look*, ed. Paul Rabinow and William M. Sullivan (Berkeley: University of California Press, 1987), 6.

19. Ibid.

20. Renée Ann Cramer, *Pregnant with the Stars: Watching and Wanting, the Pregnant Celebrity Body* (Stanford, CA: Stanford University Press, 2016), 4–5. See also Michael W. McCann, "Causal versus Constitutive Explanations (or, On the Difficulty of Being So Positive)," *Law and Social Inquiry* 21, no. 2 (1996): 457–482; and Mary Hawkesworth, "Contending Conceptions of Science and Politics: Methodology and the Constitution of the Political," in *Interpretation and Method: Empirical Research Methods and the Interpretive Turn*, ed. Dvora Yanow and Peregrine Schwartz-Shea (Armonk, NY: M. E. Sharpe, 2006), 34–41.

21. As McCann writes, "Inherited legal conventions shape the very terms of citizen understanding, aspiration, and interaction with others." McCann, *Rights at Work*, 6.

22. Corey Robin, *The Reactionary Mind: Conservatism from Edmund Burke to Sarah Palin* (New York: Oxford University Press, 2011), 9–10.

23. Burgess documents this compulsion in regard to theories of constitutional interpretation. She argues that the grounding of interpretive approaches in the supposed desires (and/or flaws) of the American founding fathers works at once to legitimize the interpretive approaches in question and limit the ability of those very approaches to

respond in a persuasive fashion to contemporary dilemmas in American constitutional law. Susan Burgess, *The Founding Fathers, Pop Culture, and Constitutional Law: Who's Your Daddy?* (Burlington, VT: Ashgate, 2008).

24. Zillah R. Eisenstein, *The Female Body and the Law* (Berkeley: University of California Press, 1988), 9.

25. Ibid., 6–13; Judith Butler, *Bodies That Matter: On the Discursive Limits of "Sex"* (New York: Routledge, 1993), 224–230. Jeffrey R. Dudas, *The Cultivation of Resentment: Treaty Rights and the New Right* (Stanford, CA: Stanford University Press, 2008), 11–13.

26. See generally Jessica Benjamin, *The Bonds of Love: Psychoanalysis, Feminism, and the Problem of Domination* (New York: Pantheon, 1988); Judith Butler, *Gender Trouble: Feminism and the Subversion of Identity* (New York: Routledge, [1990] 1999); Williams, *The Alchemy of Race and Rights*; Judith Butler, *The Psychic Life of Power: Theories in Subjection* (Stanford, CA: Stanford University Press, 1997); Rasmussen, *The Autonomous Animal.*

27. Projection, writes Erik Erikson, occurs when "people see over-clearly in [others] what they wish not to recognize in themselves." Erik Erikson, *Childhood and Society, 2nd Edition* (New York: Norton, 1963), 353. See also Benjamin's penetrating analysis of how subject-object intersubjective dynamics, which first emerge in early childhood, constitute identity. Insisting on how identity depends on these dynamics of mutual recognition, Benjamin affirms how "we recognize ourselves in the other." Benjamin, *The Bonds of Love,* 21. Or, as Julia Kristeva puts it, "The other is in me. It is my unconscious. And instead of searching for a scapegoat in the foreigner, I [should] try to tame the demons that are in me." Julia Kristeva, "Cultural Strangeness and the Subject in Crisis," in *Julia Kristeva Interviews*, ed. Ross Mitchell Guberman (New York: Columbia University Press, 1996), 41.

28. Jane Caputi, *Goddesses and Monsters: Women, Myth, and Popular Culture* (Madison: University of Wisconsin Press, 2004), 14.

29. Christine DiStefano, *Configurations of Masculinity: A Feminist Perspective on Modern Political Theory* (Ithaca, NY: Cornell University Press, 1991), 30–55; see also Caputi, *Goddesses and Monsters*; Rasmussen, *The Autonomous Animal*; and Mary Caputi, *A Kinder, Gentler America: Melancholia and the Mythical 1950's* (Minneapolis: University of Minnesota Press, 2005), 43. Richard Slotkin's discussion of the Moira-Themis tension plots this dynamic in early American literature, *Regeneration through Violence: The Mythology of the American Frontier, 1600–1860* (Norman: University of Oklahoma Press, [1973] 2000), 6–14, while Michael Rogin's *Fathers and Children: Andrew Jackson and the Subjugation of the American Indian* (New York: Transaction Publishers, [1975] 1991), 19–37, exposes the gendered dynamics of early American political thought.

30. See Benjamin, *The Bonds of Love,* generally; and Caputi, *Goddesses and Monsters*, 6–14.

31. See, for example, Steven Mintz, *Huck's Raft: A History of American Childhood* (Cambridge, MA: Belknap Press of Harvard University Press, 2004), 276–287.

32. Boys, according to Benjamin, "develop [their] gender[s] and [identities] by means of establishing discontinuity and difference from the person to whom [they are] most attached. This process of disidentification explains the repudiation of the mother that

underlies conventional masculine identity formation, and results in a kind of 'fault line' running through the male achievement of individuality." Benjamin, *The Bonds of Love*, 75–76.

33. DiStefano, *Configurations of Masculinity*, 54.

34. Indeed, modern conservatives, according to Lakoff, imagine themselves as strong, stern fathers, and they envision liberals as weak, permissive parents. George Lakoff, *Moral Politics*, 2nd ed. (Chicago: University of Chicago Press, 2004). See also Natasha Zaretsky, *No Direction Home: The American Family and the Fear of National Decline, 1968–1980* (Chapel Hill: University of North Carolina Press, 2007); and Dominic Sandbrook, *Mad as Hell: The Crisis of the 1970's and the Rise of the Populist Right* (New York: Knopf, 2011), 65–79.

35. Buckley Jr., "Our Mission Statement," 1.

Portions of this chapter are adapted, with significant revisions, from Jeffrey R. Dudas, "Alchemical Histories: Understanding Contemporary American Conservatism," *Choice*, October 2012, 1, and "Subversives All! Ronald Reagan and the Paternal Roots of 'Law & Order' at Home and Abroad," *Law, Culture, and the Humanities* 8 (2012): 119.

Chapter 2

1. See Michael Coulter's comprehensive bibliography, "Conservatism, 1995 to the Present." *Choice Magazine* 44, no. 3 (2006): 409–417.

2. Corey Robin, *The Reactionary Mind: Conservatism from Edmund Burke to Sarah Palin* (New York: Oxford University Press, 2011), 36.

3. Michael Rogin's analyses of the countersubversive tradition place it at the heart of American politics writ large, not simply as the province of American conservatism. My analysis in this book—in both method and substance—is indebted to Rogin's distinctive interrogations of the imagined monsters and demons that are barely submerged below the supposedly rational, democratic veneer of the American nation. See especially Michael Paul Rogin, *Ronald Reagan, the Movie: And Other Episodes in Political Demonology* (Berkeley: University of California Press, 1987); Rogin, *Fathers and Children*; and Rogin, *Independence Day, or How I Learned to Stop Worrying and Love the Enola Gay* (London: British Film Institute, 1998).

4. Lauren Berlant, *The Queen of America Goes to Washington City: Essays on Sex and Citizenship* (Durham, NC: Duke University Press, 1997), 2.

5. Ibid., 3.

6. Scheingold's *The Politics of Rights* remains the entry point for this claim. Stuart A. Scheingold, *The Politics of Rights: Lawyers, Public Policy, and Political Change*, 2nd ed. (Ann Arbor: University of Michigan Press, 2004).

7. D. H. Lawrence, *Studies in Classic American Literature* (Garden City, NY: Doubleday, [1923] 1951), 18.

8. Kim Phillips-Fein, *Invisible Hands: The Making of the Conservative Movement from the New Deal to Reagan* (New York: Norton, 2009); Kathryn S. Olmsted, *Real Enemies: Conspiracy Theories and American Democracy, World War I to 9/11* (New York: Oxford

University Press, 2009); Jennifer Burns, *Goddess of the Market: Ayn Rand and the American Right* (New York: Oxford University Press, 2009).

9. Thomas W. Evans, *The Education of Ronald Reagan: The General Electric Years and the Untold Story of His Conversion to Conservatism* (Ithaca, NY: Cornell University Press, 2007).

10. Jeffrey Hart's *The Making of the American Conservative Mind* is the standard treatment of the *National Review*'s founding and its long-term importance within modern American conservatism. Jeffrey Hart, *The Making of the American Conservative Mind: National Review and Its Times* (Wilmington, DE: ISI Books, 2005); see also John B. Judis, *William F. Buckley, Jr.: Patron Saint of the Conservatives* (New York: Simon & Schuster, 1988); Kevin Mattson, *Rebels All! A Short History of the Conservative Mind in Postwar America* (New Brunswick, NJ: Rutgers University Press, 2008), 42–56; and David Farber, *The Rise and Fall of Modern American Conservatism: A Short History* (Princeton, NJ: Princeton University Press, 2010), 39–76.

11. Kristol's *The Neoconservative Persuasion* features a representative selection of Kristol's writing for the *Public Interest* and other prominent conservative periodicals of the era (such as *American Spectator*). Irving Kristol, *The Neoconservative Persuasion: Selected Essays, 1942–2009*, ed. Gertrude Himmelfarb (New York: Basic Books, 2011).

12. Mark C. Henrie, ed. *Arguing Conservatism: Four Decades of the Intercollegiate Review* (Wilmington, DE: ISI Books, 2008).

13. Lizabeth Cohen, *A Consumer's Republic: The Politics of Mass Consumption in Postwar America* (New York: Knopf, 2003); Ira Katznelson, *When Affirmative Action Was White: An Untold History of Racial Inequality in Twentieth-Century America* (New York: Norton, 2005); Andrew Hurley, *Diners, Bowling Alleys, and Trailer Parks: Chasing the American Dream in the Postwar Consumer Culture* (New York: Basic Books, 2002).

14. Dwight D. Eisenhower, "Farewell Radio and Television Address to the American People," January 17, 1961. http://www.presidency.ucsb.edu/ws/?pid=12086.

15. Lisa McGirr, *Suburban Warriors: The Origins of the New American Right* (Princeton, NJ: Princeton University Press, 2001); Rick Perlstein, *Before the Storm: Barry Goldwater and the Unmaking of the American Consensus* (New York: Hill and Wang, 2001).

16. The general outlines of Nixon's plan are ably sketched in many books. See, for example, Garry Wills, *Nixon Agonistes: The Crisis of the Self-Made Man* (Boston: Mariner Books, [1970] 2002), 258–275; Rick Perlstein, *Nixonland: The Rise of a President and the Fracturing of America* (New York: Scribner, 2008), 463–468.

17. Diane McWhorter, *Carry Me Home: Birmingham, Alabama: The Climactic Battle of the Civil Rights Revolution* (New York: Simon & Schuster, 2001); Dan Carter, *The Politics of Rage: George Wallace, the Origins of the New Conservatism, and the Transformation of American Politics* (New York: Simon & Schuster, 1995).

18. See, for example, Stuart A. Scheingold, *The Politics of Law and Order: Street Crime and Public Policy* (New York: Longman, 1984); Michael Flamm, *Law and Order: Street Crime, Civil Unrest, and the Crisis of Liberalism in the 1960's* (New York: Columbia University Press, 2007); Jonathan Simon, *Governing through Crime: How the War on Crime*

Transformed American Democracy and Created a Culture of Fear (New York: Oxford University Press, 2007).

19. Joseph Lowndes, *From the New Deal to the New Right: Race and the Southern Origins of Modern Conservatism* (New Haven, CT: Yale University Press, 2008); Anders Walker, *The Ghost of Jim Crow: How Southern Moderates Used Brown v. Board of Education to Stall Civil Rights* (New York: Oxford University Press, 2009); Kevin Kruse, *White Flight: Atlanta and the Making of Modern Conservatism* (Princeton, NJ: Princeton University Press, 2005); Jason Sokol, *There Goes My Everything: White Southerners in the Age of Civil Rights, 1945–1975* (New York: Knopf, 2006); Joseph Crespino, *In Search of Another Country: Mississippi and the Conservative Counterrevolution* (Princeton, NJ: Princeton University Press, 2007); George Lewis, *The White South and the Red Menace: Segregationists, Anticommunism, and Massive Resistance, 1945–1965* (Gainesville: University of Florida Press, 2004).

20. Matthew D. Lassiter, *The Silent Majority: Suburban Politics in the Sunbelt South* (Princeton, NJ: Princeton University Press, 2006).

21. Dan Carter, *From George Wallace to Newt Gingrich: Race in the Conservative Counterrevolution, 1963–1994* (Baton Rouge: LSU Press, 1999).

22. Richard A. Viguerie and David Franke, *America's Right Turn: How Conservatives Used Old and New Media to Take Power* (Chicago: Bonus Books, 2004).

23. Perlstein, *Before the Storm*, generally.

24. Ronald Reagan, "Televised Nationwide Address on Behalf of Senator Barry Goldwater," in Ronald Reagan, *Speaking My Mind: Selected Speeches* (New York: Simon & Schuster, 1989), 22–36.

25. Jonathan M. Schoenwald, *A Time for Choosing: The Rise of Modern American Conservatism* (New York: Oxford University Press, 2001), 198–220.

26. Richard Nixon, "Gentlemen, This Is My Last Press Conference," in *Nixon: Speeches, Writings, Documents*, ed. Rick Perlstein (Princeton, NJ: Princeton University Press, 2008), 105–112.

27. Perlstein, *Nixonland*, 64–69, 115–117, 277–304.

28. Natasha Zaretsky, *No Direction Home: The American Family and the Fear of National Decline, 1968–1980* (Chapel Hill: University of North Carolina Press, 2007); Kevin Mattson, *"What the Heck Are You Up To, Mr. President?" Jimmy Carter, America's "Malaise," and the Speech That Should Have Changed the Country* (New York: Bloomsbury USA, 2009).

29. Andrew E. Busch, *Reagan's Victory: The Presidential Election of 1980 and the Rise of the Right* (Lawrence: University Press of Kansas, 2005).

30. Representative examples include Sean Wilentz, *The Age of Reagan: A History, 1974–2008* (New York: Harper Perennial, 2009); and Gil Troy, *Morning in America: How Ronald Reagan Invented the 1980's* (Princeton, NJ: Princeton University Press, 2005).

31. Jean Stefancic and Richard Delgado, *No Mercy: How Conservative Think Tanks and Foundations Changed America's Social Agenda* (Philadelphia: Temple University Press, 1996); Steven Teles, *The Rise of the Conservative Legal Movement: The Battle for the Control of Law* (Princeton, NJ: Princeton University Press, 2010); Ann Southworth, *Lawyers of*

the Right: Professionalizing the Conservative Coalition (Chicago: University of Chicago Press, 2008).

32. Dan Gilgoff, *The Jesus Machine: How James Dobson, Focus on the Family, and Evangelical America Are Winning the Culture War* (New York: St. Martin's Press, 2007).

33. Daniel K. Williams, *God's Own Party: The Making of the Christian Right* (New York: Oxford University Press, 2010).

34. Allan J. Lichtman, *White Protestant Nation: The Rise of the American Conservative Movement* (New York: Atlantic Monthly Press, 2008), 399.

35. Robin, *The Reactionary Mind*, 36.

36. Scheingold, *The Politics of Rights*, 3.

37. Dudas, *The Cultivation of Resentment: Treaty Rights and the New Right* (Stanford, CA: Stanford University Press, 2008).

38. Scheingold, *The Politics of Rights,* xlix.

39. Ibid., 17, 62–79.

40. Ibid., 5.

41. Ibid., 131.

42. See, for example, Joel F. Handler, *Social Movements and the Legal System: A Theory of Law Reform and Social Change* (Madison, WI: Academic Press, 1979); Elizabeth Schneider, "The Dialectic of Rights and Politics: Perspectives from the Women's Movement," *New York University Law Review* 61, no. 4 (1986): 589–652; Michael W. McCann, *Rights at Work: Pay Equity Reform and the Politics of Legal Mobilization* (Chicago: University of Chicago Press, 1994).

43. Jonathon Goldberg-Hiller, *The Limits to Union: Same-Sex Marriage and the Politics of Civil Rights* (Ann Arbor: University of Michigan Press, 2002); William Haltom and Michael W. McCann, *Distorting the Law: Politics, Media, and the Litigation Crisis* (Chicago: University of Chicago Press, 2004); Dudas, *The Cultivation of Resentment*; Joseph Mello, "Rights Discourse and the Mobilization of Bias: Exploring the Institutional Dynamics of the Same-Sex Marriage Debates in America," *Studies in Law, Politics, and Society* 66, no. 1 (2015): 1–34.

44. The outstanding example of this scholarship is Patricia Williams, *The Alchemy of Race and Rights: Diary of a Law Professor* (Cambridge, MA: Harvard University Press, 1991). See also Ian Haney López, *White by Law: The Legal Construction of Race,* 10th anniversary ed. (New York: New York University Press, 2006).

45. Philip A. Klinkner and Rogers M. Smith, *The Unsteady March: The Rise and Decline of Racial Equality in America* (Chicago: University of Chicago Press, 1999), 202–241; Mary L. Dudziak, *Cold War, Civil Rights: Race and the Image of American Democracy* (Princeton, NJ: Princeton University Press, 2000); Thomas Borstelmann, *The Cold War and the Color Line: American Race Relations in the Global Arena* (Cambridge, MA: Harvard University Press, 2001), generally; Gary Gerstle, *American Crucible: Race and Nation in the Twentieth Century* (Princeton, NJ: Princeton University Press, 2001), 187–227.

46. See the works cited in note 18.

47. Naomi Murakawa, "The Origins of the Carceral Crisis: Racial Order as 'Law and Order' in Postwar American Politics," in *Race and American Political Development,* ed. Joseph Lowndes, Julie Novkov, and Dorian Warren (New York: Routledge, 2008), 238.

48. Winthrop D. Jordan, *White over Black: American Attitudes toward the Negro, 1550–1812* (Chapel Hill: University of North Carolina Press, 1968), 457–481.

49. Murakawa, "Origins of the Carceral Crisis," 237–244; see also Crespino, *In Search of Another Country,* 49–63.

50. Katherine Beckett, *Making Crime Pay: Law and Order in Contemporary America* (New York: Oxford University Press, 1999), 31–33, 86–88.

51. See, for example, Richard M. Weaver, "Integration Is Communization," *National Review,* July 13, 1957, 67.

52. Crespino, *In Search of Another Country,* 52; see also Lowndes, *From the New Deal to the New Right,* generally. On Cold War–era mass anxiety, see T. Jackson Lears, "A Matter of Taste: Corporate Cultural Hegemony in a Mass-Consumption Society," in *Recasting America: Culture and Politics in the Age of Cold War,* ed. Lary May (Chicago: University of Chicago Press, 1989), 38–57; Warren Susman, "Did Success Spoil the United States? Dual Representations in Postwar America," in May, *Recasting America,* 19–37; and Gerstle, *American Crucible,* 238–267.

53. Jeff R. Woods, *Black Struggle, Red Scare*: *Segregation and Anti-Communism in the South, 1948–1968* (Baton Rouge: Louisiana State University Press, 2003).

54. William F. Buckley Jr., *The Jeweler's Eye: A Book of Irresistible Political Reflections* (New York: Putnam, 1968), 156–158.

55. US Department of Labor, *The Negro Family: The Case for National Action* (Washington, DC, March 1965).

56. Ibid., 6.

57. Ibid., 28, 15, 31. The consequences of black familial pathology extended even to the armed forces and the opportunities for training and employment offered there. Decrying the poor performance of young black men on the Armed Forces Qualification Test, Moynihan fretted that black men missed out on the salutary effects of "an utterly masculine world." Indeed, "given the strains of the disorganized and matrifocal family life in which so many Negro youth come of age, the armed forces are a dramatic and desperately needed change: a world away from women, a world run by strong men of unquestioned authority, where discipline, if harsh, is nonetheless orderly and predictable, and rewards, if limited, are granted on the basis of performance." Ibid., 34.

58. Ibid., 8, 39, 7.

59. Richard M. Nixon, "The Present Welfare System Has to Be Judged a Colossal Failure," in Perlstein, *Nixon: Speeches, Writing, Documents,* 165.

60. Reagan paid Gilder one his highest compliments in a 1986 radio address, referring to him as a "pioneer of economic growth." Ronald Reagan, "Radio Address to the Nation on Tax Reform," June 7, 1986.

61. George Gilder, *Wealth and Poverty* (New York: Basic Books, 1981), 70–71.

62. Rogin, *Ronald Reagan, the Movie*, 134–168; Richard Slotkin, *Gunfighter Nation: The Myth of the Frontier in Twentieth-Century America* (New York: Atheneum, 1992), generally.

63. The insistence on self-discipline as the marker of personal virtue reflects what Lears calls the American "zeal for control . . . the faith that we can master fate through force of will, and that rewards will match merits." Jackson Lears, *Something for Nothing: Luck in America* (New York: Viking, 2003), 2.

64. Ronald Reagan, "The Republican Party and the Conservative Movement: On Losing," *National Review*, December 1, 1964.

65. Wills, *Nixon Agonistes*, 164–167; Claire E. Rasmussen, *The Autonomous Animal: Self-Governance and the Modern Subject* (Minneapolis: University of Minnesota Press, 2011), generally.

66. Leslie Fiedler, *Love and Death in the American Novel* (New York: Delta/Dell, 1966), 296–320; Jordan, *White over Black*, 469–475; Richard Slotkin, *Regeneration through Violence: The Myth of the Frontier in Twentieth-Century America* (Norman: University of Oklahoma Press, [1973] 2000), 42–56; Robert F. Berkhofer Jr., *The White Man's Indian: Images of the American Indian from Columbus to the Present* (New York: Vintage, 1979), 5–31; Rogin, *Ronald Reagan, the Movie*, 49–52.

67. Ronald Reagan, "Letter to the Editor of the *Pegasus*," in *Reagan, in His Own Hand: The Writings of Ronald Reagan that Reveal His Revolutionary Vision for America*, ed. Kiron Skinner, Annelise Anderson, and Martin Anderson (New York: Simon & Schuster, 2001), 449.

68. Jordan, *White over Black*, 101–268; Rogin, *Fathers and Children*, 168–169; Francis Paul Prucha, *The Great Father: The United States Government and the American Indians* (Lincoln: University of Nebraska Press, 1986); Jeffrey R. Dudas, "Of Savages and Sovereigns: Tribal Self-Administration and the Legal Construction of Dependence," *Studies in Law, Politics, and Society* 23 (2001): 12–17.

69. Peter Goodrich, "Maladies of the Legal Soul: Psychoanalysis and Interpretation in Law," *Washington and Lee Law Review* 54, no. 3 (1997): 1044.

70. Peter Goodrich, "Maladies of the Legal Soul: Psychoanalysis and Interpretation in Law," *Washington and Lee Law Review* 154 no. 3 (1997): 1045; see also Austin Sarat, "Imagining the Law of the Father: Loss, Dread, and Mourning in *The Sweet Hereafter*," *Law and Society Review* 34, no. 1 (2000): 10–14; Susan Burgess, *The Founding Fathers, Pop Culture, and Constitutional Law: Who's Your Daddy?* (Burlington: VT: Ashgate, 2008), generally.

71. Ronald Reagan, "The Morality Gap at Berkeley," in Ronald Reagan, *The Creative Society: Some Comments on Problems Facing America* (New York: Devin-Adair, 1968), 126.

72. Mark Feeney, *Nixon at the Movies: A Book about Belief* (Chicago: University of Chicago Press, 2004), 229–235; Perlstein, *Nixonland*, 374–393.

73. Ronald Reagan, "What Is Academic Freedom?" in Reagan, *The Creative Society*, 121–122.

74. Wills, *Nixon Agonistes*, 184–186.

75. Zaretsky, *No Direction Home*, 187.

76. Ibid.

77. Ibid., 183–222.

78. Jeffrey R. Dudas, "Little Monsters, Wild Animals, and Welfare Queens: Ronald Reagan and the Legal Constitution of American Politics," *Studies in Law, Politics, and Society* 49 (2009): 157 generally.

79. Ronald Reagan, "America's Strength," in Skinner et al., *Reagan, in His Own Hand*, 12–13.

80. William F. Buckley, Jr., "The New Conservatism," in *Athwart History: Half a Century of Polemics, Animadversions, and Illuminations: A William F. Buckley, Jr. Omnibus*, ed. Linda Bridges and Roger Kimball (New York: Encounter Books, 2010), 35–36.

81. Irving Kristol, "Republican Virtue versus Servile Institutions," in Kristol, *The Neoconservative Persuasion*, 64–76.

82. Irving Kristol, "The Old Politics, the New Politics, the *New*, New Politics," *New York Times Magazine*, November 24, 1968, SM49. See also "A Conversation with Irving Kristol," *Alternative* 2, no. 5 (1969): 7.

83. Kristol, "The Old Politics," 177.

84. Ibid.

85. Kristol, "Servile Institutions," 76.

86. Buckley Jr., "Did You Ever See a Dream Walking?" in *Did You Ever See a Dream Walking? American Conservative Thought in the Twentieth Century* (New York: Bobbs-Merrill, 1970), xxxviii.

87. Buckley Jr., "The New Conservatism," 35.

88. Dudas, "Little Monsters, Wild Animals, and Welfare Queens," 168–193;

89. Clarence Thomas, "Speech by Clarence Thomas before the Pacific Research Institute," San Francisco, August 10, 1987.

90. Cyrus Ernesto Zirakzadeh, *Social Movements in Politics, Expanded Edition: A Comparative Study* (New York: Palgrave Macmillan, 2006), 3–20.

Chapter 3

1. Lee Edwards, "William F. Buckley, Jr.: Conservative Icon," *First Principles*, December 17, 2012, 7.

2. Carl Bogus, "William F. Buckley, Father of American Conservatism," *National Public Radio*, December 17, 2011.

3. Evan Thomas, "He Knew He Was Right," *Newsweek* 153, no. 10 (2008): 26–33; "William F. Buckley, Jr., R.I.P.," *National Review Online*, February 27, 2008.

4. Bart Barnes, "Erudite Voice of the Conservative Movement," *Washington Post*, February 28, 2008, A01; Douglas Martin, "William F. Buckley Jr. Is Dead at 82," *New York Times* February 27, 2008.

5. Thomas, "He Knew He Was Right."

6. Ibid.

7. Ronald Reagan, "The Defense of Freedom and the Metaphysics of Fun," in *Tear Down This Wall: The Reagan Revolution—A National Review History*, ed. National Review (New York: Continuum, 2004), 75.

8. Stephen Miller, "William F. Buckley, Jr., 82, Godfather of Modern Conservatism," *New York Sun*, February 28, 2008; Judis, *William F. Buckley, Jr.: Patron Saint of the Conservatives* (New York: Simon & Schuster, 1988), 372.

9. William F. Buckley Jr. and Charles R. Kesler, eds., *Keeping the Tablets: Modern American Conservative Thought* (New York: Harper & Row, 1988).

10. William F. Buckley Jr., "Triumph of the Republican Ideal," *Goodlife* (October 1983): 19.

11. Corey Robin, *The Reactionary Mind: Conservatism from Edmund Burke to Sarah Palin* (New York: Oxford University Press, 2011); William F. Meehan III, ed., *Conversations with William F. Buckley, Jr.* (Jackson: University Press of Mississippi, 2009), 132.

12. William F. Buckley Jr., *Who's on First* (Garden City, NY: Doubleday, 1980), 50.

13. Leslie Fiedler, *Love and Death in the American Novel* (New York: Delta/Dell, 1966), 362–363.

14. Buckley Jr., "Did You Ever See a Dream Walking?" in *Did You Ever See a Dream Walking? American Conservative Thought in the Twentieth Century*, ed. William F. Buckley Jr., 19–36 (New York: Bobbs-Merrill, 1970), xxxviii.

15. Judis, *William F. Buckley, Jr.*, 372–375, 393–395.

16. William F. Buckley Jr., *Miles Gone By: A Literary Autobiography* (Washington, DC: Regnery, 2004), ix.

17. Sydney Pollack, Dir., *Three Days of the Condor* Paramount (1975).

18. Buckley Jr. was himself a virulent critic of Allende's regime and a strong defender of the coup that brought the vile Augusto Pinochet to power. Buckley consistently denied conclusive, eyewitness testimony of Pinochet's death squads and was a key figure in developing a public relations and lobbying presence for Pinochet on American soil. See, for example, the following by William F. Buckley Jr.: *Inveighing We Will Go* (New York: Putnam, 1972), 168–170; "Point Counterpoint," *On the Right*, November 18, 1971; "The Chilean Refugees," *On the Right*, September 27, 1973; "Playing with Torture," *On the Right*, December 21–22, 1974; "Pinochet and Human Rights," *On the Right*, February 19–20, 1977; "Marx, Engels, Lenin and Pinochet," *On the Right*, January 26, 1978; "Pinochet? Why Him?" *On the Right*, October 20, 1998. See also Judis, *William F. Buckley, Jr.*, 369–371.

19. Jeffrey R. Dudas, "'A Madman Full of Paranoid Guile': The Myth of Rights in the Modern American Mind," *Studies in Law, Politics, and Society* 59 (2012): 39–56; Feeney, *Nixon at the Movies: A Book about Belief* (Chicago: University of Chicago Press, 2004).

20. William F. Buckley Jr., *The Blackford Oakes Reader* (Kansas City, MO: Andrews and McMeel, 1995), xiii-xvi. See also Buckley's disgust over a 1975 article in the *New Yorker* that associated the tactics of the FBI and the CIA with those of the American mafia and the KGB. William F. Buckley Jr., *A Hymnal: The Controversial Arts* (New York: Putnam, 1978), 63–65.

21. William F. Meehan III, ed., *Conversations with William F. Buckley, Jr.* (Jackson: University Press of Mississippi, 2009), 96, emphasis preserved.

22. Buckley Jr., *Blackford Oakes Reader*, xxxiii.

23. William F. Buckley Jr., *See You Later, Alligator* (New York: Doubleday, 1985), 74.

24. Buckley Jr., *Who's On First*, 35.

25. William F. Buckley Jr. *The Reagan I Knew* (New York: Basic Books, 2008), 241.

26. Richard Slotkin, *Regeneration through Violence: The Mythology of the American Frontier, 1600–1860* (Norman: University of Oklahoma Press, [1973] 2000); generally; Michael Paul Rogin, *Ronald Reagan, the Movie: And Other Episodes in Political Demonology* (Berkeley: University of California Press, 1987), generally.

27. "Great Elm," affirmed Buckley's older sister Priscilla, "provided us with everything good and exciting any child could desire." Priscilla L. Buckley, "Buckley Branches: Splitting Up a Family Home in Order to Preserve It," *Town Vibe Litchfield* (March–April 2011), http://www.townvibe.com/Litchfield/March-April-2011/Buckley-Branches/

28. Buckley Jr., *Miles Gone By*, 17–21.

29. Ibid., 20.

30. Ibid., 51–52.

31. William F. Buckley Jr., *The Jeweler's Eye: A Book of Irresistible Political Reflections* (New York: Putnam, 1968), 262.

32. Ibid., 48.

33. Meehan III, *Conversations*, 84.

34. Buckley Jr., *Miles Gone By*, 48–49.

35. Ibid., 12, 4.

36. Ibid., 16, 12.

37. Buckley Jr., *The Jeweler's Eye*, 263–264.

38. Ibid. *Happy Days Were Here Again: Reflections of a Libertarian Journalist* (New York: Basic Books, 1993), 5.

39. Oakes's absent father, in fact, reminded Buckley of then-presidential nominee Jimmy Carter, whom Buckley regarded as a weak-willed "hypocrite" willing to "humiliate" himself for the votes of the nation's electorate. William F. Buckley Jr., "The Selling of William F. Buckley, Jr.," *Esquire* (July 1976): 141; William F. Buckley Jr., "What They Are Doing to Carter," *On the Right*, April 8, 1976.

40. Buckley Jr., *Miles Gone By*, 50.

41. Ibid., 25.

42. William F. Buckley Jr., *Saving the Queen* (New York: Doubleday, 1976), 77.

43. Ibid., 70.

44. Ibid., 71.

45. Meehan, *Conversations*, 78. According to Buckley, "I heard that for extreme acts of misbehavior the birch rod was used on the buttocks, but I never knew any boy who received this punishment at St. John's." Buckley Jr., *Miles Gone By*, 31.

46. Buckley, Jr., *Miles Gone By*, 30–31.

47. Indeed, Buckley will later reveal in the pages of *Moongoose R.I.P.*, in a gratuitous aside, that Anthony Trust was raped by an older prefect during his days at Greyburn College. William F. Buckley Jr., *Moongoose R.I.P.* (New York: Random House, 1987), 4–5.

48. Buckley Jr., *Saving the Queen*, 87.

49. Buckley Jr., *Blackford Oakes Reader*, xx.

50. Herman Melville, *Billy Budd, Sailor (An Inside Narrative)*, ed. Harrison Hayford and Merton M. Sealts Jr. (Chicago: University of Chicago Press, 1962).

51. The 1994 penultimate Blackford Oakes novel, *A Very Private Plot*, is the first in which Oakes and Sally appear as husband and wife; Buckley Jr. there explains that they were married in 1965. William F. Buckley Jr., *A Very Private Plot* (New York: Morrow, 1994).

52. Meehan III, *Conversations*, 149.

53. Ibid., 91.

54. Ibid.

55. Buckley's tampering with series chronology did not go unnoticed by critics, but it did go unappreciated. *Kirkus*, for example, called *High Jinx* "contrived and disjointed . . . one of the series' weaker installments . . . [it] lacks the stylish wit and sly charm of Buckley at his brightest." *Kirkus Reviews*, February 15, 1986. Nor was the *New York Times* impressed, as evidenced by Ruth Rendell's stinging review. Ruth Rendell, "Oakes against the Spooks," *New York Times* (April 6, 1986). Nevertheless, High Jinx sold 100,000 copies and again was on the New York Times best-seller list. Bob Mack, "The Boys Who Would be Buckley," *Spy* (July 1989): 71.

56. Meehan III, *Conversations*, 129.

57. Ibid., 106.

58. Ibid., 117, 97, 128; Robin, *The Reactionary Mind*.

59. Meehan III, *Conversations*, 79.

60. Ibid., 100.

61. Ibid., 75; 132, emphasis added.

62. "Gloria Steinem on Population, Sexual Pleasure, and Creating Better Fathers," *Grist*, December 24, 2010.

63. William F. Buckley Jr., "Linda's Crusade," *National Review*, May 21, 1968. 518.

64. William F. Buckley Jr., *Let Us Talk of Many Things: The Collected Speeches* (New York: Forum, 2000), 440, 438.

65. Buckley Jr., *The Jeweler's Eye* 156–158.

66. George Gilder, *Wealth and Poverty* (New York: Basic Books, 1981), 70–71.

67. William F. Buckley Jr., "Zounds! Enforcing the Law in Idaho!" *On the Right*, January 9, 1996.

68. Catharine A. MacKinnon, *Toward a Feminist Theory of the State* (Cambridge, MA: Harvard University Press, 1989).

69. Buckley Jr., *Saving the Queen*, 45.

70. Ibid., 15.

71. Meehan III, *Conversations*, 149.

72. William F. Buckley Jr., "A Handsome Man Is Not the Equivalent of a Beautiful Woman, He Is the Complement," *Vogue* (April 1978): 291.

73. Buckley had already vilified the name *Peregrine* on both aesthetic and substantive grounds, in a 1966 *On the Right* column regarding the efforts of the British House of Commons to repeal antisodomy laws. Buckley's column fixated on the advocacy efforts of "Mr. Peregrine Worsthorne," an English journalist who possessed Buckley's

"favorite name this side of the Pickwick Papers." Buckley ridiculed the efforts of both the House of Commons and Worsthorne, who were advocating a "new morality that comes in to justify and even to honor th[e] abnormality [of homosexuality]." Unsurprising, then, is Buckley's intimation ten years hence that Peregrine Kirk harbors "abnormal" sexual desire for his royal cousin. William F. Buckley Jr., "The Repeal of the Homosexual Laws," *On the Right*, March 3, 1966; Buckley Jr., *Saving the Queen*, 165.

74. George Roy Hill, Dir., *The Great Waldo Pepper,* Universal Pictures (1975).

75. Buckley Jr., *Saving the Queen*, 148, 144.

76. Ibid., 150.

77. Chase's assault was, Trust knew, a "primal experience" that left Oakes with "scar tissue." Ibid., 25.

78. Ibid., 134–138.

79. Ibid., 191–192.

80. Ibid., 199–200.

81. Meehan III, *Conversations*, 79.

82. Buckley Jr., *Saving the Queen*, 215–218.

83. Ibid., 218–220.

84. Buckley Jr., "The Selling of William F. Buckley, Jr.," 140.

85. Ibid., *Saving the Queen*, 265.

86. Oakes's travails, in this sense, recall less those of Melville's Billy Budd and more those of Ronald Reagan's character Drake McHugh from the 1942 movie *King's Row*. Reagan's most celebrated role (in both his and the general estimation), McHugh's legs are unnecessarily amputated by the sadistic, incestuous father of his paramour, leading McHugh, upon the grisly discovery, to exclaim, "Where's the rest of me?!" Buckley's political hero, Reagan, would later borrow the line for the title of the 1965 memoir that was designed to bolster his coming 1966 California gubernatorial candidacy. Ronald Reagan, with Richard G. Hubler, *Where's the Rest of Me?* (New York: Katz Publishers, [1981] 1965).

87. Thomas Jefferson, *Jefferson: Writings* (New York: Library of America, 1984), 19.

88. Paul A. Passavant, *No Escape: Freedom of Speech and the Paradox of Rights* (New York: New York University Press, 2002), 25–31.

89. Bernard Bailyn, *The Ideological Origins of the American Revolution,* enlarged ed. (Cambridge, MA: Belknap Press of Harvard University Press, 1992).

90. Rogin, *Ronald Reagan, the Movie*, 44–80.

91. Edwin G. Burrows and Michael Wallace, "The American Revolution: The Ideology and Psychology of National Liberation," *Perspectives in American History* 6 (1972): 167–305.

92. Jefferson, *Jefferson*, 23.

93. Michael Paul Rogin, *Fathers and Children: Andrew Jackson and the Subjugation of the American Indian* (New York: Transaction Publishers, [1975] 1991), 25.

94. Buckley Jr., *Saving the Queen*, 84, 87.

95. Buckley had begun to sense his limits as early as 1983's *The Story of Henri Tod*, the fifth installment in the Oakes series. There he has Oakes worry that he "was . . . becoming a bore." William F. Buckley Jr., *The Story of Henri Tod* (New York: Dell, 1983), 40.

96. Buckley Jr., *A Very Private Plot*, 272.

97. Josh Rubins, "Blackford Oakes, One Stand-Up Guy," *New York Times*, February 6, 1994.

98. Buckley Jr., *The Reagan I Knew*, 241, 4, 240, 1; Ron Reagan, *My Father at 100: A Memoir* (New York: Viking, 2011), 115–139; Meehan III, *Conversations*, 91.

99. Buckley Jr., *The Reagan I Knew*, 1.

100. Rogin, *Ronald Reagan, the Movie*, 1–43.

101. Gregory Katz, "Keep Queen Elizabeth II Waiting? Ronald Reagan Got Away with It, Newly Released Papers Show," Associated Press, December 28, 2012; Ronald Reagan, "Toasts of the President and Queen Elizabeth II at a Dinner Honoring the President at Windsor Castle in England," June 8, 1982.

102. "Reagan Now a Knight But Not a Sir: Queen Bestows Title—No Dubbing, No Kneeling Required," *Los Angeles Times*, June 14, 1989.

A portion of this chapter appears, with significant revision, as "Subversives All! Ronald Reagan and the Paternal Roots of 'Law & Order' at Home and Abroad," *Law, Culture, and the Humanities* 8 (2012): 119–152.

Chapter 4

1. John Patrick Diggins, *Ronald Reagan: Fate, Freedom, and the Making of History* (New York: Norton, 2007), xvii, 16.

2. Lou Cannon, "Remembering Reagan," *Washington Post*, June 7, 2004, A23.

3. Shalaigh Murray, "Obama's Reagan Comparison Sparks Debate," *Washington Post*, January 17, 2008.

4. Ronald Reagan, with Richard G. Hubler, *Where's the Rest of Me?* (New York: Katz Publishers, [1981] 1965), 54.

5. Victor Davis Hanson, "Reagan and the National Psyche," in *Tear Down This Wall: The Reagan Revolution—A National Review History*, ed. *National Review* (New York: Continuum, 2004), 188.

6. Linda Chavez, "The Ghost of Ronald Reagan," Townhall.com, February 1, 2008.

7. Sean Wilentz, *The Age of Reagan: A History, 1974–2008* (New York: Harper Perennial, 2009), 8.

8. Ronald Reagan, "Letter to Mrs. Gail E. Foyt," in *Reagan: A Life in Letters*, ed. Kiron K. Skinner, Annelise Anderson, and Martin Anderson (New York: Free Press, 2003), 622.

9. Ronald Reagan, "Televised Nationwide Address on Behalf of Senator Barry Goldwater," in Reagan, *Speaking My Mind: Selected Speeches* (New York: Simon & Schuster, 1989), 26, emphasis added.

10. Ronald Reagan, "Letter to the Editor of the *Pegasus*," in *Reagan, in His Own Hand: The Writings of Ronald Reagan that Reveal His Revolutionary Vision for America*, ed. Kiron K. Skinner, Annelise Anderson, and Martin Anderson (New York: Touchstone, 2001), 467.

11. Ronald Reagan, *The Creative Society: Some Comments on Problems Facing America* (New York: Devin-Adair, 1968), 138.

12. See, for example, Jane S. Schacter, "The Gay Civil Rights Debate in the States: Decoding the Discourse of Equivalents," *Harvard Civil Rights–Liberties Law Review* 29, no. 2 (1994): 283–317, and "Skepticism, Culture, and the Gay Rights Debate in a Post-Civil-Rights Era," *Harvard Law Review* 110, no. 3 (1997): 684–731; Jonathan Goldberg-Hiller, *The Limits to Union: Same-Sex Marriage and the Politics of Civil Rights* (Ann Arbor: University of Michigan Press, 2002); Jonathan Goldberg-Hiller and Neal Milner, "Rights as Excess: Understanding the Politics of Special Rights," *Law and Social Inquiry* 28, no. 4 (2003): 1075–1118; Jeffrey R. Dudas, "In the Name of Equal Rights: 'Special' Rights and the Politics of Resentment in Post–Civil Rights America," *Law and Society Review* 39, no. 4 (2005): 723–758, and *The Cultivation of Resentment: Treaty Rights and the New Right* (Stanford, CA: Stanford University Press, 2008).

13. William F. Buckley Jr., "The Prayer Amendment and Its Critics," *On the Right*, May 22–23, 1982.

14. Reagan, "Televised Nationwide Address," 26.

15. See, for example, Anne Edwards, *Early Reagan: The Rise to Power* (London: Taylor Trade Publishing, [1987] 2012), 32–46; Lou Cannon, *President Reagan: The Role of a Lifetime* (New York: Touchstone, 1991), 173–176; Robert Dallek, *Ronald Reagan: The Politics of Symbolism* (Cambridge, MA: Harvard University Press, 1984), generally; Garry Wills, *Reagan's America: Innocents at Home* (New York: Penguin, [1987] 2000), 15–19; Edmund Morris, *Dutch: A Memoir of Ronald Reagan* (New York: Random House, 1999), 24–43; Rick Perlstein, *The Invisible Bridge: The Fall of Nixon and the Rise of Reagan* (New York: Simon & Schuster, 2014), 28–31; H. W. Brands, *Reagan: The Life* (New York: Doubleday, 2015), part I, generally.

16. Reagan, with Hubler, *Where's the Rest of Me?* 9.

17. "[Jack] was restless, always ready to pull up stakes and move on in search of a better life for himself and his family. . . . During one period of four years, I attended four different schools. We moved to wherever my father's ambition took him. " Ronald Reagan, *An American Life* (New York: Simon & Schuster, 1990), 22–23.

18. Reagan, with Hubler, *Where's the Rest of Me?* 54.

19. Reagan, *An American Life*, 26.

20. Ibid., 7–8, 33.

21. Rasmussen, *The Autonomous Animal: Self-Governance and the Modern Subject* (Minneapolis: University of Minnesota Press, 2011), generally.

22. Reagan, with Hubler, *Where's the Rest of Me?* 8.

23. Reagan revised his self-narrative for his 1990 memoir. In that later account, Jack's physical abuse is replaced by an emphasis on how "kind and loving" Jack was, at least when he was sober. Reagan, *An American Life*, 33–34. This late-life revision accords with the suspicion of Ron Reagan (Ronald and Nancy's son) that Dutch's tales of paternal abuse were "a bit of hyperbole . . . whatever other faults may have been Jack's, there is no evidence that he physically abused his children." Ron Reagan, *My Father at 100*, 63. Ron Reagan's biography is incisive; his sense, accordingly, that his father exaggerated Jack's

punishments should be credited. Even so, Dutch's multiple accounts of self consistently make it clear that Jack's legacy—no matter whether it included the disputed physical abuse—was the major impediment to finding "the rest of me," to becoming the figure of political destiny to which he aspired.

24. Reagan, with Hubler, *Where's the Rest of Me?* 8.

25. Ibid., 11.

26. Ibid., 14.

27. Ibid., 14–15.

28. Reagan, *An American Life*, 22; see also Reagan, with Hubler, *Where's the Rest of Me?* 8.

29. Reagan, with Hubler, *Where's the Rest of Me?* 8.

30. Jack was "adorned with the gift of blarney and the charm of a leprechaun. No one I ever met could tell a story better than he could." Reagan, *An American Life*, 21.

31. Reagan, with Hubler, *Where's the Rest of Me?* 8.

32. Lou Cannon, one of Reagan's first and still best biographers, was nevertheless skeptical of Dutch's literary redemptions of Jack, chalking them up to Reagan's skill at "softening hard memories with happy stories." Cannon: "While [Reagan's] portrayal of his father is drawn to show much light among the shadows, the recollections of Jack Reagan's drunkenness are infinitely more dramatic and convincing than the collection of anecdotes the son selects to display the father's virtues." Cannon, *President Reagan*, 173–174.

33. "Nothing," Reagan wrote to a citizen in 1983, "has frustrated me more than the unfounded propaganda" that claimed he was a racist. With apparent sincerity, Reagan insisted that "our record with regard to blacks is probably better than any previous administration." That same year, Reagan defended himself in another letter against accusations of being a "closet racist." Reagan recited the influence of Jack's antiracism, claimed that he had campaigned against Major League Baseball's color line in the 1930s, and noted that when he was governor of California, he had "appointed more blacks to executive and policymaking positions than all the previous governors of California put together." Reagan, "Letter to Dina Merrill," in Skinner et al., *Reagan: A Life in Letters*, 625–626; Ronald Reagan., "Letter to Leonard Kirk," in Skinner et al., *Reagan: A Life in Letters*, 13. As was characteristic, Reagan's responses to these claims of racism emphasized his personal antiracism, but they never betrayed any cognition of, or responsibility for, the structural forms of racism that were intensified by the policies of his administration. See, for example, Cannon, *President Reagan*, 457–463, and Hugh Heclo, "Ronald Reagan and the American Public Philosophy," in *The Reagan Presidency: Pragmatic Conservatism and Its Legacies*, ed. W. Elliot Brownlee and Hugh Graham Davis (Lawrence: University Press of Kansas, 2003), 34–35.

34. See, generally, Kiron K. Skinner, Annelise Anderson, and Martin Anderson, eds., *Reagan's Path to Victory: The Shaping of Ronald Reagan's Vision: Selected Writings* (New York: Free Press, 2004).

35. Edwards, *Early Reagan*, 143.

36. Ibid, generally; Morris, *Dutch*, 111–310; Reagan, with Hubler, *Where's the Rest of Me?* 49–261; Reagan, *An American Life*, 62–94, 126–131; Thomas W. Evans, *The Education*

of Ronald Reagan: The General Electric Years and the Untold Story of His Conversion to Conservatism (Ithaca, NY: Cornell University Press, 2007, generally.

37. Reagan, with Hubler, *Where's the Rest of Me?* 42–43; Reagan, *An American Life,* 60–61.

38. Reagan, with Hubler, *Where's the Rest of Me?* 25–27, 31–39; Reagan, *An American Life,* 47–52; Reagan, *My Father at 100,* 145–163.

39. Reagan, Nationwide Address," 26.

40. Wills, *Reagan's America,* 205–212.

41. Edwards, *Early Reagan,* 289–317; Wills, *Reagan's America,* 255–285; Perlstein, *The Invisible Bridge,* 354–371.

42. Edwards, *Early Reagan,* 322–337; Wills, *Reagan's America,* 294–297; Morris, *Dutch,* 252–262.

43. Morris, *Dutch,* 277–283, 302–310; Evans, *The Education of Ronald Reagan,* generally.

44. Jules Tygiel, *Ronald Reagan and the Triumph of American Conservatism,* 2nd ed. (New York: Pearson, 2006), 99–101.

45. Ronald Reagan, "Encroaching Control: An Address by Ronald Reagan" (1961), 12.

46. Ronald Reagan, "California Young Republican Convention," in *Actor, Ideologue, Politician: The Public Speeches of Ronald Reagan,* ed. Davis W. Houck and Amos Kiewe (Westport, CT: Greenwood Press, 1993), 91.

47. Reagan, "Televised Nationwide Address," 26.

48. Ronald Reagan, "America's Strength," in Skinner et al., *Reagan, In His Own Hand,* 13.

49. Reagan, "Letter to the Editor of the Pegasus," in Skinner et al., *Reagan, In His Own Hand,* 449.

50. Reagan, "Televised Nationwide Address," 26; Rick Perlstein, *Nixonland: The Rise of a President and the Fracturing of America* (New York: Scribner, 2008), 385.

51. Reagan, "Have We Been Out of Touch with Reality?" in Reagan, *The Creative Society,* 13–14.

52. Reagan, *The Creative Society,* 138.

53. Reagan, "What Is Academic Freedom?" in Reagan, *The Creative Society,* 121–122.

54. Reagan, "Encroaching Control," 12.

55. See, for example, ibid., 11–12; Reagan, "Television Address," in Houck and Kiewe, *Actor, Ideologue, Politician,* 27–35; Reagan, "Televised Nationwide Address," 22–36; Reagan, "What Is Academic Freedom?" 119–123; Reagan, "Property Rights," in Skinner et al., *Reagan: In His Own Hand,* 341; Reagan, "OSHA," in Skinner et al., *Reagan's Path to Victory,* 109–110; Reagan, "More about OSHA," in Skinner et al., *Reagan's Path to Victory,* 111; Reagan, "Man's Castle," in Skinner et al., *Reagan: In His Own Hand,* 291–292; and Reagan, "Treaties," in *Reagan's Path to Victory,* 273.

56. Reagan,, *An American Life,* 197; Reagan, "What Is Academic Freedom?" 122.

57. Reagan, "Televised Nationwide Address," 26, 33.

58. Reagan, "Letter to Mrs. Gail E. Foyt," 622.

59. Reagan did not originate the term "forgotten American." And the logic that the appellation expresses—there is a virtuous majority population whose rights and interests

are abused by a tiny but powerful minority—is a lasting feature of American populism. See, generally, Michael Kazin, *The Populist Persuasion: An American History* (Ithaca, NY: Cornell University Press, 1998). Reagan's use of the term and the concept was likely indebted to Barry Goldwater and Richard Nixon, each of whom employed it consistently in their attempts to break apart the New Deal governing coalition. Richard Nixon, "Presidential Nomination Acceptance Speech," Miami, FL, August 8, 1968; Barry M. Goldwater, *The Conscience of a Majority* (Englewood Cliffs, NJ: Prentice Hall, 1970).

60. Reagan, "YMCA Model Legislature," in *Actor, Ideologue, Politician*, 84.

61. Reagan, "The Republican Party and the Conservative Movement: On Losing." See also Reagan, "A Moment of Truth: Our Rendezvous with Destiny," *Vital Speeches of the Day*, September 1, 1965, 685; Reagan "The Average Man," in *Reagan's Path to Victory: The Shaping of Ronald Reagan's Vision: Selected Writings*, 355–356; Reagan "Inaugural Address," 63.

62. Ibid., *The Creative Society*, 138

63. See, for example, Reagan, "Televised Nationwide Address," 29.

64. Ibid.

65. Reagan, "Inaugural Address," 62.

66. Reagan, "Televised Nationwide Address," 27.

67. Reagan, *The Creative Society*, 16.

68. Dudas, "Little Monsters, Wild Animals, and Welfare Queens: Ronald Reagan and the Legal Constitution of American Politics," *Studies in Law, Politics, and Society* 49 (2009): 157–210.

69. Gerald J. De Groot, "Ronald Reagan and Student Unrest in California, 1966–1970," *Pacific Historical Review* 65, no. 1 (1996): 107–129; Lou Cannon, *Governor Reagan: His Rise to Power* (New York: Public Affairs, 2003), 271–296.

70. Reagan, "Letter to the Honorable Jack Williams," in *Reagan: A Life in Letters*, 190; see also Reagan, *An American Life*, 180.

71. De Groot, "Ronald Reagan and Student Unrest in California," 111, 120–122.

72. Reagan, "Eisenhower College Fund-Raiser," in *Speaking My Mind*, 42.

73. Reagan, *The Creative Society*, 126.

74. Reagan, "Letter to the Editor of the *Pegasus*," 448–449.

75. Ibid., 446, 448.

76. Reagan, "Eisenhower College Fund-Raiser," 41.

77. Reagan,, "People's Park I," in *Reagan's Path to Victory*, 448.

78. Reagan urged the University of California's board of trustees to dismiss Davis from her teaching post at UCLA for several years before finally succeeding in 1970. Davis was ultimately fired for her opposition to Reagan's conduct of the Battle of People's Park (see below). Wallace Turner, "California Regents Drop Communist from Faculty," *New York Times*, June 20, 1970.

79. Reagan, "What Is Academic Freedom?" 122.

80. Reagan claimed that many campus radicals were not actually students, but were instead amateur agitators from elsewhere. See, for example, Reagan, "People's Park II," in *Reagan's Path to Victory*, 449–450, and his *An American Life*, 180.

81. Reagan, "People's Park II," 449; Reagan, "What Is Academic Freedom?" 74; see also Reagan, "Missing Person," in *Reagan: In His Own Hand*, 411–412.

82. *Regents of the University of California-Davis v. Bakke*, 438 U.S. 265.

83. Reagan, "Bakke," in *Reagan's Path to Victory*, 274–275.

84. Reagan, "The 'People's Park,'" in *Actor, Ideologue, Politician*, 81.

85. Ibid., 82.

86. Reagan, "What Is Academic Freedom?" 120–121.

87. Reagan's rendering of the liberal professoriate and the multiple dangers that its employment of the equal outcomes logic of rights inflicted—on academic freedom, on the university's traditional mission to ensure national order and growth, and on the rights and interests of ordinary university students—had lasting influence. Reagan's image of the university under siege from a noxious vision of individual rights is, in fact, both the discursive cornerstone of culture war battles against the presence of political correctness on university campuses and a widely shared conviction that animates recent policy trends in higher education. See, for example, Dinesh D'Souza, *Illiberal Education: The Politics of Race and Sex on Campus* (New York: Free Press, 1991); Arthur M. Schlesinger Jr., *The Disuniting of America: Reflections on a Multicultural Society* (New York: Norton, 1991).

88. Ronald Reagan, "The Generation Gap," in *The Creative Society*, 60–63.

89. Ibid., 63; see also Reagan, "Eisenhower College Fund Raiser," 43–44.

90. Reagan, "The Generation Gap," 63.

91. Ibid.

92. Reagan, "Letter to the Editor of the *Pegasus*," 448–449.

93. Cited in Cannon, *Governor Reagan*, 287.

94. Ibid., 285; Reagan, "Letter to the Editor of the *Pegasus*," 447.

95. Reagan, "Letter to the Editor of the *Pegasus*," 447.

96. Reagan, "People's Park I," 449.

97. Reagan, 448–449, and his "People's Park II," 449–450.

98. Reagan, "What Is Academic Freedom?" 122.

99. Reagan, "The Generation Gap," 61.

100. Ibid., 59–63, and his "What Is Academic Freedom?" 122.

101. Rogin, *Ronald Reagan, the Movie*, 238.

102. Reagan, "The Morality Gap at Berkeley," in *The Creative Society*, 125–126.

103. Ibid, 126.

104. Reagan, "Eisenhower College Fund Raiser," 42.

105. Reagan, "Letter to the Honorable Jack Williams," 190.

106. Reagan, *Speaking My Mind*, 38.

107. Reagan, "Inaugural Address," 43.

108. Reagan, "Letter to the Editor of the *Pegasus*," 447.

109. Morris, *Dutch*, 343–344.

110. Cannon, *Governor Reagan*, 271–296; John Brigham, *Material Law: A Jurisprudence of What's Real* (Philadelphia: Temple University Press, 2009), 11–12.

111. Langdon Winner, "The Battle of People's Park," *Rolling Stone*, June 14, 1969; Cannon, *Governor Reagan*, 291–293.

112. Morris, *Dutch*, 362–365; Perlstein, *Nixonland*, 383–386.

113. Cited in ibid., 385.

114. Reagan, "The People's Park," 75–76.

115. Ibid., 78.

116. Ibid, 78–79.

117. Ibid, 79.

118. Reagan, "Letter to Samuel Hayakawa," in *Reagan: A Life in Letters*, 189.

119. Reagan, "Letter to the Honorable Jack Williams," 190.

120. Cited in Cannon, *Governor Reagan*, 295.

121. Ibid., 293.

122. Rogin, *Ronald Reagan, the Movie*, 1–43.

123. Cited in Perlstein, *Nixonland*, 385.

124. Cannon, *Governor Reagan*, generally; Tygiel, *Ronald Reagan*, 119–133; Perlstein, *The Invisible Bridge*, 408–413, 434–442.

125. The transcripts of a great many of these radio broadcasts are contained in Skinner et al., *Reagan's Path to Victory*.

126. See, generally, Ronald Reagan, *The Reagan Diaries*, ed. Douglas Brinkley (New York: Harper, 2007).

127. Reagan, *Speaking My Mind*, 145–146.

128. Ronald Reagan, "Remarks at a Fund-Raising Dinner for the Nicaragua Refugee Fund," April 15, 1985.

129. Ibid.

130. Reagan, "Address on Central America before a Joint Session of the Congress," in *Speaking My Mind*, 147.

131. Reagan, "Remarks at the Quadrennial Convention of the International Longshoreman's Association in Hollywood, Florida," July 18, 1983.

132. Ibid., "Interview with Allan Dale of WOAI-Radio in San Antonio, Texas, on Domestic and Foreign Policy Issues," May 5, 1983; Reagan, "Remarks at a Fund-Raising Dinner." See also Ronald Reagan, "Question-and-Answer Session with High School Students on Domestic and Foreign Policy Issues," January 21, 1983; Reagan, "Remarks on Central America and El Salvador at the Annual Meeting of the National Association of Manufacturers," March 10, 1983; and Reagan, "Remarks at Cinco de Mayo Ceremonies in San Antonio, Texas," May 5, 1983.

133. Reagan, "Remarks at the Quadrennial Convention."

134. Ibid.

135. Reagan, "Address to the Nation on Central America," April 14, 1984.

136. Reagan, "Address to the Nation on the Situation in Nicaragua," March 16, 1986.

137. Reagan, "Address to the Nation on United States Policy in Central America," May 9, 1984, and his "Remarks at a Fund-Raising Dinner."

138. Reagan, "Address before a Joint Session of Congress on the State of the Union," February 4, 1986.

139. Reagan, "Remarks and a Question-and-Answer Session with Regional Editors and Broadcasters on United States Assistance for the Nicaraguan Democratic Resistance," March 11, 1986.

140 Ibid., "Address to the Nation on the Situation in Nicaragua"; see also Reagan, "Question-and-Answer Session with Reporters on Domestic and Foreign Policy Issues," March 29, 1983; his "Remarks and a Question-and-Answer Session with Reporters on Domestic and Foreign Policy Issues," April 14, 1983; and his "Address to the Nation on United States Policy in Central America."

141. William M. Leogrande, "The Contras and Congress," in *Reagan versus the Sandinistas: The Undeclared War on Nicaragua*, ed. Thomas Walker (Boulder, CO: Westview Press, 1987), 425–427; Robert Kagan, *Twilight Struggle: American Power and Nicaragua, 1977–1990* (New York: Free Press, 1996), 124–133.

142. Ronald Reagan, "Remarks to Elected Officials during a White House Briefing on United States Assistance for the Nicaraguan Democratic Resistance," March 14, 1986.

143. Reagan, "Radio Address to the Nation on Grenada and Nicaragua," February 22, 1986.

144. Reagan, "Remarks and a Question-and-Answer Session," and "Address on Central America before a Joint Session of the Congress," 152.

145. Reagan, "Remarks and a Question-and-Answer Session."

146. Roy Gutman, *Banana Diplomacy: The Making of American Policy in Nicaragua, 1981–1987* (New York: Simon & Schuster, 1988), 35–38.

147. Gutman, *Banana Diplomacy*, 38; Stephen Kinzer, *Blood of Brothers: Life and War in Nicaragua* (Cambridge, MA: Harvard University Press, 2007), 96–97.

148. Reagan, *The Reagan Diaries*, 314, and his *Speaking My Mind*, 145.

149. Reagan, "Address to the Nation on the Situation in Nicaragua."

150. Reagan, "Remarks at a White House Briefing for Supporters of United States Assistance for the Nicaraguan Democratic Resistance," March 10, 1986, and *The Reagan Diaries*, 308, 330.

151. Cannon, *President Reagan*, 310–313; Reagan, *The Reagan Diaries*, 383.

152. Leogrande, "The Contras and Congress," 431–435; Gutman, *Banana Diplomacy*, 39–57.

153. Ronald Reagan, "The President's News Conference," June 28, 1983.

154. Reagan, "Radio Address to the Nation on the Situation in Central America," August 13, 1983, and "Remarks at a Fund-Raising Dinner."

155. Reagan, "Address to the Nation on the Situation in Nicaragua."

156. Reagan, "Remarks and a Question-and-Answer Session," and his "Remarks at a Fund-Raising Dinner."

157. Reagan, "Remarks to Elected Officials."

158. Reagan, "Radio Address to the Nation on United States Assistance for the Nicaraguan Democratic Resistance," March 22, 1986; Reagan, "Remarks and an Informal Exchange with Reporters on United States Assistance for the Nicaraguan Democratic Resistance," February 18, 1986; Reagan, *Speaking My Mind*, 145.

159. Reagan, "Address to the Nation."

160. Reagan, *Speaking My Mind*, 145; Reagan, "Interview with Allan Dale"; Reagan, *The Reagan Diaries*, 304, 402.

161. Leslie Cockburn, *Out of Control: The Story of the Reagan Administration's Secret War in Nicaragua* (New York: Atlantic Monthly Press, 1987), 6–9; Kagan, *Twilight Struggle*, 240–241, 250–251, 355–356; Kinzer, *Blood of Brothers*, 199–206.

162. Cockburn, *Out of Control*, 152–188.

163. See, for example, Reagan, *Speaking My Mind*, 145–146.

164. Reagan, "Remarks at a Fund-Raising Dinner."

165. Cited in Perlstein, *Nixonland*, 385.

166. See, for example, Reagan, *The Reagan Diaries*, 496.

167. Cannon, *President Reagan*, 336–337; David M. Abshire, *Saving the Reagan Presidency: Trust Is the Coin of the Realm* (Lawrence: University of Kansas Press, 2005), 57–59.

168. Cannon, *President Reagan*, 335–336; Kagan, *Twilight Struggle*, 339–341; Reagan, *The Reagan Diaries*, 301.

169. Abshire, *Saving the Reagan Presidency*, 59.

170. Cannon, *President Reagan*, 338.

171. "Excerpts from Interview with Nixon about Domestic Effects of Indochina War," *New York Times*, May 20, 1977. Mary Dudas suggested this formulation.

172. Reagan, "Letter to the Honorable Jack Williams," 190.

173. See, for example, Woodrow Wilson, "The Ideals of America," *Atlantic Monthly* (December 1902): 721–722; Michael Paul Rogin, "Max Weber and Woodrow Wilson: The Iron Cage in Germany and America," *Polity* 3, no. 3 (1971): 562–575.

174. Ronald Reagan, "Letter to Richard Nixon," in *Reagan: A Life in Letters*, 714.

175. Juan Williams, "Black Conservatives, Center Stage," *Washington Post*, December 16, 1980, A21.

176. Shelby Steele, "The Freest Black Man in America," *National Review*, October 22, 2007, 36.

A portion of this chapter appears, with significant revision, as "All the Rage: Clarence Thomas, Paternal Authority, and Conservative Desire," *Law, Culture, and the Humanities* 12 (2016): 70–105.

Chapter 5

1. Andrew Peyton Thomas, "America's Leading Conservative," *Weekly Standard*, August 30, 1999, 23; Quin Hillyer, "There's No Doubting Thomas," *American Spectator*, September 9, 2007; "A Model Justice," *National Review*, October 22, 2007, 14; Rich Lowry, "A Great American Story," *National Review Online*, October 2, 2007; Henry Mark Holzer, "His Grandfather's Miracle," *Front Page Magazine,* October 10, 2007; Rush Limbaugh, "Rush Interviews Justice Clarence Thomas," *Rush Limbaugh Show*, October 1, 2007; *Meet the Press*, October 16, 2011.

2. R. Emmett Tyrell, "A Good Man," *American Spectator*, November 8, 2007.

3. Claire E. Rasmussen, *The Autonomous Animal: Self-Governance and the Modern Subject* (Minneapolis: University of Minnesota Press, 2011), 23–95.

4. Rod Dreher, "Clarence Thomas' Story Is the Real American Dream," *Dallas Morning News*, October 14, 2007.

5. Clarence Thomas, "Be Not Afraid," 2001 Francis Boyer Lecture American Enterprise Institute Annual Dinner, February 13, 2001; Shelby Steele, "The Freest Black Man in America," *National Review* 59, no. 19 (2007): 36–39.

6. To acknowledge that Clarence Thomas has repressed the basic elements of his identity (race, class, and family status) is not, of course, to say that he has overcome or left

them behind. "In repression certain psychic 'contents' (or representations) are strongly cathected with emotional energy but denied access to consciousness because of an inner conflict. Indeed, if these items were *not* deeply cathected, these items would not be repressed in the first place." Daniel Burston, *Erik Erickson and the American Psyche: Ego, Ethics, and Evolution* (Lanham, MD: Aronson, 2007), 199.

7. John Yoo, "The Real Clarence Thomas," *Wall Street Journal,* October 9, 2007.

8. Timothy Sandefur, "Clarence Thomas's Jurisprudence Unexplained," *New York Journal of Law and Liberty* 4, no. 3 (2009): 535–556; "A Model Justice," *National Review,* October 22, 2007; Emmett R. Tyrell, "A Good Man," *American Spectator* (October 2007).

9. Jane Flax, *The American Dream in Black and White: The Clarence Thomas Hearings* (Ithaca, NY: Cornell University Press, 1998).

10. See, for example, A. Leon Higginbotham Jr., "An Open Letter to Justice Clarence Thomas from a Federal Judicial Colleague," *University of Pennsylvania Law Review* 140, no. 3 (1992): 1005–1028; Toni Morrison, "Introduction: Friday on the Potomac," in *Racing Justice, En-gendering Power,* ed. Toni Morrison (New York: Random House, 1992), vii–xxx; Alvin Wyman Walker, "The Conundrum of Clarence Thomas: An Attempt at a Psychodynamic Understanding" (n.d.), http://www.raceandhistory.com/historicalviews/clarencethomas.htm; Molefi K. Asante and Ronald E. Hall, *Rooming in the Master's House: Power and Privilege in the Rise of Black Conservatism* (Boulder, CO: Paradigm Publishers, 2011), 127–133.

11. Rick Perlstein, *Nixonland: The Rise of a President and the Fracturing of America* (New York: Scribner, 2008), 382–386.

12. Thomas is thus, according to self-proclamation, "a strict law and order man." Quoted in Andrew Peyton Thomas, *Clarence Thomas: A Biography* (San Francisco: Encounter Books, 2001), 223.

13. See, for example, Christopher E. Smith and Joyce A. Baugh, *The Real Clarence Thomas: Confirmation Veracity Meets Performance Reality* (New York: Peter Lang, 2000).

14. See, for example, the works cited in note 10 above. Nor am I interested in the familiar, hoary accusation that Thomas lacks the basic intellectual capabilities to be a viable Supreme Court justice. The "evidence" of his supposed incapacity—that Thomas characteristically refuses to question attorneys during oral arguments and that his jurisprudence is broadly consistent with that of his late fellow justice, Antonin Scalia—is weak at best and unserious at worst. See Angela Onwuachi-Willig, "Just Another Brother on the SCT? What Justice Clarence Thomas Teaches Us about the Influence of Racial Identity," *Iowa Law Review* 90, no. 3 (2005): 931–996.

15. I thus take inspiration from Hartog's illuminating study of Abigail Bailey. Like Hartog, my interest in the depictions that animate Clarence Thomas's self-narrative is not whether they are "truthful," but rather in their "roles in giving meaning to actions." I thus aim to "recover something of the meanings" that Clarence Thomas gives "to the events of [his] life through [his direct and indirect] use of the language and the symbols of law." Hendrik Hartog, "Abigail Bailey's Coverture: Law in a Married Woman's Consciousness," in *Law in Everyday Life,* ed. Austin Sarat and Thomas R. Kearns (Ann Arbor: University of Michigan Press, 1993), 69.

16. Clarence Thomas, *My Grandfather's Son: A Memoir* (New York: Harper Perennial, 2007): 1.

17. Ibid., 5. See also Clarence Thomas, "The Necessity of Moral Absolutes in a Free Society," *Religion and Liberty* (January and February 1996): 6–8. Thomas's nostalgia for a childhood that was, by any measure, undesirable mirrors a similar nostalgia employed by Ronald Reagan (one of Thomas's surrogate fathers). As with Thomas, Reagan's nostalgia highlights, even as it means to diminish, the importance of missing paternal authority on the constitution of his later self. See Chapter 4.

18. Thomas, *My Grandfather's Son*, 6–8.

19. Ibid., 8. During this time Thomas "can remember spending countless hours alone, wandering the streets, or looking out the window on the dirt streets below," Peyton Thomas, *Clarence Thomas*, 63. Merida and Fletcher confirm that Thomas "disparaged [his mother] before friends and colleagues" and that he "carried his resentment of his mother for a long time." Kevin Merida and Michael Fletcher, *Supreme Discomfort: The Divided Soul of Clarence Thomas* (New York: Broadway Books, 2007), 87. See also Juan Williams, "A Question of Fairness," *Atlantic Monthly* (February 1987).

20. Thomas, *My Grandfather's Son*, 7–9.

21. Ibid., 8–9.

22. Peyton Thomas, *Clarence Thomas*, 64.

23. Merida and Fletcher confirm Peyton Thomas's account, noting that "one former Thomas aide . . . recalled his boss saying that 'his mother dumped him and his brother on the grandfather because she'd met some man.'" Merida and Fletcher, *Supreme Discomfort*, 87; see also 56–57. Similarly, Williams's fawning account of Thomas notes that "his mother had remarried, and her new husband didn't want children from the previous marriage around." Williams, "A Question of Fairness," 5.

24. Thomas, *My Grandfather's Son*, 12.

25. Erik Erickson, *Childhood and Society,* 2nd ed. (New York: Norton, 1963), generally.

26. Thomas, *My Grandfather's Son*, 12.

27. Clarence Thomas, "The New Intolerance" (Mercer University, May 1993).

28. George Lakoff, *Moral Politics*, 2nd ed. (Chicago: University of Chicago Press, 2004), generally.

29. Thomas, *My Grandfather's Son*, 11–12, 26.

30. Clarence Thomas, "Keynote Address at the Bill of Rights Institute's *Being an American* Awards Gala," March 31, 2009; Clarence Thomas, "Address by Justice Clarence Thomas," 15th Annual Ashbrook Memorial Dinner," Ashland, Ohio, February 5, 1999.

31. See, for example, Thomas, "The Necessity of Moral Absolutes," 8; Merida and Fletcher, *Supreme Discomfort*, 241–242.

32. Elizabeth Kantor, "A Conversation with Clarence Thomas," *Human Events*, October 9, 2007.

33. For example, when Daddy removed the heater from a new delivery truck because he believed that it would lead Clarence and Myers to sit in the warmth rather than work hard during winter deliveries, Clarence clandestinely warmed his hands by setting scrap pieces of newspaper aflame. Thomas, *My Grandfather's Son*, 21.

34. Jan Crawford Greenburg, "Clarence Thomas: A Silent Justice Speaks Out: Part II: The Integrator," *ABC News*, September 30, 2007.

35. Thomas, *My Grandfather's Son*, 45–48.

36. Clarence Thomas, "Speech to the National Bar Association," Memphis, TN, July 28, 1998.

37. Quoted in Merida and Fletcher, *Supreme Discomfort*, 143; see also Bill Kaufman, "Clarence Thomas," *Reason*, November 1, 1987.

38. Clarence Thomas, "Climb the Jagged Mountain," *New York Times*, July 17, 1991, A21.

39. Clarence Thomas, "Speech to the Centenary U.M.C.," June 17, 1984, quoted in Peyton Thomas, *Clarence Thomas*, 255–256.

40. It is thus unsurprising that Thomas's many accounts of his own childhood minimize the role that Daddy Anderson's wife, Tina, played in his upbringing, in spite of the dispassionate accounts of Thomas's biographers that affirm her presence and importance. See, generally, Merida and Fletcher, *Supreme Discomfort*, and Peyton Thomas, *Clarence Thomas*.

41. Thomas, *My Grandfather's Son*, 135

42. Juan Williams, "Black Conservatives, Center Stage," *Washington Post*, December 16, 1980, A21.

43. Thomas, ignoring that his sister, Emma Mae, had received public assistance only temporarily and while unable to work because she was caring for a terminally ill relative, accused his sister of getting "mad when the mailman is late with her welfare check. That is how dependent she is. What's worse is that now her kids feel entitled to the check too. They have no motivation for doing better or getting out of that situation." Ibid. See also Joel F. Handler, "The Judge and His Sister: Growing Up Black," *New York Times* July 23, 1991; Katherine Tate, "Invisible Woman," *American Prospect* (Winter 1992): 74–81.

44. Kaufman, "Clarence Thomas."

45. Thomas, *My Grandfather's Son*, 137–138.

46. For example, Thomas famously battled with William Bradford Reynolds, then assistant attorney general for civil rights, over many of Thomas's decisions while he served as head of the Equal Employment Opportunity Commission. Reynolds would eventually publicly "hail" Thomas as "the epitome of the right kind of affirmative action working in the right way," a comment for which Thomas has never forgiven him. Williams, "A Question of Fairness"; Thomas, *My Grandfather's Son*, 176–178.

47. Kaufman, "Clarence Thomas."

48. *Bob Jones University v. United States*, 461 U.S. 574 (1983).

49. Thomas, *My Grandfather's Son*, 162, 146–147.

50. Williams, "A Question of Fairness."

51. Clarence Thomas, "Speech by Clarence Thomas before the Pacific Research Institute," San Francisco, August 10, 1987; see also Thomas, "Keynote Address."

52. Alan Freeman's seminal work on contemporary American antidiscrimination law and ideology envisions the antidiscrimination logic as a contest between a structural, "victim"-based perspective on racial inequality and an individualistic, "perpetrator"-based

one that is especially persuasive for American conservatives, among others. Although Clarence Thomas does not subscribe to this perpetrator model of racial hierarchy (for he acknowledges that racial inequality is a historical and structural force), he does, paradoxically, endorse the perpetrator model's solution to racial inequality: a practice of rights that envisions them as limited guarantors of an "equal opportunity" to participate in a pre-existing, market-based economy. Alan D. Freeman, "Antidiscrimination Law: A Critical Review," in *The Politics of Law: A Progressive Critique* ed. David Kairys (New York: Pantheon Books, 1982), 96–116. See also Kimberlé Willams Crenshaw, "Race, Reform, and Retrenchment: Transformation and Legitimation in Antidiscrimination Law," *Harvard Law Review* 101, no. 7 (1988): 1331–1387.

53. Williams, "A Question of Fairness."

54. Greenburg, "Clarence Thomas."

55. Thomas, "Speech by Clarence Thomas," emphasis preserved.

56. Ibid.

57. Thomas, "Climb the Jagged Mountain."

58. Ibid.

59. Thomas, "Speech by Clarence Thomas."

60. Thomas, *My Grandfather's Son*, 145–146.

61. Peyton Thomas, *Clarence Thomas*, 209.

62. Thomas, *My Grandfather's Son*, 193. "I never really wanted to be on the court," Thomas told Rush Limbaugh in a 2007. Limbaugh, "Rush Interviews."

63. Thomas, *My Grandfather's Son*, 231–232.

64. Ibid., 216. Eventually Thomas accepted the explanation of a Bush administration official that "the president had been looking for someone who was not only competent at doing the job but who had also been tested in political battle and thus could be counted on not to cave in under the pressure of a confirmation battle, or to change his views after being appointed to the Court. I definitely qualified on that score." Ibid., 216–217.

65. Ibid., 197, 202; Merida and Fletcher, *Supreme Discomfort*, 167–169.

66. Thomas, *My Grandfather's Son*, 207–208, 211.

67. Ibid., 212–215.

68. Ibid., 211.

69. Ibid., 168, 173–174, 234–236, 245–246, 260, 257, 251–252.

70. Jan Crawford Greenburg, "Clarence Thomas: A Silent Justice Speaks Out, Part VII: 'Traitorous' Adversaries: Anita Hill and the Senate Democrats," *ABC News*, September 30, 2007.

71. Kaufman, "Clarence Thomas."

72. Fox News, "Cable Exclusive: Justice Clarence Thomas Sits Down with Sean Hannity," *Fox News*, October 3, 2007.

73. Thomas, "The New Intolerance."

74. Thomas, "Speech by Clarence Thomas."

75. "Grandfather's Son Speaks Off the Bench," *Wisconsin Law Journal*, October 29, 2007.

76. Ibid.

77. Peter Fitzpatrick, *The Mythology of Modern Law* (New York: Routledge, 1992).

78. Richard Slotkin, *Regeneration through Violence: The Mythology of the American Frontier, 1600–1860* (Norman: University of Oklahoma Press, [1973] 2000), 3.

79. Eve Darian-Smith, *Religion, Race, Rights: Landmarks in the History of Modern Anglo-American Law* (Portland, OR: Hart Publishing, 2010), generally.

80. Fitzpatrick, *The Mythology of Modern Law*, 20.

81. Stuart A. Scheingold, *The Politics of Rights: Lawyers, Public Policy, and Political Change*, 2nd ed. (Ann Arbor: University of Michigan Press, 2004), 39–79; Darian-Smith, *Religion, Race, Rights* 10–16.

82. Thomas, "Be Not Afraid."

83. John Brigham, *The Cult of the Court* (Philadelphia: Temple University Press, 1987), 63–91.

84. Peter Goodrich, "Maladies of the Legal Soul: Psychoanalysis and Interpretation in Law," *Washington and Lee Law Review* 54, no. 3 (1997): 1044–1045; see also Austin Sarat, "Imagining the Law of the Father: Loss, Dread, and Mourning in *The Sweet Hereafter*," *Law and Society Review* 34, no. 1 (2000): 10–14; Susan Burgess, *The Founding Fathers, Pop Culture, and Constitutional Law: Who's Your Daddy?* (Burlington, VT: Ashgate, 2008), generally.

85. Jeffrey R. Dudas, "Subversives All! Ronald Reagan and the Paternal Roots of 'Law and Order' at Home and Abroad," *Law, Culture, and the Humanities* 8 (2012): 119–152.

86. Jonathan Goldberg-Hiller and Neal Milner, "Rights as Excess: Understanding the Politics of Special Rights," *Law and Social Inquiry* 28, no. 4 (2003), generally; Jeffrey R. Dudas, *The Cultivation of Resentment: Treaty Rights and the New Right* (Stanford, CA: Stanford University Press, 2008), 140–152.

87. Dudas, "Subversives All!" 140–142.

88. Peyton Thomas, *Clarence Thomas*, 223.

89. Thomas, "Address by Justice Clarence Thomas"; Clarence Thomas, "Remarks to Oklahoma Council of Public Affairs," June 1, 2000.

90. During his testimony before the Senate Judiciary Committee that evaluated his candidacy for the Supreme Court, Thomas frequently invoked the image of a long-distance runner, who "strips down" to the bare essentials in order to run a marathon. Like such a runner, Thomas claimed, his own jurisprudence would be devoid of any accoutrements or affectations, such as those embodied in his own personal and political experiences. See, generally, *Hearings before the Committee on the Judiciary, United States Senate, 102nd Cong., 1st sess. on the Nomination of Clarence Thomas to be Associate Justice of the Supreme Court of the United States, September 10, 11, 12, 13, and 16, 1991* (Washington, DC: Government Printing Office, 1993).

91. Thomas, "Keynote Address."

92. Thomas, "Address by Justice Clarence Thomas." See also Thomas, "Keynote Address": It takes "discipline, that even when you think strongly about something you have no authority to make some of those decisions."

93. Clarence Thomas, "Remarks to Oklahoma Council of Public Affairs," June 1, 2000.

94. While Thomas tends to employ "original understanding" and "original intent" as synonyms, such usage is not uncontested. Pamela Brandwein, *Reconstructing Reconstruction: The Supreme Court and the Production of Historical Truth* (Durham, NC: Duke University Press, 1999), 14–17. Maggs's analysis of Thomas's originalism is, in this regard, useful. Gregory E. Maggs, "Which Original Meaning of the Constitution Matters to Justice Thomas?" *New York University Journal of Law and Liberty* 4, no. 3 (2009): 494–516. See also Gerber's lucid account of Thomas's "liberal" originalism on civil rights and "conservative" originalism on civil liberties and federalism. Scott Douglas Gerber, *First Principles: The Jurisprudence of Clarence Thomas* (New York: New York University Press, 1999), 69–187.

95. "Grandfather's Son Speaks Off the Bench."

96. Thomas, "Be Not Afraid."

97. "Grandfather's Son Speaks Off the Bench."

98. Thomas, "Keynote Address." See also Clarence Thomas, "How to Read the Constitution," *Wall Street Journal*, October 20, 2008, A19: "No matter how ingenious, imaginative, or artfully put, unless interpretive methodologies are tied to the original intent of the framers, they have no more basis in the Constitution than the latest football scores."

99. Matt Kelley, "Justice Clarence Thomas Speaks in Western Iowa," *Radio Iowa*, September 16, 2011.

100. Thomas, "Speech to the National Bar Association."

101. Lally Weymouth, "A Justice's Candid Opinions," *Newsweek* , October 14, 2007, 50.

102. Limbaugh, "Rush Interviews."

103. *Lawrence et al. v. Texas*, 539 U.S. 558 (2003)

104. *Hudson v. McMillian*, 503 U.S. 1 (1992)

105. See, for example, "The Youngest, Cruelest Justice," *New York Times*, February 27, 1992, A24.

106. Thomas, "Speech to the National Bar Association."

107. Thomas, "Remarks to Oklahoma Council of Public Affairs."

108. Marla Jo Fisher, "Justice Clarence Thomas Reveals Personal Side at Chapman," *Orange County Register*, December 18, 2007.

109. Kelley, "Justice Clarence Thomas Speaks."

110. Ibid.

111. Thomas, "Necessity of Moral Absolutes in a Free Society."

112. Thomas, "Remarks to Oklahoma Council of Public Affairs."

113. Thomas, "Speech to the National Bar Association."

114. "I have returned to my grandfather," Thomas related in a 2007 interview, "and to the way that he raised me. And I think that's home, and that's where I'll stay." Steve Kroft, "The Justice Nobody Knows; Justice Clarence Thomas Discusses His Childhood, His Career, Anita Hill and His Book," *60 Minutes II*, September 30, 2007.

115. Merida and Fletcher, *Supreme Discomfort*, 35–45.

116. Rasmussen, *The Autonomous Animal*, 95.

117. Steele, "The Freest Black Man in America."

118. Merida and Fletcher, *Supreme Discomfort*, 283; Thomas, "Address by Justice Clarence Thomas."

Chapter 6

1. Charles R. Epp, *The Rights Revolution: Lawyers, Activists, and Supreme Courts in Comparative Perspective* (Chicago: University of Chicago Press, 1998); Steven Teles, *The Rise of the Conservative Legal Movement: The Battle for the Control of Law* (Princeton, NJ: Princeton University Press, 2010); Anne Southworth, *Lawyers of the Right: Professionalizing the Conservative Coalition* (Chicago: University of Chicago Press, 2008); Amanda Hollis-Brusky, *Ideas with Consequences: The Federalist Society and the Conservative Counterrevolution* (New York: Oxford University Press, 2015).

2. Jeffrey Dudas, *The Cultivation of Resentment: Treaty Rights and the New Right* (Stanford, CA: Stanford University Press, 2008).

3. Joshua C. Wilson, *The Street Politics of Abortion: Speech, Violence, and America's Culture Wars* (Stanford, CA: Stanford University Press, 2013).

4. Mello, "Rights Discourse and the Mobilization of Bias: Exploring the Institutional Dynamics of the Same-Sex Marriage Debates in America," *Studies in Law, Politics, and Society* 66, no. 1 (2015): 1–34.

5. Linda Bridges and John R. Coyne Jr., *Strictly Right: William F. Buckley Jr. and the American Conservative Movement* (Hoboken, NJ: Wiley, 2007), 33–34.

6. "Did You Ever See a Dream Walking?" music by Harry Revel, lyrics by Mack Gordon, 1933.

7. Leslie Fiedler, *Love and Death in the American Novel* (New York: Delta/Dell Publishing, 1966), 338.

8. Ibid.

9. Karl Marx, "The 18th Brumaire of Louis Bonaparte," in *The Marx-Engels Reader,* 2nd ed., ed. Robert C. Tucker (New York: Norton, 1978), 595.

10. Colin Dayan, *The Law Is a White Dog: How Legal Rituals Make and Unmake Persons* (Princeton, NJ: Princeton University Press, 2011), 40.

11. Maria Aristodemou, *Law, Psychoanalysis, Society: Taking the Unconscious Seriously* (New York: Routledge, 2014): 3.

12. "Rather than seek the meaning of despair," writes Kristeva, "let us acknowledge that there is meaning only in despair." There is, accordingly, "no imagination that is not, overtly or secretly, melancholy." Julia Kristeva, *Black Sun: Depression and Melancholia*, trans. Leon S. Roudiez (New York: Columbia University Press, 1989), 5–6.

13. Walter Sobchak—the lunatic Vietnam War veteran played to comic effect by John Goodman in 1998's *The Big Lebowski*—articulates the modern horror of nihilism. Aghast at the nihilism of the German tormentors of his best friend, the Dude ("they kept saying they believe in nothing"), the converted Jew Sobchak proclaims even the Nazis more admirable: "Nihilists! Fuck me. I mean, say what you want about the tenets of National Socialism, Dude, at least it's an ethos." Joel and Ethan Cohen, Dir., *The Big Lebowski* (Polygram Filmed Entertainment, 1998).

14. William E. Connolly, *Political Theory and Modernity* (Ithaca, NY: Cornell University Press, [1988] 1993), 1–15; Peter Fitzpatrick, *The Mythology of Modern Law* (London: Routledge, 1992), generally.

15. Robert Cover, "Nomos and Narrative," in *Narrative, Violence, and the Law: The Essays of Robert Cover*, ed. Martha Minow, Michael Ryan, and Austin Sarat (Ann Arbor: University of Michigan Press, 1993), 140.

16. Jane Caputi, *A Kinder, Gentler America: Melancholia and the Mythical 1950's* (Minneapolis: University of Minnesota Press, 2005), 18.

17. Ibid., 22.

18. Ibid., 43. Kristeva links paternal desire to childhood loss of the maternal connection ("dual unity") and, thus, to the root of individuation and eventual subjectivity. "Beginning with [maternal] separation . . . the child produces or uses objects or vocalizations that are the symbolic equivalents of what is lacking . . . what makes such a triumph over sadness possible is the ability of the self to identify no longer with the lost object [mother] but with a third party—father, form, schema . . . such an identification . . . insures the subject's entrance into the universe of signs and creation. The supporting father of such a symbolic triumph is not the oedipal father but truly that 'imaginary father,' 'father in individual prehistory,' according to Freud, who guarantees primary identification." Julia Kristeva, *Black Sun: Depression and Melancholia*, trans. Leon S. Roudiez (New York: Columbia University Press, 1989), 23–24.

19. Caputi, *A Kinder, Gentler America*, 95.

20. Ibid., 47.

21. Ibid., 46.

22. Kennan Ferguson, *All in the Family: On Community and Incommensurability* (Durham, NC: Duke University Press, 2012), 29.

23. Caputi, *A Kinder, Gentler America*, 46.

24. Caputi, *Goddesses and Monsterss: Women, Myth, and Popular Culture* (Madison: University of Wisconsin Press, 2004), 166.

25. Ibid., 137, 139.

26. Aristodemou, *Law, Psychoanalysis, Society*, 5.

27. Jack Sholder, Dir., *A Nightmare on Elm Street 2: Freddy's Revenge* (New Line Cinema, 1985).

28. Rogin, *Ronald Reagan, the Movie: And Other Episodes in Political Demonology* (Berkeley: University of California Press, 1987), generally.

29. Brendan James, "Rand Paul: Baltimore Violence Is about 'Lack of Fathers' and Morals," *Talking Points Memo*, April 28, 2015.

30. Reena Flores, "Ted Cruz: 'Government Must Preserve the Peace," *CBS News*, April 29, 2015.

31. Reena Flores, "Chris Christie Provides State Police Support," *CBS News*, April 29, 2015.

32. Marina Fang, "Rand Paul Blames 'Lack of Fathers' for Baltimore Protests," *Huffington Post*, April 28, 2015.

33. Jessica Durando, "Donald Trump Slams 'African American President' on Riots," *USA Today*, April 28, 2015.

34. Dara Lind, "The Problem with Violence at Trump Rallies Starts with Trump Himself: Trump Is Not Just Condoning Violence. He Is Encouraging It," *Vox*, March 13, 2016.

35. Perlstein, *Nixonland: The Rise of a President and the Fracturing of America* (New York: Scribner, 2008), 383–386.

36. William F. Buckley Jr., "Yes, Hang Them," *On the Right*, August 12, 1985; "Pinochet and Chilean Rights," *On the Right*, March 1, 1977.

37. William F. Buckley Jr., "Unscrambling Pinochet," *On the Right*, March 7, 2000.

38. William F. Buckley Jr., "Up Again: Capital Punishment," *National Review*, June 27, 1994 .

39. Clarence Thomas, "Address by Justice Clarence Thomas," Fifteenth Annual Ashbrook Memorial Dinner, Ashland, OH, February 5, 1999

40. *Lawrence et al. v. Texas*, 539 U.S. 558 (2003).

41. Linda Chavez, "The Ghost of Ronald Reagan," Townhall.com, February 1, 2008, http://townhall.com/columnists/lindachavez/2008/02/01/the_ghost_of_ronald_reagan/page/full.

42. Michael Walsh, "At Reagan Library, Republican Presidential Hopefuls Vie to Be the Most Reaganesque," *Yahoo News*, September 16, 2015.

43. Jeffrey Vallance, "The Gipper's Ghost," *L.A. Weekly*, December 15, 2005.

44. George Will, "Donald Trump Is an Affront to Anyone Devoted to William F. Buckley's Legacy," *National Review*, August 12, 2015.

45. Dayan, *The Law Is a White Dog*, 16–17.

46. Lauren Carroll, "Getting the Facts Straight about the Founding Fathers," PolitFact.com, July 3, 2014.

47. Lucy Morgan, "After 2010 Campaign, Gov. Rick Scott Gave Back Reagan the Dog," *Tampa Bay Times*, January 14, 2013.

References

Abshire, David M. *Saving the Reagan Presidency: Trust Is the Coin of the Realm.* Lawrence: University of Kansas Press, 2005.

Aristodemou, Maria. *Law, Psychoanalysis, Society: Taking the Unconscious Seriously.* New York: Routledge, 2014.

Asante, Molefi K., and Ronald E. Hall. *Rooming in the Master's House: Power and Privilege in the Rise of Black Conservatism.* Boulder, CO: Paradigm Publishers, 2011.

Associated Press. "Reagan Now a Knight But Not a Sir: Queen Bestows Title—No Dubbing, No Kneeling Required." *Los Angeles Time,* June 14, 1989. http://articles.latimes.com/1989–06–14/news/mn-2281_1_knighthood-british-empire- queen-s-warning.

Bailyn, Bernard. *The Ideological Origins of the American Revolution,* enlarged ed. Cambridge, MA: Belknap Press of Harvard University Press, 1992.

Barnes, Bart. "Erudite Voice of the Conservative Movement." *Washington Post,* February 28, 2008, A01

Beckett, Katherine. *Making Crime Pay: Law and Order in Contemporary America.* New York: Oxford University Press, 1999.

Benjamin, Jessica. *The Bonds of Love: Psychoanalysis, Feminism, and the Problem of Domination.* New York: Pantheon, 1988.

Berkhofer, Jr., Robert F. *The White Man's Indian: Images of the American Indian from Columbus to the Present.* New York: Vintage, 1979.

Berlant, Lauren. *The Queen of America Goes to Washington City: Essays on Sex and Citizenship.* Durham, NC: Duke University Press, 1997.

Bogus, Carl. "William F. Buckley, Father of American Conservatism." National Public Radio, December 17, 2011.

Borstelmann, Thomas. *The Cold War and the Color Line: American Race Relations in the Global Arena.* Cambridge, MA: Harvard University Press, 2001.

Brands, H. W. *Reagan: The Life.* New York: Doubleday, 2015.

Brandwein, Pamela. *Reconstructing Reconstruction: The Supreme Court and the Production of Historical Truth.* Durham, NC: Duke University Press, 1999.

Bridges, Linda, and John R. Coyne Jr. *Strictly Right: William F. Buckley Jr. and the American Conservative Movement.* Hoboken, NJ: Wiley, 2007.

Brigham, John. *The Cult of the Court.* Philadelphia: Temple University Press, 1987.

————. *Material Law: A Jurisprudence of What's Real*. Philadelphia: Temple University Press, 2009.

Buckley, Priscilla L. "Buckley Branches: Splitting Up a Family Home in Order to Preserve It." *TownVibe Litchfield* (March–April 2011). http://www.townvibe.com/Litchfield/March-April-2011/Buckley-Branches/.

Buckley Jr., William F. *The Blackford Oakes Reader*. Kansas City, MO: Andrews and McMeel, 1995.

————. "The Chilean Refugees." *On the Right*, September 27, 1973.

————. "Did You Ever See a Dream Walking?" in *Did You Ever See a Dream Walking? American Conservative Thought in the Twentieth Century*, ed. William F. Buckley Jr., 19–36. New York: Bobbs-Merrill, 1970.

————. "A Handsome Man Is Not the Equivalent of a Beautiful Woman, He Is the Complement." *Vogue* (April 1978): 291.

————. *Happy Days Were Here Again: Reflections of a Libertarian Journalist*. New York: Basic Books, 1993.

————. *A Hymnal: The Controversial Arts*. New York: Putnam, 1978.

————. *Inveighing We Will Go*. New York: Putnam, 1972.

————. *The Jeweler's Eye: A Book of Irresistible Political Reflections*. New York: Putnam, 1968.

————. *Let Us Talk of Many Things: The Collected Speeches*. New York: Forum, 2000.

————. "Linda's Crusade." *National Review* 20, no. 2 (1968): 518.

————. "Marx, Engels, Lenin and Pinochet." *On the Right*, January 26, 1978.

————. *Miles Gone By: A Literary Autobiography*. Washington, DC: Regnery, 2004.

————. *Moongoose R.I.P.* New York: Random House, 1987.

————. "The New Conservatism," in *Athwart History: Half a Century of Polemics, Animadversions, and Illuminations: A William F. Buckley Jr. Omnibus*, ed. Linda Bridges and Roger Kimball, 35–36. New York: Encounter Books, 2010.

————. "Our Mission Statement." *National Review* 1, no. 1 (1955): 1.

————. "Pinochet and Chilean Rights." *On the Right*, March 1, 1977.

————. "Pinochet and Human Rights." *On the Right*, February 19–20, 1977.

————. "Pinochet? Why Him?" *On the Right*, October 20, 1998.

————. "Playing with Torture." *On the Right*, December 21–22, 1974.

————. "Point Counterpoint." *On the Right*, November 18, 1971.

————. "The Prayer Amendment and Its Critics." *On the Right*, May 22–23, 1982.

————. *The Reagan I Knew*. New York: Basic Books, 2008.

————. "The Repeal of the Homosexual Laws." *On the Right*, March 3, 1966.

————*Saving the Queen*. New York: Doubleday, 1976.

————. *See You Later, Alligator*. New York: Doubleday, 1985.

————. "The Selling of William F. Buckley Jr." *Esquire* (July 1976): 141.

————. *The Story of Henri Tod*. New York: Dell, 1983.

————. "Triumph of the Republican Ideal." *Goodlife* (October 1983): 19.

————. "Unscrambling Pinochet." *On the Right*, March 7, 2000).

————. "Up Again: Capital Punishment." *National Review* 46, no. 12 (1994): 71.

———. *A Very Private Plot*. New York: Morrow, 1994.

———. "What They Are Doing to Carter." *On the Right*, April 8, 1976.

———. *Who's on First*. Garden City, NY: Doubleday, 1980.

———. "Yes, Hang Them." *On the Right*, August 12, 1985.

———. "Zounds! Enforcing the Law in Idaho!" *On the Right*, January 9, 1996.

Buckley Jr., William F., and Charles R. Kesler, eds. *Keeping the Tablets: Modern American Conservative Thought*. New York: Harper & Row, 1988.

Burgess, Susan. *The Founding Fathers, Pop Culture, and Constitutional Law: Who's Your Daddy?* Burlington, VT: Ashgate, 2008.

Burns, Jennifer. *Goddess of the Market: Ayn Rand and the American Right*. New York: Oxford University Press, 2009.

Burrows, Edwin G., and Michael Wallace. "The American Revolution: The Ideology and Psychology of National Liberation." *Perspectives in American History* 6 (1972): 167–305.

Burston, Daniel. *Erik Erickson and the American Psyche: Ego, Ethics, and Evolution*. Lanham, MD: Aronson, 2007.

Busch, Andrew E. *Reagan's Victory: The Presidential Election of 1980 and the Rise of the Right*. Lawrence: University Press of Kansas, 2005.

Butler, Judith. *Bodies That Matter: On the Discursive Limits of "Sex."* New York: Routledge, 1993.

———. *Gender Trouble: Feminism and the Subversion of Identity*. New York: Routledge, [1990] 1999.

———. *The Psychic Life of Power: Theories in Subjection*. Stanford, CA: Stanford University Press, 1997.

Cannon, Lou. *Governor Reagan: His Rise to Power*. New York: Public Affairs, 2003.

———. *President Reagan: The Role of a Lifetime*. New York: Touchstone, 1991.

———. "Remembering Reagan," *Washington Post*, June 7, 2004, A23.

Caputi, Jane. *Goddesses and Monsters: Women, Myth, and Popular Culture*. Madison: University of Wisconsin Press, 2004.

Caputi, Mary. *A Kinder, Gentler America: Melancholia and the Mythical 1950's*. Minneapolis: University of Minnesota Press, 2005.

Carroll, Lauren. "Getting the Facts Straight about the Founding Fathers." PolitFact.com, July 3, 2014. http://www.politifact.com/truth-o-meter/article/2014/jul/03/fact-checking-founding-fathers-misquoting/.

Carter, Dan. *From George Wallace to Newt Gingrich: Race in the Conservative Counterrevolution, 1963–1994*. Baton Rouge: LSU Press, 1999.

———. *The Politics of Rage: George Wallace, the Origins of the New Conservatism, and the Transformation of American Politics*. New York: Simon & Schuster, 1995.

Chavez, Linda. "The Ghost of Ronald Reagan." Townhall.com, February 1, 2008. http://townhall.com/columnists/lindachavez/2008/02/01/the_ghost_of_ronald_reagan/page/full.

Cockburn, Leslie. *Out of Control: The Story of the Reagan Administration's Secret War in Nicaragua*. New York: Atlantic Monthly Press, 1987.

Cohen, Joel, and Ethan Cohen, Dir. *The Big Lebowski*. Polygram Filmed Entertainment, 1998.

Cohen, Lizabeth. *A Consumer's Republic: The Politics of Mass Consumption in Postwar America*. New York: Knopf, 2003.

Comaroff, John L., and Jean Comaroff. *Of Revelation and Revolution: The Dialectics of Modernity on a South African Frontier*, vol. 2. Chicago: University of Chicago Press, 1997.

Connolly, William E. *Political Theory and Modernity*. Ithaca, NY: Cornell University Press, [1993] 1988.

Coulter, Michael. "Conservatism, 1995 to the Present." *Choice Magazine* 44, no. 3 (2006): 409–417.

Cover, Robert. "Nomos and Narrative." In *Narrative, Violence, and the Law: The Essays of Robert Cover*, ed. Martha Minow, Michael Ryan, and Austin Sarat, 95–172. Ann Arbor: University of Michigan Press, 1993.

Cramer, Renée Ann. *Pregnant with the Stars: Watching and Wanting, the Pregnant Celebrity Body*. Stanford, CA: Stanford University Press, 2016.

Crawford Greenburg, Jan. "Clarence Thomas: A Silent Justice Speaks Out, Part VII: 'Traitorous' Adversaries: Anita Hill and the Senate Democrats." *ABC News*, September 30, 2007.

———. "Clarence Thomas: A Silent Justice Speaks Out: Part II: The Integrator." *ABC News*, September 30, 2007.

Crespino, Joseph. *In Search of Another Country: Mississippi and the Conservative Counter-revolution*. Princeton, NJ: Princeton University Press, 2007.

D'Souza, Dinesh. *Illiberal Education: The Politics of Race and Sex on Campus*. New York: Free Press, 1991.

Dallek, Robert. *Ronald Reagan: The Politics of Symbolism*. Cambridge, MA: Harvard University Press, 1984.

Darian-Smith, Eve. *Religion, Race, Rights: Landmarks in the History of Modern Anglo-American Law*. Oxford: Hart Publishing, 2010.

Dayan, Colin. *The Law Is a White Dog: How Legal Rituals Make and Unmake Persons*. Princeton, NJ: Princeton University Press, 2011.

De Groot, Gerald J. "Ronald Reagan and Student Unrest in California, 1966–1970." *Pacific Historical Review* 65, no. 1 (1996): 107–129.

Diggins, John Patrick. *Ronald Reagan: Fate, Freedom, and the Making of History*. New York: Norton, 2007.

DiStefano, Christine. *Configurations of Masculinity: A Feminist Perspective on Modern Political Theory*. Ithaca, NY: Cornell University Press, 1991.

Dreher, Rod. "Clarence Thomas' Story Is the Real American Dream." *Dallas Morning News*, October 14, 2007.

Dudas, Jeffrey R. *The Cultivation of Resentment: Treaty Rights and the New Right*. Stanford, CA: Stanford University Press, 2008.

———. "Little Monsters, Wild Animals, & Welfare Queens: Ronald Reagan & the Legal Constitution of American Politics." *Studies in Law, Politics, and Society* 49 (2009): 157-210.

——. "In the Name of Equal Rights: 'Special' Rights and the Politics of Resentment in Post–Civil Rights America." *Law and Society Review* 39, no. 4 (2005): 723–758.

——. "'A Madman Full of Paranoid Guile': The Myth of Rights in the Modern American Mind." *Studies in Law, Politics, and Society* 59 (2012): 31–63.

——. "Of Savages and Sovereigns: Tribal Self-Administration and the Legal Construction of Dependence." *Studies in Law, Politics, and Society* 23 (2001): 3–44.

Dudas, Jeffrey R., Jonathan Goldberg-Hiller, and Michael W. McCann. "The Past, Present, and Future of Rights Scholarship." In *The Handbook of Law and Society*, ed. Austin Sarat and Patricia Ewick, 367–381. Hoboken, NJ: Wiley-Blackwell, 2015.

Dudziak, Mary L. *Cold War, Civil Rights: Race and the Image of American Democracy.* Princeton, NJ: Princeton University Press, 2000.

Durando, Jessica. "Donald Trump Slams 'African American President' on Riots." *USA Today*, April 28, 2015. http://www.usatoday.com/story/news/nation-now/2015/04/28/donald-trump-barack-obama-tweets-baltimore-riots/26500879/.

Edwards, Anne. *Early Reagan: The Rise to Power.* London: Taylor, [1987] 2012.

Edwards, Lee. "William F. Buckley Jr.: Conservative Icon." *First Principles*, December 17, 2012, 7.

Eisenhower, Dwight D. "Farewell Radio and Television Address to the American People," January 17, 1961. http://www.presidency.ucsb.edu/ws/?pid=12086.

Eisenstein, Zillah R. *The Female Body and the Law.* Berkeley: University of California Press, 1988.

Engel, David M., and Frank W. Munger. *Rights of Inclusion: Law and Identity in the Life Stories of Americans with Disabilities.* Chicago: University of Chicago Press, 2003.

Epp, Charles R. *The Rights Revolution: Lawyers, Activists, and Supreme Courts in Comparative Perspective.* Chicago: University of Chicago Press, 1998.

Erikson, Erik. *Childhood and Society,* 2nd ed. New York: Norton, 1963.

Evans, Thomas W. *The Education of Ronald Reagan: The General Electric Years and the Untold Story of His Conversion to Conservatism.* Ithaca, NY: Cornell University Press, 2007.

"Excerpts from Interview with Nixon about Domestic Effects of Indochina War," *New York Times*, May 20, 1977, A16-A20.

Ewick, Patricia, and Susan S. Silbey. *The Common Place of Law: Stories from Everyday Life.* Chicago: University of Chicago Press, 1998.

Fang, Marina. "Rand Paul Blames 'Lack of Fathers' for Baltimore Protests." *Huffington Post*, April 28, 2015. http://www.huffingtonpost.com/2015/04/28/rand-paul-baltimore_n_7162630.html.

Farber, David. *The Rise and Fall of Modern American Conservatism: A Short History.* Princeton, NJ: Princeton University Press, 2010.

Feeney, Mark. *Nixon at the Movies: A Book about Belief.* Chicago: University of Chicago Press, 2004.

Ferguson, Kennan. *All in the Family: On Community and Incommensurability.* Durham, NC: Duke University Press, 2012.

Fiedler, Leslie. *Love and Death in the American Novel.* New York: Delta/Dell Publishing, 1966.

Fisher, Marla Jo. "Justice Clarence Thomas Reveals Personal Side at Chapman." *Orange County Register*, December 18, 2007.

Fitzpatrick, Peter. *The Mythology of Modern Law*. London: Routledge, 1992.

Flamm, Michael. *Law and Order: Street Crime, Civil Unrest, and the Crisis of Liberalism in the 1960's*. New York: Columbia University Press, 2007.

Flax, Jane. *The American Dream in Black and White: The Clarence Thomas Hearings*. Ithaca, NY: Cornell University Press, 1998.

Flores, Reena. "Chris Christie Provides State Police Support." *CBS News*, April 29, 2015. http://www.cbsnews.com/media/2016-candidates-on-baltimore-riots/3/.

——. "Ted Cruz: 'Government Must Preserve the Peace." *CBS News*, April 29, 2015. http://www.cbsnews.com/media/2016-candidates-on-baltimore-riots/2/.

Fox News, "Cable Exclusive: Justice Clarence Thomas Sits Down with Sean Hannity." *Fox News*, October 3, 2007. http://www.foxnews.com/story/2007/10/03/cable-exclusive-justice-clarence-thomas-sits-down-with-sean-hannity.html.

Freeman, Alan D. "Antidiscrimination Law: A Critical Review." In *The Politics of Law: A Progressive Critique*, ed. David Kairys, 96–116. New York: Pantheon Books, 1982.

Gerber, Scott Douglas. *First Principles: The Jurisprudence of Clarence Thomas*. New York: New York University Press, 1999.

Gerstle, Gary. *American Crucible: Race and Nation in the Twentieth Century*. Princeton, NJ: Princeton University Press, 2001.

Gilder, George. *Wealth and Poverty*. New York: Basic Books, 1981.

Gilgoff, Dan. *The Jesus Machine: How James Dobson, Focus on the Family, and Evangelical America Are Winning the Culture War*. New York: St. Martin's Press, 2007.

Glendon, Mary Ann. *Rights Talk: The Impoverishment of Political Discourse*. New York: Free Press, 1991.

Goldberg-Hiller, Jonathan. *The Limits to Union: Same-Sex Marriage and the Politics of Civil Rights*. Ann Arbor: University of Michigan Press, 2002.

Goldberg-Hiller, Jonathan, and Neal Milner. "Rights as Excess: Understanding the Politics of Special Rights." *Law and Social Inquiry* 28, no. 4 (2003): 1075–1118. Goldwater, Barry M. *The Conscience of a Majority*. Englewood Cliffs, NJ: Prentice Hall, 1970.

Goodrich, Peter. "Maladies of the Legal Soul: Psychoanalysis and Interpretation in Law." *Washington and Lee Law Review* 54, no. 3 (1997): 1035–1074.

"Grandfather's Son Speaks Off the Bench." *Wisconsin Law Journal*, October 29, 2007. http://wislawjournal.com/2007/10/29/grandfathers-son-speaks-off-the-bench/.

Gutman, Roy. *Banana Diplomacy: The Making of American Policy in Nicaragua, 1981–1987*. New York: Simon & Schuster, 1988.

Haltom, William, and Michael W. McCann. *Distorting the Law: Politics, Media, and the Litigation Crisis*. Chicago: University of Chicago Press, 2004.

Handler, Joel F. "The Judge and His Sister: Growing Up Black." *New York Times*, July 23, 1991, A20.

——. *Social Movements and the Legal System: A Theory of Law Reform and Social Change*. Madison, WI: Academic Press., 1979.

Haney López, Ian. *White by Law: The Legal Construction of Race,* 10th anniversary ed. New York: New York University Press, 2006.

Hanson, Victor Davis. "Reagan and the National Psyche." In *Tear Down This Wall: The Reagan Revolution—A National Review History,* ed. National Review, 188. New York: Continuum, 2004.

Hart, Jeffrey. *The Making of the American Conservative Mind: National Review and Its Times.* Wilmington, DE: ISI Books, 2005.

Hartog, Hendrik. "Abigail Bailey's Coverture: Law in a Married Woman's Consciousness." In *Law in Everyday Life,* ed. Austin Sarat and Thomas R. Kearns, 63–108. Ann Arbor: University of Michigan Press, 1993.

Hawkesworth, Mary. "Contending Conceptions of Science and Politics: Methodology and the Constitution of the Political." In *Interpretation and Method: Empirical Research Methods and the Interpretive Turn,* ed. Dvora Yanow and Peregrine Schwartz-Shea, 34–41. Armonk, NY: M. E. Sharpe, 2006.

Hearings before the Committee on the Judiciary, United States Senate, 102nd Cong., 1st Sess., on the Nomination of Clarence Thomas to Be Associate Justice of the Supreme Court of the United States, September 10, 11, 12, 13, and 16, 1991. Washington, DC: Government Printing Office, 1993.

Heclo, Hugh. "Ronald Reagan and the American Public Philosophy." In *The Reagan Presidency: Pragmatic Conservatism and Its Legacies,* ed. W. Elliot Brownlee and Hugh Graham Davis, 17–39. Lawrence: University Press of Kansas, 2003.

Henrie, Mark C., ed. *Arguing Conservatism: Four Decades of the Intercollegiate Review.* Wilmington, DE: ISI Books, 2008.

Herman, Didi. *Rights of Passage: Struggles for Lesbian and Gay Legal Equality.* Toronto, Ontario, Canada: University of Toronto Press, 1994.

Higginbotham, Jr., A. Leon. "An Open Letter to Justice Clarence Thomas from a Federal Judicial Colleague." *University of Pennsylvania Law Review* 140, no. 3 (1992): 1005–1028.

Hill, George Roy, Dir. *The Great Waldo Pepper.* Universal Pictures, 1975.

Hillyer, Quin. "There's No Doubting Thomas." *American Spectator,* September 9, 2007.

Hollis-Brusky, Amanda. *Ideas with Consequences: The Federalist Society and the Conservative Counterrevolution.* New York: Oxford University Press, 2015.

Holzer, Henry Mark. "His Grandfather's Miracle." *Front Page Magazine,* October 10, 2007.

Hurley, Andrew. *Diners, Bowling Alleys, and Trailer Parks: Chasing the American Dream in the Postwar Consumer Culture.* New York: Basic Books, 2002.

James, Brendan. "Rand Paul: Baltimore Violence Is about 'Lack of Fathers' and Morals." *Talking Points Memo,* April 28, 2015. http://talkingpointsmemo.com/livewire/rand-paul-freddie-gray-baltimore-morals.

Jefferson, Thomas. *Jefferson: Writings.* New York: Library of America, 1984.

Jordan, Winthrop D. *White over Black: American Attitudes toward the Negro, 1550–1812.* Chapel Hill: University of North Carolina Press, 1968.

Judis, John B. *William F. Buckley Jr.: Patron Saint of the Conservatives.* New York: Simon & Schuster, 1988.

Kagan, Robert. *Twilight Struggle: American Power and Nicaragua, 1977–1990*. New York: Free Press,1996.

Kantor, Elizabeth. "A Conversation with Clarence Thomas." *Human Events*, October 9, 2007.

Katz, Gregory. "Keep Queen Elizabeth II Waiting? Ronald Reagan Got Away with It, Newly Released Papers Show." Associated Press, December 28, 2012.

Katznelson, Ira. *When Affirmative Action Was White: An Untold History of Racial Inequality in Twentieth-Century America*. New York: Norton, 2005.

Kaufman, Bill. "Clarence Thomas." *Reason*, November 1, 1987.

Kazin, Michael. *The Populist Persuasion: An American History*. Ithaca, NY: Cornell University Press, 1998.

Kelley, Matt. "Justice Clarence Thomas Speaks in Western Iowa." *Radio Iowa*, September 16, 2011.

Kinzer, Stephen. *Blood of Brothers: Life and War in Nicaragua*. Cambridge, MA: Harvard University Press, 2007.

Kirkus Reviews. "High Jinx." *Kirkus Reviews*, February 15, 1986. https://www.kirkusreviews.com/book-reviews/william-f-buckley-jr/high-jinx/.

Klinkner, Philip A., and Rogers M. Smith, *The Unsteady March: The Rise and Decline of Racial Equality in America*. Chicago: University of Chicago Press, 1999.

Kornbluh, Felicia A. *The Battle for Welfare Rights: Politics and Poverty in Modern America*. Philadelphia: University of Pennsylvania Press, 2007.

Kristeva, Julia. *Black Sun: Depression and Melancholia*. Translated by Leon S. Roudiez. New York: Columbia University Press, 1989.

———. "Cultural Strangeness and the Subject in Crisis." In *Julia Kristeva Interviews*, ed. Ross Mitchell Guberman, 35–58. New York: Columbia University Press, 1996.

Kristol, Irving. *The Neoconservative Persuasion: Selected Essays, 1942–2009*. Edited by Gertrude Himmelfarb. New York: Basic Books, 2011.

———. "The Old Politics, the New Politics, the *New*, New Politics." *New York Times Magazine*, November 24, 1968, SM49.

———. "Republican Virtue versus Servile Institution." In Irving Kristol, *The Neoconservative Persuasion: Selected Essays, 1942–2009*, ed. Gertrude Himmelfarb, 64–76. New York: Basic Books, 2011.

Kroft, Steve. "The Justice Nobody Knows; Justice Clarence Thomas Discusses His Childhood, His Career, Anita Hill and His Book." *60 Minutes II*, September 30, 2007.

Kruse, Kevin. *White Flight: Atlanta and the Making of Modern Conservatism*. Princeton, NJ: Princeton University Press, 2005.

Lakoff, George. *Moral Politics*, 2nd ed. Chicago: University of Chicago Press, 2004.

Lassiter, Matthew D. *The Silent Majority: Suburban Politics in the Sunbelt South*. Princeton, NJ: Princeton University Press, 2006.

Lawrence, D. H. *Studies in Classic American Literature*. Garden City, NY: Doubleday, [1923] 1951.

Lears, Jackson. "A Matter of Taste: Corporate Cultural Hegemony in a Mass-Consumption Society." In *Recasting America: Culture and Politics in the Age of Cold War*, ed. Lary May, 38–57. Chicago: University of Chicago Press, 1989.

———. *Something for Nothing: Luck in America*. New York: Viking, 2003.

Leogrande, William M. "The Contras and Congress." In *Reagan versus the Sandinistas: The Undeclared War on Nicaragua*, ed. Thomas Walker, 202–227. Boulder, CO: Westview Press, 1987.

Lewis, George. *The White South and the Red Menace: Segregationists, Anticommunism, and Massive Resistance, 1945–1965*. Gainesville: University of Florida Press, 2004.

Lichtman, Allan J. *White Protestant Nation: The Rise of the American Conservative Movement*. New York: Atlantic Monthly Press, 2008.

Limbaugh, Rush. "Rush Interviews Justice Clarence Thomas." *Rush Limbaugh Show*, October 1, 2007.

Lind, Dara. "The Problem with Violence at Trump Rallies Starts with Trump Himself: Trump Is Not Just Condoning Violence. He's Encouraging It." *Vox*, March 13, 2016.

Lowndes, Joseph. *From the New Deal to the New Right: Race and the Southern Origins of Modern Conservatism*. New Haven, CT: Yale University Press, 2008.

Lowry, Rich. "A Great American Story." *National Review Online*, October 2, 2007.

Mack, Bob. "The Boys Who Would Be Buckley." *Spy* (July 1989): 69–78.

MacKinnon, Catharine A. *Toward a Feminist Theory of the State*. Cambridge, MA: Harvard University Press, 1989.

Maggs, Geoffrey E. "Which Original Meaning of the Constitution Matters to Justice Thomas?" *New York University Journal of Law and Liberty* 4, no. 3 (2009): 494–516.

Martin, Douglas. "William F. Buckley Jr., 82, Dies; Sesquipedalian Spark of Right." *New York Times*, February 28, 2008, A1.

Marx, Karl. "The 18th Brumaire of Louis Bonaparte." In *The Marx-Engels Reader*, 2nd ed., ed. Robert C. Tucker, 594–617. New York: Norton, 1978.

Mattson, Kevin. *Rebels All! A Short History of the Conservative Mind in Postwar America*. New Brunswick, NJ: Rutgers University Press, 2008.

———. *"What the Heck Are You Up To, Mr. President?" Jimmy Carter, America's "Malaise," and the Speech That Should Have Changed the Country*. New York: Bloomsbury, 2009.

May, Lary, ed. *Recasting America: Culture and Politics in the Age of Cold War*. Chicago: University of Chicago Press, 1989.

McCann, Michael W. "Causal versus Constitutive Explanations (or, On the Difficulty of Being So Positive)." *Law and Social Inquiry* 21, no. 2 (1996): 457–482.

———. *Rights at Work: Pay Equity Reform and the Politics of Legal Mobilization*. Chicago: University of Chicago Press, 1994.

McGirr, Lisa. *Suburban Warriors: The Origins of the New American Right*. Princeton, NJ: Princeton University Press, 2001.

McWhorter, Diane. *Carry Me Home: Birmingham, Alabama: The Climactic Battle of the Civil Rights Revolution*. New York: Simon & Schuster, 2001.

Meehan III, William F., ed. *Conversations with William F. Buckley Jr.* Jackson: University Press of Mississippi, 2009.

Meet the Press, October 16, 2011. "Interview with Herman Cain."

Mello, Joseph. "Rights Discourse and the Mobilization of Bias: Exploring the Institutional Dynamics of the Same-Sex Marriage Debates in America." *Studies in Law, Politics, and Society* 66, no. 1 (2015): 1–34.

Melville, Herman. *Billy Budd, Sailor (An Inside Narrative)*, ed. Harrison Hayford and Merton M. Sealts Jr. Chicago: University of Chicago Press, 1962.

Merida, Kevin, and Michael Fletcher. *Supreme Discomfort: The Divided Soul of Clarence Thomas*. New York: Broadway Books, 2007.

Miller, Stephen. "William F. Buckley Jr., 82, Godfather of Modern Conservatism." *New York Sun*, February 28, 2008.

Mintz, Steven. *Huck's Raft: A History of American Childhood*. Cambridge, MA: Belknap Press of Harvard University Press, 2004.

"A Model Justice." *National Review* 59, no. 19 (2007): 14.

Morgan, Lucy. "After 2010 Campaign, Gov. Rick Scott Gave Back Reagan the Dog," *Tampa Bay Times*, January 14, 2013.

Morris, Edmund. *Dutch: A Memoir of Ronald Reagan*. New York: Random House, 1999.

Morrison, Toni. "Introduction: Friday on the Potomac." In *Race-ing Justice, Engendering Power*, ed. Toni Morrison, vii-xxx. New York: Random House, 1992.

Murakawa, Naomi. "The Origins of the Carceral Crisis: Racial Order as 'Law and Order' in Postwar American Politics." In *Race and American Political Development*, ed. Joseph Lowndes, Julie Novkov, and Dorian Warren, 234–255. New York: Routledge, 2008.

Murray, Shalaigh. "Obama's Reagan Comparison Sparks Debate." *Washington Post*, January 17, 2008. http://voices.washingtonpost.com/44/2008/01/17/obamas_reagan_comparison_spark_1.html.

"William F. Buckley Jr., R.I.P." *National Review* 60, no. 5 (2008): 14.

Nixon, Richard M. "Gentlemen, This Is My Last Press Conference." In *Nixon: Speeches, Writings, Documents*, ed. Rick Perlstein, 105–112. Princeton, NJ: Princeton University Press, 2008.

———. "The Present Welfare System Has to Be Judged a Colossal Failure." In *Nixon: Speeches, Writings, Documents*, ed. Rick Perlstein, 163–169. Princeton, NJ: Princeton University Press, 2008.

———. "Presidential Nomination Acceptance Speech." Miami, Florida, August 8, 1968. http://www.presidency.ucsb.edu/ws/?pid=25968.

Olmsted, Kathryn S. *Real Enemies: Conspiracy Theories and American Democracy, World War I to 9/11*. New York: Oxford University Press, 2009.

Onwuachi-Willig, Angela. "Just Another Brother on the SCT? What Justice Clarence Thomas Teaches Us about the Influence of Racial Identity." *Iowa Law Review* 90, no. 3 (2005): 931-996.

Passavant, Paul A. *No Escape: Freedom of Speech and the Paradox of Rights*. New York: New York University Press, 2002.

Perlstein, Rick. *Before the Storm: Barry Goldwater and the Unmaking of the American Consensus.* New York: Hill and Wang, 2001.

——— *The Invisible Bridge: The Fall of Nixon and the Rise of Reagan.* New York: Simon & Schuster, 2014.

———. *Nixonland: The Rise of a President and the Fracturing of America.* New York: Scribner, 2008.

Perlstein, Rick, ed. *Nixon: Speeches, Writings, Documents.* Princeton, NJ Princeton University Press, 2008.

Peyton Thomas, Andrew. "America's Leading Conservative." *Weekly Standard,* August 30, 1999, 23.

———. *Clarence Thomas: A Biography.* San Francisco: Encounter Books, 2001.

Phillips-Fein, Kim. *Invisible Hands: The Making of the Conservative Movement from the New Deal to Reagan.* New York: Norton, 2009.

Pollack, Sydney, Dir. *Three Days of the Condor.* Paramount, 1975.

Polletta, Francesca. "The Structural Context of Novel Rights Claims: Southern Civil Rights Organizing, 1961–1966." *Law and Society Review* 34, no. 2 (2000): 367–406.

Population Media Center. "Gloria Steinem on Population, Sexual Pleasure, and Creating Better Fathers." *Grist,* December 23, 2010. http://grist.org/article/2010–12–23-gloria-steinem-on-population-sexual-pleasure-men-parents/.

Prucha, Francis Paul. *The Great Father: The United States Government and the American Indians.* Lincoln: University of Nebraska Press, 1986.

Rabinow, Paul, and William M. Sullivan, "The Interpretive Turn: A Second Look." In *Interpretive Social Science: A Second Look,* ed. Paul Rabinow and William M. Sullivan, 1–30. Berkeley: University of California Press, 1987.

Rasmussen, Claire E. *The Autonomous Animal: Self-Governance and the Modern Subject.* Minneapolis: University of Minnesota Press, 2011.

Reagan, Ron. *My Father at 100: A Memoir.* New York: Viking, 2011.

Reagan, Ronald. "Address before a Joint Session of Congress on the State of the Union." February 4, 1986. http://www.presidency.ucsb.edu/ws/?pid=36646.

———. "Address on Central America before a Joint Session of the Congress." In Ronald Reagan, *Speaking My Mind: Selected Speeches,* 145–160. New York: Simon & Schuster, 1989.

———. "Address to the Nation on Central America." April 14, 1984. http://www.presidency.ucsb.edu/ws/?pid=39777.

———. "Address to the Nation on the Situation in Nicaragua." March 16, 1986. http://www.presidency.ucsb.edu/ws/?pid=36999.

———. "Address to the Nation on United States Policy in Central America." May 9, 1984. http://www.presidency.ucsb.edu/ws/?pid=39901.

———. *An American Life.* New York: Simon & Schuster, 1990.

———. "America's Strength." In *Reagan, In His Own Hand: The Writings of Ronald Reagan That Reveal His Revolutionary Vision for America,* ed. Kiron K. Skinner, Annelise Anderson, and Martin Anderson, 12–13. New York: Touchstone, 2001.

———. "Bakke." In *Reagan's Path to Victory: The Shaping of Ronald Reagan's Vision: Selected Writings* ed. Kiron K. Skinner, Annelise Anderson, and Martin Anderson, 274–275. New York: Free Press, 2004.

———. "California Young Republican Convention." In *Actor, Ideologue, Politician: The Public Speeches of Ronald Reagan*, ed. Davis W. Houck and Amos Kiewe, 86–92. Westport, CT: Greenwood Press, 1993.

———. *The Creative Society: Some Comments on Problems Facing America*. New York: Devin-Adair, 1968.

———. "The Defense of Freedom and the Metaphysics of Fun." In *Tear Down This Wall: The Reagan Revolution—A National Review History*, ed. National Review, 75. New York: Continuum, 2004.

———. "Eisenhower College Fund-Raiser." In Ronald Reagan, *Speaking My Mind: Selected Speeches*, 37–45. New York: Simon & Schuster, 1989.

———. "Encroaching Control: An Address by Ronald Reagan." https://archive.org/details/RonaldReagan-EncroachingControl

———. "The Generation Gap," in Reagan, *The Creative Society*: 60–63.

———. "Have We Been Out of Touch with Reality?" in Reagan, *The Creative Society*, 13–14.

———. "Interview with Allan Dale of WOAI-Radio in San Antonio, Texas, on Domestic and Foreign Policy Issues." May 5, 1983. http://www.presidency.ucsb.edu/ws/?pid=41281.

———. "Letter to Dina Merrill." In *Reagan: A Life in Letters*, ed. Kiron K. Skinner, Annelise Anderson, and Martin Anderson, 625–626. New York: Free Press, 2003.

———. "Letter to the Editor of the *Pegasus*." In *Reagan, in His Own Hand: The Writings of Ronald Reagan That Reveal His Revolutionary Vision for America*, ed. Kiron K. Skinner, Annelise Anderson, and Martin Anderson, 467–469. New York: Touchstone, 2001.

———. "Letter to the Honorable Jack Williams." In *Reagan: A Life in Letters*, ed. Kiron K. Skinner, Annelise Anderson, and Martin Anderson, 190. New York: Free Press, 2003.

———. "Letter to Leonard Kirk." In *Reagan: A Life in Letters*, ed. Kiron K. Skinner, Annelise Anderson, and Martin Anderson, 13. New York: Free Press, 2003.

———. "Letter to Mrs. Gail E. Foyt." In *Reagan: A Life in Letters*, ed. Kiron K. Skinner, Annelise Anderson, and Martin Anderson, 622. New York: Free Press, 2003.

———. "Letter to Richard Nixon." In *Reagan: A Life in Letters*, ed. Kiron K. Skinner, Annelise Anderson, and Martin Anderson, 714. New York: Free Press, 2003.

———. "Letter to Samuel Hayakawa." In *Reagan: A Life in Letters*, ed. Kiron K. Skinner, Annelise Anderson, and Martin Anderson, 189. New York: Free Press, 2003.

———. "Man's Castle." In *Reagan, in His Own Hand: The Writings of Ronald Reagan That Reveal His Revolutionary Vision for America*, ed. Kiron K. Skinner, Annelise Anderson, and Martin Anderson, 291–292. New York: Touchstone, 2001.

———. "Missing Person." In *Reagan, in His Own Hand: The Writings of Ronald Reagan That Reveal His Revolutionary Vision for America*, ed. Kiron K. Skinner, Annelise Anderson, and Martin Anderson, 411–412. New York: Touchstone, 2001.

———. "A Moment of Truth: Our Rendezvous with Destiny." In *Vital Speeches of the Day*, September 1, 1965, 681–685.

———. "The Morality Gap at Berkeley," in Reagan, *The Creative Society*: 125–127.

———. "More about OSHA." In *Reagan's Path to Victory: The Shaping of Ronald Reagan's Vision: Selected Writings* ed. Kiron K. Skinner, Annelise Anderson, and Martin Anderson, 111. New York: Free Press, 2004.

———. "OSHA." In *Reagan's Path to Victory: The Shaping of Ronald Reagan's Vision: Selected Writings* ed. Kiron K. Skinner, Annelise Anderson, and Martin Anderson, 109–110. New York: Free Press, 2004.

———. "The 'People's Park.'" In *Actor, Ideologue, Politician: The Public Speeches of Ronald Reagan*, ed. Davis W. Houck and Amos Kiewe, 73–82. Westport, CT: Greenwood Press, 1993.

———. "People's Park I." In *Reagan's Path to Victory: The Shaping of Ronald Reagan's Vision: Selected Writings*, ed. Kiron K. Skinner, Annelise Anderson, and Martin Anderson, 448. New York: Free Press, 2004.

———. "People's Park II." In *Reagan's Path to Victory: The Shaping of Ronald Reagan's Vision: Selected Writings* ed. Kiron K. Skinner, Annelise Anderson, and Martin Anderson, 449–450. New York: Free Press, 2004.

———. "The President's News Conference." June 28, 1983. http://www.presidency.ucsb.edu/ws/?pid=41535.

———. "Property Rights." In *Reagan, in His Own Hand: The Writings of Ronald Reagan That Reveal His Revolutionary Vision for America*, ed. Kiron K. Skinner, Annelise Anderson, and Martin Anderson, 341. New York: Touchstone, 2001.

———. "Question-and-Answer Session with High School Students on Domestic and Foreign Policy Issues." January 21, 1983. http://www.presidency.ucsb.edu/ws/?pid=41598.

———. "Question-and-Answer Session with Reporters on Domestic and Foreign Policy Issues." March 29, 1983. http://www.presidency.ucsb.edu/ws/?pid=41112.

———. "Radio Address to the Nation on Grenada and Nicaragua." February 22, 1986. http://www.presidency.ucsb.edu/ws/?pid=36904.

———. "Radio Address to the Nation on Tax Reform." June 7, 1986. http://www.presidency.ucsb.edu/ws/?pid=37418.

———. "Radio Address to the Nation on the Situation in Central America." August 13, 1983. http://www.presidency.ucsb.edu/ws/?pid=41716.

———. "Radio Address to the Nation on United States Assistance for the Nicaraguan Democratic Resistance." March 22, 1986. http://www.presidency.ucsb.edu/ws/?pid=37034.

———. *The Reagan Diaries*, ed. Douglas Brinkley. New York: Harper, 2007.

———. "Remarks and an Informal Exchange with Reporters on United States Assistance for the Nicaraguan Democratic Resistance." February 18, 1986. http://www.presidency.ucsb.edu/ws/?pid=36877.

———. "Remarks and a Question-and-Answer Session with Regional Editors and Broadcasters on United States Assistance for the Nicaraguan Democratic Resistance." March 11, 1986. http://www.presidency.ucsb.edu/ws/?pid=36972.

———. "Remarks and a Question-and-Answer Session with Reporters on Domestic and Foreign Policy Issues." April 14, 1983. http://www.presidency.ucsb.edu/ws/?pid=41190.

———. "Remarks at Cinco de Mayo Ceremonies in San Antonio, Texas." May 5, 1983. http://www.presidency.ucsb.edu/ws/?pid=41282.

———. "Remarks at a Fund-Raising Dinner for the Nicaragua Refugee Fund." April 15, 1985. http://www.presidency.ucsb.edu/ws/?pid=38474.

———. "Remarks at a White House Briefing for Supporters of United States Assistance for the Nicaraguan Democratic Resistance." March 10, 1986. http://www.presidency.ucsb.edu/ws/?pid=36967.

———. "Remarks at the Quadrennial Convention of the International Longshoreman's Association in Hollywood, Florida." July 18, 1983. http://www.presidency.ucsb.edu/ws/?pid=41596.

———. "Remarks on Central America and El Salvador at the Annual Meeting of the National Association of Manufacturers." March 10, 1983. http://www.presidency.ucsb.edu/ws/?pid=41034.

———. "Remarks to Elected Officials during a White House Briefing on United States Assistance for the Nicaraguan Democratic Resistance." March 14, 1986. http://www.presidency.ucsb.edu/ws/?pid=36994.

———. "The Republican Party and the Conservative Movement: On Losing." *National Review*, December 1, 1964.

———. *Speaking My Mind: Selected Speeches*. New York: Simon & Schuster, 1989.

———. "Televised Nationwide Address on Behalf of Senator Barry Goldwater." In Ronald Reagan, *Speaking My Mind: Selected Speeches*, 22–36. New York: Simon & Schuster, 1989.

———. "Television Address." In *Actor, Ideologue, Politician: The Public Speeches of Ronald Reagan*, ed. Davis W. Houck and Amos Kiewe, 27–35. Westport, CT: Greenwood Press, 1993.

———. "Toasts of the President and Queen Elizabeth II at a Dinner Honoring the President at Windsor Castle in England." June 8, 1982. http://www.presidency.ucsb.edu/ws/?pid=42616.

———. "Treaties." In *Reagan's Path to Victory: The Shaping of Ronald Reagan's Vision: Selected Writings* ed. Kiron K. Skinner, Annelise Anderson, and Martin Anderson, 273. 275. New York: Free Press, 2004.

———. "What Is Academic Freedom?" in Reagan, *The Creative Society*: 121–122.

―――. "YMCA Model Legislature." In *Actor, Ideologue, Politician: The Public Speeches of Ronald Reagan*, ed. Davis W. Houck and Amos Kiewe, 83–85. Westport, CT: Greenwood Press, 1993.

Reagan, Ronald, with Richard G. Hubler. *Where's the Rest of Me?* New York: Katz Publishers, [1965] 1981.

Rendell, Ruth. "Oakes against the Spooks." *New York Times*, April 6, 1986, 360.

Revel, Harry, and Mack Gordon. "Did You Ever See a Dream Walking?" Sony/ATV Harmony, Chappell Co., 1933.

Robin, Corey. *The Reactionary Mind: Conservatism from Edmund Burke to Sarah Palin*. New York: Oxford University Press, 2011.

Rogin, Michael Paul. *Fathers and Children: Andrew Jackson and the Subjugation of the American Indian*. New York: Transaction Publishers, [1975] 1991.

―――. *Independence Day, or How I Learned to Stop Worrying and Love the Enola Gay*. London: British Film Institute, 1998.

―――. "Max Weber and Woodrow Wilson: The Iron Cage in Germany and America." *Polity* 3, no. 3 (1971): 562–575.

―――. *Ronald Reagan, the Movie: And Other Episodes in Political Demonology*. Berkeley: University of California Press, 1987.

Rubins, Josh. "Blackford Oakes, One Stand-Up Guy." *New York Times*, February 6, 1994, BR14.

Saada, Emmanuelle. *Empire's Children: Race, Filiation, and Citizenship in the French Colonies*. Translated by Arthur Goldhammer. Chicago: University of Chicago Press, 2012.

Sandbrook, Dominic. *Mad as Hell: The Crisis of the 1970's and the Rise of the Populist Right*. New York: Knopf, 2011.

Sandefur, Timothy. "Clarence Thomas's Jurisprudence Unexplained." *New York Journal of Law and Liberty* 4, no. 3 (2009): 535–556.

Sarat, Austin. "Imagining the Law of the Father: Loss, Dread, and Mourning in *The Sweet Hereafter*." *Law and Society Review* 34, no. 1 (2000): 3–46.

Schacter, Jane S. "The Gay Civil Rights Debate in the States: Decoding the Discourse of Equivalents." *Harvard Civil Rights–Liberties Law Review* 29, no. 2 (1994): 283–317.

―――. "Skepticism, Culture, and the Gay Rights Debate in a Post-Civil-Rights Era." *Harvard Law Review* 110, no. 3 (1997): 684–731.

Scheingold, Stuart A. *The Politics of Law and Order: Street Crime and Public Policy*. New York: Longman, 1984.

―――. *The Politics of Rights: Lawyers, Public Policy, and Political Change*, 2nd ed. Ann Arbor: University of Michigan Press, 2004.

Schlesinger, Jr., Arthur M. *The Disuniting of America: Reflections on a Multicultural Society*. New York: Norton, 1991.

Schneider, Elizabeth. "The Dialectic of Rights and Politics: Perspectives from the Women's Movement." *New York University Law Review* 61, no. 4 (1986): 589–652

Schoenwald, Jonathan M. *A Time for Choosing: The Rise of Modern American Conservatism*. New York: Oxford University Press, 2001.

Sholder, Jack. Dir. *A Nightmare on Elm Street 2: Freddy's Revenge*. New Line Cinema, 1985.

Simon, Jonathan. *Governing through Crime: How the War on Crime Transformed American Democracy and Created a Culture of Fear*. New York: Oxford University Press, 2007.

Skinner, Kiron K., Annelise Anderson, and Martin Anderson, eds. *Reagan, in His Own Hand: The Writings of Ronald Reagan That Reveal His Revolutionary Vision for America*. New York: Touchstone, 2001.

———. *Reagan: A Life in Letters*. New York: Free Press, 2003.

———. *Reagan's Path to Victory: The Shaping of Ronald Reagan's Vision: Selected Writings*. New York: Free Press, 2004.

Slotkin, Richard. *Gunfighter Nation: The Myth of the Frontier in Twentieth-Century America*. New York: Atheneum, 1992.

———. *Regeneration through Violence: The Mythology of the American Frontier, 1600–1860*. Norman, Oklahoma: University of Oklahoma Press, [1973] 2000.

Smith, Christopher E., and Joyce A. Baugh. *The Real Clarence Thomas: Confirmation Veracity Meets Performance Reality*. New York: Peter Lang, 2000.

Sokol, Jason. *There Goes My Everything: White Southerners in the Age of Civil Rights, 1945–1975*. New York: Knopf, 2006.

Southworth, Anne. *Lawyers of the Right: Professionalizing the Conservative Coalition*. Chicago: University of Chicago Press, 2008.

Steele, Shelby. "The Freest Black Man in America." *National Review* 59, no. 19 (2007): 36–39.

Stefancic, Jean, and Richard Delgado. *No Mercy: How Conservative Think Tanks and Foundations Changed America's Social Agenda*. Philadelphia: Temple University Press, 1996.

Susman, Warren. "Did Success Spoil the United States? Dual Representations in Post-war America." In *Culture and Politics in the Age of Cold War*, ed. Lary May, 19–37. Chicago: University of Chicago Press, 1989.

Tate, Katherine. "Invisible Woman." *American Prospect*, no. 8 (1992): 74–81.

Taylor, Charles. "Interpretation and the Sciences of Man." *Review of Metaphysics* 25, no. 1 (1971): 3–51.

Teles, Steven. *The Rise of the Conservative Legal Movement: The Battle for the Control of Law*. Princeton, NJ: Princeton University Press, 2010.

Thomas, Clarence. "Address by Justice Clarence Thomas." Fifteenth Annual Ashbrook Memorial Dinner, Ashland, OH, February 5, 1999. http://ashbrook.org/events/thomas-transcript/

———. "Be Not Afraid." 2001 Francis Boyer Lecture American Enterprise Institute, February 13, 2001. https://www.aei.org/publication/be-not-afraid/

———. "Climb the Jagged Mountain." *New York Times*, July 17, 1991, A21.

———. "How to Read the Constitution." *Wall Street Journal*, October 20, 2008. A19.

———. "Keynote Address at the Bill of Rights Institute's Being an American Awards Gala." March 31, 2009. http://www.billofrightsinstitute.org/files/essays/thomas_keynote.pdf

———. "The Necessity of Moral Absolutes in a Free Society." *Religion and Liberty* (January & February 1996): 6–8.

———. "The New Intolerance." Mercer University, May 1993. http://www.american-rhetoric.com/speeches/clarencethomasthenewintolerance.htm

———. *My Grandfather's Son: A Memoir.* New York: Harper Perennial, 2007.

———. "Remarks to Oklahoma Council of Public Affairs." June 1, 2000. http://justice-thomas.blogspot.com/2007/09/oklahoma-council-of-public-affairs-2000.html

———. "Speech by Clarence Thomas before the Pacific Research Institute." San Francisco, August 10, 1987. Hearings before the Committee on the Judiciary, United States Senate. Nomination of Judge Clarence Thomas to be Associate Justice of the United States Supreme Court, September 1991, 1378-1395.

———. "Speech to the Centenary U.M.C. June 17, 1984." In *Clarence Thomas: A Biography* , ed. Andrew Peyton Thomas, 255–256. San Francisco: Encounter Books, 2001.

———. "Speech to the National Bar Association." Memphis, Tennessee, July 28, 1998. http://teachingamericanhistory.org/library/document/speech-to-the-national-bar-association/

Thomas, Evan. "He Knew He Was Right." *Newsweek* 153, no. 10 (2008): 26–33.

Troy, Gil. *Morning in America: How Ronald Reagan Invented the 1980's.* Princeton, NJ: Princeton University Press, 2005.

Turner, Wallace. "California Regents Drop Communist from Faculty." *New York Times,* June 20, 1970, 32.

Tygiel, Jules. *Ronald Reagan and the Triumph of American Conservatism,* 2nd ed. New York: Pearson, 2006.

Tyrrell, Emmett R. "A Conversation with Irving Kristol." *Alternative* 2, no. 5 (1969): 7.

Tyrell, Jr., R. Emmett. "A Good Man." *American Spectator,* November 8, 2007.

US Department of Labor, *The Negro Family: The Case for National Action.* Washington, DC, March 1965.

Vallance, Jeffrey. "The Gipper's Ghost." *L.A. Weekly,* December 15, 2005.

Viguerie, Richard A., and David Franke. *America's Right Turn: How Conservatives Used Old and New Media to Take Power.* Chicago: Bonus Books, 2004.

Walker, Anders. *The Ghost of Jim Crow: How Southern Moderates Used Brown v. Board of Education to Stall Civil Rights.* New York: Oxford University Press, 2009.

Walsh, Michael. "At Reagan Library, Republican Presidential Hopefuls Vie to Be the Most Reaganesque." *Yahoo News,* September 16, 2015. https://www.yahoo.com/news/at-reagan-library-republican-presidential-129247682571.html.

Weaver, Richard M. "Integration Is Communization." *National Review* 4, no. 28 (1957): 67–68.

Weymouth, Lally. "A Justice's Candid Opinions." *Newsweek* 150, no. 17 (2007): 50.

Wilentz, Sean. *The Age of Reagan: A History, 1974–2008.* New York: Harper Perennial, 2009.

Will, George. "Donald Trump Is an Affront to Anyone Devoted to William F. Buckley's Legacy." *National Review*, August 12, 2015.

"William F. Buckley Jr., R.I.P." *National Review* 60, no. 5 (2008): 14.

Williams, Daniel K. *God's Own Party: The Making of the Christian Right.* New York: Oxford University Press, 2010.

Williams, Juan. "Black Conservatives, Center Stage." *Washington Post*, December 16, 1980, A21.

———. "A Question of Fairness." *Atlantic Monthly* 259, no. 2 (1987): 70–82.

Williams, Patricia J. *The Alchemy of Race and Rights: Diary of a Law Professor.* Cambridge, MA: Harvard University Press, 1991.

Williams Crenshaw, Kimberlé. "Race, Reform, and Retrenchment: Transformation and Legitimation in Antidiscrimination Law." *Harvard Law Review* 101, no. 7 (1988): 1331–1387.

Wills, Garry. *Nixon Agonistes: The Crisis of the Self-Made Man.* Boston: Mariner Books, [1970] 2002.

———. *Reagan's America: Innocents at Home.* New York: Penguin, [1987] 2000.

Wilson, Joshua C. *The Street Politics of Abortion: Speech, Violence, and America's Culture Wars.* Stanford, CA: Stanford University Press, 2013.

Wilson, Woodrow. "The Ideals of America." *Atlantic Monthly* 90 (December 1902): 721–734.

Winner, Langdon. "The Battle of People's Park." *Rolling Stone*, June 14, 1969.

Woods, Jeff R. *Black Struggle, Red Scare: Segregation and Anti-Communism in the South, 1948–1968.* Baton Rouge, LA: Louisiana State University Press, 2003.

Wyman Walker, Alvin. "The Conundrum of Clarence Thomas: An Attempt at a Psychodynamic Understanding." N.d. http://www.raceandhistory.com/historicalviews/clarencethomas.htm.

Yoo, John. "The Real Clarence Thomas," *Wall Street Journal*, October 9, 2007, A17.

"The Youngest, Cruelest Justice." *New York Times*, February 27, 1992, A24.

Zaretsky, Natasha. *No Direction Home: The American Family and the Fear of National Decline, 1968–1980.* Chapel Hill: University of North Carolina Press, 2007.

Zirakzadeh, Cyrus Ernesto. *Social Movements in Politics, Expanded Edition: A Comparative Study.* New York: Palgrave MacMillan, 2006.

Court Cases

Bob Jones University v. United States, 461 U.S. 574 (1983).

Hudson v. McMillian, 503 U.S. 1 (1992).

Lawrence et al. v. Texas, 539 U.S. 558 (2003).

Regents of the University of California-Davis v. Bakke, 438 U.S. 265.

Index

Adams, John, 63

affirmative action, 84, 116, 174n46

Affordable Care Act, 147

Allen, Woody, 45

Allende, Salvador, 45, 159n18

Alternative, 36

Altschuler, Sid, 74

American conservatism: countersubversive politics in, 9, 17, 34–38, 39, 122–23, 142, 144–46; definition of, 1–2; diversity in, 1–2, 3–4, 7, 12, 16, 22–23, 26, 38; and intimate personal relations, 31–32; legal mobilizations, 133–34; longing for stability in, 137–38, 139; origins, 16, 18–27; role of paternal rights discourse in, 2–3, 4, 7, 8–9, 15, 16, 17, 22, 27, 38, 134–35, 137, 138–40, 146–47; role of public figures in, 3–4, 7, 8, 9, 12, 16, 17, 23, 26; scholarship regarding, 16, 18, 21, 22–23, 24, 25–27, 133–34. *See also* Buckley, William F., Jr.; paternal rights discourse; Reagan, Ronald; Thomas, Clarence

American dream, 104; Reagan on, 77, 79–80

American Enterprise Institute, 25

American independence: and Buckley's Blackford Oakes novels, 61, 62, 63–64; Declaration of Independence, 62, 63, 147; as family dispute, 62–63; and individual rights, 61, 62–63

American Southwest, 18, 20–21

American Spectator, 36, 103

antiabortion protestors, 133–34

anticommunism: blacklisting, 75; of Buckley, 19, 41, 45–46; and civil rights movement, 22, 28–29; of Reagan, 30, 87, 88, 90, 91, 92–100

anti-Semitism, 73

Arizona, 18, 20

Austin, Jane, 52–53

autonomy, individual, 7, 9, 15, 17, 27, 72, 91, 107, 112, 113, 114, 119–20; as limited by paternal authority, 2–3, 18, 69, 100, 102, 105–6, 125, 128, 130–31, 136–37, 146; as precondition for individual rights, 5–6, 33, 68, 79, 142; in virtuous citizens, 10, 11, 12, 32, 34, 44, 104, 106, 130–31, 132, 136–37, 146. *See also* self-discipline

Bakke, Alan, 84

Battle of People's Park, 85, 89–92, 96, 100, 167n78

Bell, Daniel, 19

Benjamin, Jessica: on identity formation, 151nn27,32

Berlant, Lauren: on intimate public sphere, 17, 31–32

Big Lebowski, The: Walter Sobchak in, 178n13

Blackford Oakes novels: and American independence, 61, 62, 63–64; and American values, 42, 43, 46–47, 50,

124; on maternal authority, 105, 106, 107, 114, 120, 125, 129–30, 173n19; nomination to Supreme Court, 117–20, 124, 132, 176n90; during oral arguments, 172n14; as originalist, 104, 106, 125, 126, 128, 131, 177nn94,98; on paternal authority, 4, 7, 12, 13, 15, 105–7, 111–12, 113–14, 120–21, 129–30, 131–32, 136–37, 146, 173n17; on race relations, 115–16, 117, 118, 119, 175n52; on Reagan administration, 115–16, 117; relationship with Danforth, 113; relationship with Emma Mae, 115, 174n43; relationship with father, 102, 108; relationship with Hill, 119; relationship with maternal grandfather, 106, 110–13, 116, 119, 120, 129, 130, 131–32, 140, 146, 173n33, 177n114; relationship with maternal grandmother, 110–11, 129, 174n40; relationship with mother, 109–11, 112–13, 120, 173n19, 173n23; relationship with Reynolds, 174n46; relationship with surrogate fathers, 102, 113, 173n17; relationship with Juan Williams, 115, 116; on self-discipline, 38, 103, 105–6, 107, 111–12, 113, 117, 120, 122, 124–27, 128–29, 130–31, 132, 146, 176n92; as Supreme Court justice, 104, 106, 107, 124–31, 175n62; on virtuous citizenship, 103, 106, 107

Thomas, Peyton: on Thomas, 110, 173n23
Thomas, Virginia, 120, 127, 132
Thurmond, Strom, 21
Trump, Donald: on Obama as weak father, 145–46
Trust, Anthony, 52, 160n47
Tyrrel, R. Emmett, Jr.: on Thomas, 103

United States Chamber of Commerce, 19, 25
university administrators, 81, 82, 84, 88
University of California–Berkeley, 35, 87–88; Battle of People's Park, 85, 89–92, 96, 100, 167n78
University of California–Davis, 84

Vaughn, Samuel, 44, 64
Virginia, 22
virtuous citizens, 7, 13, 27, 43, 70, 85–86, 103; as autonomous, 10, 11, 12, 32, 34, 44, 104, 106, 107, 130–31, 132, 136–37, 146; as self-disciplined, 10, 11, 12, 32, 33, 34, 77, 79–80, 104, 107, 117, 130–31, 132, 136–37; Thomas on, 103, 106, 107
Vogelin, Eric, 19
Von Mises, Ludwig, 18, 19

Walker, Anders, 22
Wallace, George, 21, 28
Wallace, Michael, 62
Warner, Jack, 74, 75, 83
Washington Post, 115
Watergate, 40, 92
Weaver, Richard, 19
Weekly Standard, 103
Welch, Robert, 2
Will, George: on Buckley, 147
Williams, Daniel K., 25
Williams, Juan, 115, 116, 173n23
Wills, Gary, 2
Wilson, Joshua, 133

Yoo, John: on Thomas, 104
Young Americans for Freedom, 21, 23

Zaretsky, Natasha, 35

The Cultural Lives of Law
Edited by Austin Sarat

The Cultural Lives of Law series brings insights and approaches from cultural studies to law and tries to secure for law a place in cultural analysis. Books in the series focus on the production, interpretation, consumption, and circulation of legal meanings. They take up the challenges posed as boundaries collapse between as well as within cultures, and as the circulation of legal meanings becomes more fluid. They also attend to the ways law's power in cultural production is renewed and resisted.

Pregnant with the Stars: Watching and Wanting the Celebrity Baby Bump
Renée Ann Cramer
2015

Letters of the Law: Race and the Fantasy of Colorblindness
Sora Y. Han
2015

Our Word Is Our Bond: How Legal Speech Acts
Marianne Constable
2014

The Street Politics of Abortion: Speech, Violence, and America's Culture Wars
Joshua C. Wilson
2013

Zooland: The Institution of Captivity
Irus Braverman
2012

After Secular Law
Edited by Winnifred Fallers Sullivan, Robert A. Yelle, and Mateo Taussig-Rubbo
2011

All Judges Are Political—Except When They Are Not: Acceptable Hypocrisies and the Rule of Law
Keith J. Bybee
2010

Riding the Black Ram: Law, Literature, and Gender
Susan Sage Heinzelman
2010

Tort, Custom, and Karma: Globalization and Legal Consciousness in Thailand
David M. Engel and Jaruwan S. Engel
2010

Law in Crisis: The Ecstatic Subject of Natural Disaster
Ruth A. Miller
2009

The Affective Life of Law: Legal Modernism and the Literary Imagination
Ravit Reichman
2009

Fault Lines: Tort Law as Cultural Practice
Edited by David M. Engel and Michael McCann
2008

Lex Populi: The Jurisprudence of Popular Culture
William P. MacNeil
2007

The Cultural Lives of Capital Punishment: Comparative Perspectives
Edited by Austin Sarat and Christian Boulanger
2005